Where to watch birds in

Scotland

Where to watch birds in

Scotland

Mike Madders and Julia Welstead

Fourth edition

Christopher Helm

A & C Black · London

© 2002 Mike Madders and Julia Welstead
Line drawings by Philip Snow, David Pullan and Marianne Taylor
Maps by Julia Welstead

Third edition 1997
Second edition 1993
First edition 1989

Christopher Helm, an imprint of
A & C Black Publishers Ltd,
37 Soho Square,
London W1D 3QZ

0-7136-5693-X

A CIP catalogue record for this book is available from the British Library

A & C Black uses paper produced with elemental chlorine-free pulp, harvested
from managed sustainable forests

www.acblack.com

Printed and bound by Creative Print and Design (Wales), Ebbw Vale

CONTENTS

Contents

Contents

ACKNOWLEDGEMENTS

We wish to record our especial gratitude to the many Scottish birders who contributed detailed information about their local sites. Foremost among these were: R Anderson, I Andrews, NK Atkinson, A Bachell, CO Badenoch, A Barclay, D Bell, MV Bell, Z Bhatia, CJ Booth, WR Brackenridge, A Bramhall, RA Broad, AW & LM Brown, DM Bryant, I Bullock, M Callan, ED Cameron, G Christer, T Clifford, P Collin, MJH Cook, L Cranna, C Cronin, WAJ Cunningham, I Darling, R Davis, DE Dickson, T Dix, T Dunbar, A Duncan, B Etheridge, K Fairclough, EC Fellowes, I Finlay, W Fraser, D & K Galloway, S Gibson, R Goater, PR Gordon, M Gray, J Hart, P Harvey, L Hatton, J Hawell, R Hawley, CJ Henty, A Hilton, A Hogg, J Holloway, D Jardine, AR Jennings, R Johnson, A Lauder, B Lightfoot, B Lynch, T Keating, FM Leckie, D McAllister, D Macdonald, C McGuigan, J McNish, J Malster, T Marshall, W Mattingley, E Maughan, P Mayhew, R Mearns, E Meek, C Miller, C Mitchell, C Munro, RD Murray, JS Nadin, D Nethersole-Thompson, R Nisbet, P Norman, S North, MA Ogilvie, JD Okill, ID Pennie, P Potts, D Pullan, K Rideout, RJ Robertson, M Robinson, DE Rowling, DB Sexton, T Shannon, RA Schofield, G Shaw, K Shaw, JC Sheldon, G Smith, TC Smout, J Stevenson, DR Stewart, I Strachan, D Suddaby, S Taylor, VM Thom, D Thorogood, M Trubridge, LLJ Vick, DH Walker, D Warnock, D Watson, K Watson, A Whitfield, E Wiffen, J Wiffen, KF Woodbridge, RE Youngman and B Zonfrillo.

The following organisations provided invaluable help: Borders Regional Council, Clackmannan District Council, Countryside Commission for Scotland, Forestry Commission, North East Fife Ranger Service, National Trust for Scotland, Royal Society for the Protection of Birds, Scottish Natural Heritage, Stirling District Council, Scottish Wildlife Trust and Speyside Wildlife.

The completed manuscript for each region was checked and improved by Ray Murray (Borders), Paul Collin (Dumfries and Galloway), Dougie Dickson (Fife), Ken Shaw (Grampian), Roy Dennis (Highland), Peter Gordon (Lothian), Eric Meek (Orkney), Tim Dix (Uists), Dave Okill (Shetland), Roger Broad (Strathclyde and Central)

Adult and juvenile Pied Wagtails

and Wendy Mattingley (Tayside). We are grateful to these people for their time and effort. We must stress, however, that the selection of sites included in the book and any mistakes that remain in the site accounts are entirely our own.

For the superb line drawings we thank Philip Snow, Dave Pullan and Marianne Taylor. We would also like to thank Pam Grant, Lynn North and Bill Wales for giving us some useful cartographical advice.

Mention must also be made of the support and encouragement of many friends who have proof-read scripts, researched details, lent books, provided us with accommodation or been otherwise invaluable: our thanks to you all. In particular, we would like to single out: David Sexton, Fay Wilkinson, Steve Newton, John-the-Post, Ken & Kathy Shaw, Cathy MacLean, Alan Stewart and Jamie, Diane, Megan & Hannah Welstead.

Finally, special thanks are due to Susan Campbell for her invaluable assistance in updating and checking the text for this fourth edition.

The authors will be pleased to receive any information and ideas that might be usefully incorporated into future editions of this guide. Any correspondence should be addressed c/o Christopher Helm (Publishers) Ltd, 37 Soho Square, London W1D 3QZ and marked for the attention of the authors. (Please enclose a SAE if a reply is required.)

INTRODUCTION

Scotland is a country of varied landscapes: covering approximately 30,000 square miles (48,000 km²), it ranges from the scenic splendour of mountain and moorland in the highlands to the subtle charm of lowland vales and rolling hills in the border country. There is over 6400 miles (10,300 km) of coastline, characterised by the rocky and heavily indented north and west coast with its steep-sided sea lochs and bold sea cliffs, and the broad estuarine firths typical of the east coast. A galaxy of islands lies off the west and north coasts, varying from fertile, low-lying ones like Tiree to the rugged and mountainous, such as Rum, and from small stacks and skerries to the large inhabited archipelagos of Orkney and Shetland.

More than 60 per cent of Scotland can be considered upland habitat and this hill ground is predominantly used for sheep grazing, although some is maintained as grouse moor or inhabited by deer. An increasing acreage of these upland tracts is being planted with commercial forest, which currently accounts for about ten per cent of land use in Scotland. About 20 per cent of the country is given over to more intensive agricultural use with the most productive areas being concentrated along the east coast, especially adjacent to the estuarine firths. The southern uplands of Dumfries & Galloway and the Borders are also quite fertile.

A large proportion of the country's human population lives in the lowlands, in particular the central industrial belt which includes the two major cities of Edinburgh and Glasgow. Areas north and south of this are predominantly rural and the highlands and islands are but sparsely populated, with only 126 of Scotland's 790 islands currently inhabited.

Over 450 species of bird have been recorded in Scotland and 175 or so regularly breed. Clearly, Scotland is an important place for birds, with many of the species that occur achieving breeding or wintering population levels that exceed those necessary to qualify for international importance (seabirds and raptors for instance). Scotland's northerly location and the presence of large tracts of relatively undisturbed ground enable a number of species to breed which would otherwise be

Peregrine and Hooded Crows

11

absent from Britain: a total of 19 British breeding birds nest only north of the border.

The northern isles and the east mainland coast are well placed to receive continental migrants, and rarities are regularly recorded among these every year. North American vagrants are occasionally recorded on the west coast and Hebrides and many more must go unnoticed. In winter, divers and sea duck gather offshore; Scotland hosts large numbers of offshore divers, wildfowl and waders, as well as important populations of thrushes, finches and buntings.

To do adequate justice to such a huge area and such diversity of birdlife in a single volume is scarcely possible. The selection of sites has been a major problem and ultimately, whatever criteria for inclusion are used the final choice tends to be subjective. We have taken into consideration the views of many local birdwatchers around the country in an effort to select sites that are both good birding locations and that are suitable for public access. Inevitably, we encountered a wide and often conflicting range of advice and probably the best we can hope is that everyone will be displeased equally with our final selection! Foremost among considerations when deciding whether or not to include a particular site were: (1) Is its inclusion likely to be in any way detrimental to the birdlife of the area? (2) Are there any problems relating to the site's access which may be exacerbated by increased visitor pressure? (3) Are there adequate vantage points, parking areas and accessible routes (either driveable or walkable) within or overlooking the area of interest?

The sites that survived this selection procedure were then graded according to their overall bird interest, importance and suitability and then assigned to either 'main site' or 'additional site' status. We make no apologies for having ensured a reasonable distribution of sites, even if this means that a site in northwest Scotland with a more restricted bird interest has usurped a good birding site in southeast Scotland. A few sites have been included for no better reason than that they are personal favourites.

Certain aspects of birdwatching are outside the scope of this guide. The most obvious is bird identification: there are many good field guides available and we therefore do not include any identification advice here. Similarly, information concerning individual species' behaviour, feeding methods, breeding cycle, distribution, migration, etc. is left to the wide range of books available on these subjects.

HOW TO USE THIS BOOK

The site accounts in this book are divided into the regions of Argyll & Bute, Ayrshire & Clyde, Borders & Lothians, Central Scotland, Dumfries & Galloway, Highland, and Northeast Scotland, with Orkney, Shetland and the Western Isles completing the picture. Due to the changes in local government districts in 1996, the names and areas of some of the regions have been altered since previous editions. Each region's heading is followed by a list of the new council areas which the region now contains.

For the most part each site is described under the subheadings of 'Habitat', 'Species', 'Access', 'Timing' and 'Calendar', using the same format as in other guides in this series. Instead of applying this system rigidly, however, we have adapted both the order and the layout to suit the site, where appropriate. This was particularly necessary in the case of island sites, where a large number of disparate access points are often grouped together under one site heading. Also, for several sites we have amalgamated the Species and Calendar sections in order to reduce repetition in the text. We trust that readers will find these changes logical.

At the end of each regional section is a list of additional sites with information relating to habitat, bird interest and timing given in note form. Unfortunately, lack of space prevents us presenting detailed access instructions for these sites, so the pertinent Ordnance Survey Landranger map is given together with a grid reference.

Following the site accounts is a 'Systematic List of Scottish Birds'. This lists birds recorded in Scotland from 1900 to the present, with a very brief indication of each species' status and distribution. For species of local or restricted distribution a selection of sites where they are likely to be found is listed.

Habitat

Here a short general description of the area is given with the emphasis on the major bird habitat regions. The size of the area is given, where appropriate, and its status quoted (for instance: Site of Special Scientific Interest, National Nature Reserve, Scottish Wildlife Trust Reserve,

Sand Martins—nest site, late spring

13

RSPB Reserve, etc.). Any relevant botanical, geological, historical or other information concerning the area completes this section.

Species

This details the species for which the site is primarily of interest with an indication of their abundance/occurrence. This is by no means an exhaustive list of all the species that may be seen, but an attempt to summarise the area's specialities and where they might be found.

Access

The most practicable routes to the site from nearby towns or main roads are detailed here. Accessible tracks and available parking in the area are noted and any available public transport to the site mentioned. Many of the main sites have an accompanying map showing access routes. In cases where there are several areas of interest, each one is listed with numbers corresponding to those on the site map.

For each site we have detailed any access restrictions known to us—these may be seasonal or perhaps applicable just to specific areas. Within some reserves sanctuary zones are often established to prevent disturbance to breeding birds and others are only accessible by prior arrangement with the warden. Many of the hides on Scottish Wildlife Trust reserves are kept locked and the keys are made available only to its members. In a few cases the area of interest is also used for military purposes and occasional access restrictions are imposed. An important point to bear in mind when visiting upland areas is that access may be severely curtailed by stalking activities (red deer stalking is between 1 August and 30 April). We trust that readers will comply with whatever conditions of access are required.

Timing

A badly timed visit to any site may result in disappointment so prior planning should always take this into consideration. This section outlines the optimum times to visit the site, with reference to season, weather conditions (wind direction, etc.), lighting (morning/evening sunlight can sometimes be a problem), tides at coastal sites and so on. Opening times of those reserves not permanently open and of visitor centres are also given.

However, do keep an open mind when visiting a particular site—just because the book doesn't mention that a particular time of year/direction of wind/state of tide, etc. is very good, doesn't mean that there will be nothing to see. The best birds are often the unexpected ones!

Calendar

For most of the important sites an analysis of the changing bird interest over the year is given. Again, this is not a comprehensive account of all the birds to be seen, but a selection of the highlights that are likely to occur. As with the Timing section, this should be interpreted as a guide rather than a definitive statement.

THE MAPS

Many of the site descriptions have accompanying maps. These essentially show location, with little if any attention paid to topography or vegetation. For each site, numbers on the map correspond to those in the text, where a description of that area and its bird interest is given. As a rule, maps have not been included for sites at which there is an information notice board or for reserves with visitor centres, as it was felt that these would be superfluous. A general key to the maps is provided below.

The use of an Ordnance Survey map is recommended, especially where walks in remote upland areas are suggested. At the head of each site account reference is made to the relevant Ordnance Survey Landranger Series (1:50,000) sheet. A four- or six-figure grid reference is also given to locate the site on that sheet. (Guidance on the use of grid references can be found on the side panel of all Ordnance Survey 1:50,000 series maps.)

In addition to individual site maps, general maps at the beginning of each regional section locate the sites described for that region. Encircled numbers correspond to main sites while lower-case letters correspond to additional sites. Finally, the map of Scotland on page 17 locates each region.

Motorways, A and B roads are labelled appropriately on each map.

Key to Maps

————————	Unclassified road	*SZ*	Sanctuary Zone
– – – – – –	Track	✛	Church
· · · · · · ·	Path	⚑	Golf course
+·+·●·+·+·+	Railway line	rd	Rubbish dump
+ + + +	Railway line (disused)	⊕	Hide
– × – × – × –	Reserve boundary	℗	Parking area
(open water)	Open water/river course	*MLW*	Mean low-water
(mud/sandflats)	Mud/sandflats	*MHW(S)*	Mean high-water (spring)
(rocky shoreline)	Rocky shoreline		

SOME NOTES FOR VISITORS

Ring Ouzel

Accommodation and Transport

Detailed information concerning accommodation and transport is well beyond the scope of this book. Bus and train routes, if available, are mentioned in the Access section of each site account, and accommodation suggestions are given for some islands where this is very restricted. The best overall advice that we can give regarding both accommodation and transport is for the reader to contact the relevant tourist information centre.

General

Scotland's climate is extremely unpredictable and at any season visitors should be prepared for a wide range of conditions. For those venturing into the hills warm and waterproof clothing is essential, even if most of it remains packed in a rucksack all day. Strong, comfortable footwear is also important, with wellingtons often being necessary in the wetter terrain characteristic of northwestern Scotland. Hill walkers will also require spare food, the relevant Ordnance Survey map and a compass. If possible leave word of your intended route and estimated time of return with someone, and if conditions are against you, turn back.

With increasing numbers of people taking an interest in Scotland's wildlife and especially birdlife, care is needed to ensure that the pursuit of these interests does not in itself conflict with wildlife conservation. Please refer to the 'Code of Conduct for Birdwatchers' on page 289 and follow the good advice which is given there in order to make your visit responsible as well as pleasurable.

As a final plea, can we stress the importance of sending details of bird sightings to the local/county recorder (see page 283). Even sightings which you consider of little note in your own area can be important elsewhere. Visiting birdwatchers can undoubtedly provide valuable information on areas that may be visited only on an irregular basis by local watchers.

REGIONAL MAP OF SCOTLAND

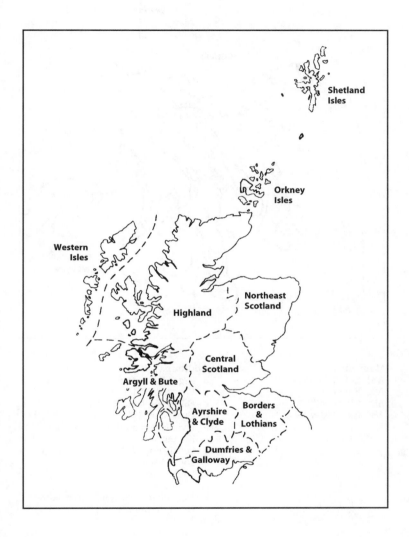

ARGYLL & BUTE

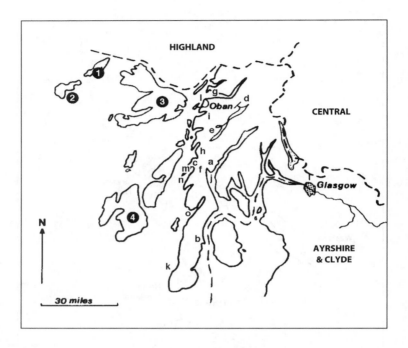

Main sites

AB1 Coll RSPB Reserve
AB2 Isle of Tiree
AB3 Isle of Mull
AB4 Isle of Islay

Additional sites

a Argyll Forest Park
b Carradale Point
c Fairy Isles, Loch Sween
d Glen Nant
e Inverliever Forest
f Knapdale
g Ledaig Point
h Loch Craignish
i Loch Feochan
j Loch Gilp
k Machrihanish Seabird Observatory
l Oban Harbour
m Taynish
n Ulva Lagoons
o West Loch Tarbert

Please note that for convenience, sites within the administrative area of Argyll & Bute and which are located along the north shore of the Clyde estuary are dealt with in the Ayrshire & Clyde section.

AB1 COLL RSPB RESERVE

Habitat

This 1221-ha reserve was acquired by the RSPB in 1991. It is situated at the west end of the Isle of Coll, a rugged, largely heather-covered island that lies 54 miles (10 km) northwest of Mull. The reserve comprises two huge dune systems, large areas of herb-rich grazing, heather moorland and some of the best hay meadows on the island. The moorland area occupies the central part of the reserve and in places grades into machair, forming a low-lying marshy habitat favoured by many breeding waders. The machair itself once formed sand dunes, and are composed of finely ground shell sand, which have stabilised and turfed over. It is by far the most fertile habitat on the island and holds a number of unusual plants, including bloody cranesbill.

The extensive dune system in the western part of the reserve separates two wide bays, both with superb sandy beaches flanked by rocky headlands: Feall Bay to the north and Crossapol Bay to the south. These are important resorts for wintering seafowl.

Species

The RSPB established the reserve specifically for Corncrake, which depend upon carefully managed grassland and is now largely confined to a few remaining strongholds in the Hebrides and parts of Ireland. Between 1988 and 1991, the British population of the Corncrake declined by a third, while over the same period, the Northern Ireland population slumped from 100 pairs to extinction by 1994. On Coll and Tiree, however, numbers have remained reasonably stable, helped by RSPB initiatives advising crofters and farmers on ways to assist the bird. Overall, Corncrake numbers have risen to 40 males in recent years, while on the RSPB reserve they have increased from six in 1991 to 28 in 1996. The Coll reserve now provides the RSPB an opportunity to experiment with different farming techniques in order to maximise the Corncrake potential here. This will probably involve removing livestock from the hay meadows earlier in the year than is currently the practice, to promote early cover for returning birds, and delaying the cutting of fields for silage until late July or early August to provide cover late in the season. In addition, fields are cut in a 'Corncrake-friendly' way to prevent the accidental mowing of adults and chicks.

Machair habitats hold some of the highest breeding densities of waders in Britain and the machair–moorland interface on the reserve supports strong populations of breeding Snipe, Dunlin, Lapwing and Redshank. Shelduck and Wheatear nest in the numerous rabbit burrows in the drier machair. Other notable breeding birds on the reserve include Rock Dove, Raven and Twite. Hen Harrier, Peregrine, Merlin and Short-eared Owl also occur.

The moorland habitats of Coll are probably best observed en route to the reserve, from the Arinagour road. Important breeding species include Red-throated Diver, native Greylag Geese, Teal and Arctic Skua. Fulmar, Shag, Eider, various gulls, Common, Arctic and Little Terns all breed on Coll, while offshore, seabird activity is likely to include plunge-diving

Gannet, marauding Arctic Skua and possibly the occasional summer-plumaged Great Northern Diver. Manx Shearwater, Razorbill, Guillemot and Puffin all breed on the nearby Treshnish Isles and are therefore frequently seen from the Coll coast. As well as birds, the coastline is also good for otters, while common seal can be watched close inshore; basking shark, porpoise, dolphin and whales are also not uncommonly seen.

In winter, Coll holds internationally important populations of Greenland White-fronted and Barnacle Geese, plus 100–300 Greylag Geese. The reserve hosts a flock of 40 or so feral Snow Geese that summer on nearby Mull. Offshore divers, mainly Great Northern, can be seen in many of the bays and elsewhere around the coast. Feall Bay is a good area for watching wintering divers and more particularly for Long-tailed Duck (up to 100 in some winters) and occasional Common Scoter and Scaup.

Access

Coll is reached by Caledonian MacBrayne ferry from Oban. The service operates four days a week in summer, plus Sundays between 28 June and 30 August. In winter there are three sailings per week. Visitors should check times with Caledonian MacBrayne, The Ferry Terminal, Gourock PA19 1QP (tel: 01475 650100). Booking is essential for vehicles. The ferry also calls at Tiree and now has a roll-on/roll-off facility. It is also possible for foot passengers to board the ferry at Tobermory (Mull). The crossing can be very good for seawatching, especially in May/June and August–early October.

Once on Coll, take the B8070 south from Arinagour, for nearly 5 miles (8 km). This road affords fine views of Coll's moorland habitats—take time to scan the roadside lochans in particular, which often have Red-throated Diver in spring/summer. The reserve is entered after turning left at Arileod. Continue for just over half a mile (1 km) or so, keeping right at the turn-off towards the Castle, then park just beyond the next cattle grid. The track continues on towards Crossapol Bay, with the dunes lying to the west.

The reserve is open year-round. Visitors are requested not to take vehicles onto the machair or to enter any of the hay meadows. There is a reception point at Totronald.

Timing

Corncrake is rarely seen and the best that most visitors can hope for is to hear one. They are present between April and September, but birds generally cease to call after late July. Calling activity is mainly confined to the hours between about 10.00 pm and 05.00 am, though in warm weather they may also call during the day. It is very important that visitors do not enter the hay meadows to try to locate birds—you are very unlikely to succeed in this way and may cause damage to vital Corncrake breeding habitat as well as to the grass crop, and creating unnecessary disturbance to the birds. Listening for calling birds from the road between Uig and Roundhouse is probably the best method. Patient watching of this area during the day may also reveal a glimpse of a bird or chicks, although it may be necessary to put in many hours!

Calendar

May–July: The best time to visit for Corncrake and other breeding birds (see Species). Young auks can be seen at sea, accompanied by single adults, from early July.

August–October: Passage waders and seabirds provide the main interest. Wintering geese generally arrive by early October.

November–April: Wintering divers, geese and sea duck present. Greylag Geese start to take up nesting territories in mid-March; White-fronted and Barnacle Geese usually depart in late April. Passage geese, duck and waders can also be seen in April.

RSPB Warden
Charlie Self, Roundhouse, Coll (tel: 01879 230301).

References
Argyll Bird Reports 1980–91. Eds. C Galbraith/SJ Petty (Argyll Bird Club). *The Birds of Coll and Tiree.* Ed. D Stroud (1989).

AB2 ISLE OF TIREE   OS Landranger 46

Habitat
Tiree is mostly a low-lying, fertile island, 15 miles (24 km) to the west of Mull. Covering approximately 8400 ha and measuring about 10 miles (16 km) from east to west and a maximum of 6 miles (9.7 km) north to south, the island has an irregular outline, much indented by a series of wide bays. These sandy beaches are interspersed with areas of rocky shoreline which generally form low headlands, although there are high-er cliffs at Ben Hynish and more especially at Ceann a' Mhara in the southwest. The shoreline is backed by dune systems in several localities, particularly those on the west-facing coast.

Inland, Tiree is characterised by a mixture of machair and wet low-land moor. The machair is extensive and is the basis for Tiree's tradi-tional and highly productive agricultural regime, which is chiefly based on cattle and sheep breeding. More than 640 ha of land are used for grass and cereal production in the summer, the livestock being put out to communal grazing areas on the moorland and permanent pasture. Despite some shift towards silage production, the herb-rich grasslands are vitally important for many breeding birds, not the least of which is the Corncrake.

There are several large inland waterbodies, such as Loch a' Phuill, Loch Bhasapol and Loch Riaghain, which are of great significance for both breeding and wintering wildfowl. In addition, several small, shal-low lochans and boggy hollows punctuate the moorland terrain.

Access
Tiree is reached by Caledonian MacBrayne ferry from Oban. The service operates five days a week in summer. In winter there are three sailings per week. Visitors should check times with Caledonian MacBrayne, The Ferry Terminal, Gourock PA19 1QP (tel: 01475 650100). Booking is

essential for vehicles. The ferry calls at Coll en route. It is also possible for foot passengers to board the ferry at Tobermory (Mull). The crossing can be very good for seawatching, especially in May/June and August–early October. British Airways Express also operates flights from Glasgow, Monday to Saturday (tel: 01345 222111).

Apart from a post-bus, there is no public transport on the island. Tiree is just too large for exploration solely on foot to be practical, although a bicycle would be a reasonable option. Both cars and bicycles may be hired locally. Although the whole island is ornithologically interesting, a number of locations are exceptional.

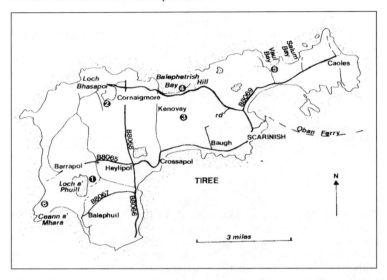

1 LOCH A' PHUILL (OS REF: NL 95/41)

This is one of the most productive inland waterbodies for wintering wild-fowl. The best viewpoint for this loch is reached from the church west of Heylipol, on the B8065, 7 miles (11.3 km) west of Scarinish. From the crossroads at the church, take the road heading south, towards Bale-martine. After 0.5 mile (0.8 km) a rough track on the right leads down to the loch shore, affording a panoramic view of all but a tiny part of the water. On clear days this vantage point is best visited in the morning, when the light will be behind you. Alternatively, walk 0.5 mile (0.8 km) along the track from Balephuil at the end of the B8067 road, 2 miles (3.2 km) from Balemartine. This gives good views of the southern half of Loch a' Phuill. A telescope is more or less essential.

The loch holds large numbers of Mute and Whooper Swans in autumn and winter; a flock of 50 or so Greenland White-fronted Geese frequents the area from October to April, while Greylag Geese are present year-round. Wintering ducks include Wigeon, Teal, Mallard, a few Pintail, occasional Shoveler, and small numbers of Pochard, Tufted Duck, Gold-eneye and Red-breasted Merganser.

2 LOCH BHASAPOL (OS REF: NL 97/46)

An easily accessible loch with a good variety of wintering wildfowl, including large numbers of Pochard and Tufted Duck. Loch Bhasapol is best viewed from the road along the north shore, just west of Cornaigmore and 6 miles (9.7 km) from Scarinish. Closer views of waterfowl in the southern half of the loch (where most of the diving duck tend to occur) can be obtained from the Kilmoluag road, to the southwest. Again, a telescope is needed.

3 THE REEF (OS REF: NM 00/45)

This area comprises the low-lying central part of the island and is an especially important area for wintering Greenland White-fronted Geese. It is a difficult area to overlook, owing to the flatness of the terrain. The only feasible vantage points are from the summit of Balephetrish Hill, reached by walking up a short track off the B8068, 2.5 miles (4 km) from Scarinish, or from Kenovay on the unclassified road between Balephetrish and Crossapol. Both afford only distant views and a telescope is essential. The B8065 road from Scarinish to Crossapol provides extensive views across the southernmost part of the reef, but the short grasslands here are perhaps the least ornithologically interesting feature of the area. It is possible to view the less cultivated eastern part of the reef either by taking the mile-long (1.6 km) tarmac road from Baugh, 2 miles (3.2 km) west of Scarinish on the B8065, or walking the 0.5-mile (0.8 km) track to the rubbish dump, 1.5 miles (2.4 km) from Scarinish on the B8068. Large groups of Raven are sometimes present at the tip.

Please note that walking onto the reef is not advised—there is no access to croft land and walking elsewhere will only result in the disturbance of nesting or wintering wildfowl.

4 BALEPHETRISH BAY (OS REF: NM 00/47)

View from the roadside at the west end of the bay. This is an excellent area for passage and wintering waders, such as Ringed Plover, Sanderling, Dunlin, Purple Sandpiper and Turnstone. Great Northern Diver, Eider and Long-tailed Duck frequent the bay in winter.

5 SALUM AND VAUL BAYS (OS REF: NM 05/48)

Take the B8069 east towards Caoles, turning off left near the telephone box beyond the Lodge Hotel. Follow this road to the end, 0.75 mile (1.2 km) later. Like Balephetrish Bay, the shoreline here is very good for feeding waders.

6 CEANN A' MHARA (OS REF: NL 93/40)

Approach from a track that leaves the B8065 at the Barrapol corner. It is possible to walk around this cliff peninsula, although the terrain is rugged and there is no obvious path. Several small headlands provide views of breeding seabirds, which include Fulmar, Shag, Kittiwake, Guillemot and Razorbill.

Timing

Tiree has year-round interest for the birdwatcher: breeding wildfowl, waders, seabirds and Corncrake are attractions during spring and summer, large numbers of passage shorebirds can be seen in spring and autumn, while a variety of wildfowl, offshore waterbirds and strong populations of waders make winter an excellent time to visit.

Calendar

Resident: Fulmar, Mute Swan, Greylag Goose (of native origin), Shelduck (except August–November), Wigeon, Teal, Pintail, Shoveler, Tufted Duck, Eider, Red-breasted Merganser, Buzzard, Kestrel, Peregrine, Moorhen, Ringed Plover, Lapwing, Dunlin, Snipe, Curlew, Redshank, Turnstone, Rock Dove, Skylark, Rock Pipit, Stonechat, Raven, Twite, Yellowhammer and Reed Bunting. Corn Bunting, once common on Tiree, is now very scarce.

April–June: Wintering geese depart in late April/early May. Gannet fish in coastal waters in May onwards. Corncrake can be heard at night (and quite frequently during the day) from May until July, with up to 100 calling birds present. Ringed Plover, Sanderling and Dunlin are prominent among spring passage waders. The machair resounds to the song of Skylark, while Sedge Warbler and Reed Bunting have territories in the denser vegetation. Large numbers of White Wagtail usually occur on passage in April.

July: At Ceann a' Mhara, breeding Fulmar, Shag, gulls and auks can be seen. Common, Arctic and Little Tern breed around the coast and are often harried by Arctic Skua in Hynish Bay and Gunna Sound. Great Skua is less common: the deck of the ferry is probably the best place from which to see one.

August–October: Manx and occasional Sooty Shearwaters, Storm and (rarely) Leach's Petrels can be seen offshore and from the ferry. Large numbers of Whooper Swan arrive in late September/early October; a small influx of Mute Swan, presumably from the Outer Hebrides, also occurs. Greenland White-fronted and Barnacle Geese generally start to arrive in mid-October. Passage Brent Geese are occasionally recorded at this time. Return passage waders can be seen in August onwards and may include small numbers of Ruff, Black-tailed Godwit and Whimbrel. In some years, very large flocks of Redwing appear in October, with smaller numbers of Fieldfare.

November–March: Red-throated, Great Northern and occasional Black-throated Divers occur offshore, especially in Gott Bay, Balephetrish Bay and Gunna Sound. A few Little Grebe, around 100 Whooper Swan, c. 1200 White-fronted and c. 1400 Barnacle Geese winter. Large populations of wintering duck include Wigeon, Teal, Mallard, Pochard, Tufted Duck and Goldeneye, with smaller numbers of Red-breasted Merganser, a few Pintail and occasional Gadwall and Shoveler. Merlin and Peregrine are regularly seen in winter. A total of between c. 3500 and c. 5600 shorebirds have been counted around the coast of Tiree in midwinter.

These are dominated by nationally important populations of Ringed Plover, Sanderling and Turnstone, though large numbers of Oyster-catcher, Lapwing, Curlew, Redshank, Dunlin and Purple Sandpiper also occur. Small numbers of Grey Plover and Bar-tailed Godwit usually over-winter. Inland, very large flocks of Lapwing and passage Golden Plover feed in the fields, where Chaffinch and Twite are also numerous. A mas-sive Starling roost at Scarinish sometimes attracts Merlin and Peregrine at dusk. Recent rarities have included American Golden Plover and Broad-billed Sandpiper.

References
Argyll Bird Reports 1980–95 (Argyll Bird Club).
The Birds of Coll and Tiree. Ed. D Stroud (1989).

AB3 ISLE OF MULL
OS Landranger 47, 48 & 49

Habitat
Mull is essentially a mountainous island. The highest of the peaks in the central body of the island, Ben More, is over 950 m. A long, low-lying moorland peninsula—the Ross of Mull—extends into the Atlantic to the southwest. To the north, the island is characterised by fairly gentle, ter-raced moorlands, separated from the rest of Mull by only a narrow nexus of land between Salen Bay and Loch na Keal. Another isthmus connects the smaller, but more rugged, landmass of Laggan. Three large glens divide the island: the steep-sided valleys of Glen More and Glen Forsa in the southern part and the more gently profiled Glen Aros in the north. Loch Ba and Loch Frisa are the only substantial freshwater bod-ies.
    The coastline is heavily indented, with four major west-facing sea lochs: Loch Tuath, Loch na Keal, Loch Scridain and Loch Buie, plus sev-eral more sheltered lochs and inlets elsewhere. Off the west coast lies a plethora of islands, ranging from semi-submerged rocks and skerries to large inhabited islands such as Iona and Ulva. Mull is approximately 25 miles (40 km) from north to south and varies from 3 to about 20 miles in width (4.8 to 32 km).

Access
Caledonian MacBrayne operate car and passenger ferries throughout the year from Oban to Craignure, Lochaline to Fishnish and between Tobermory and Kilchoan (on the Ardnamurchan peninsula). If approaching from the south, it is more convenient to take the ferry from Oban. The 40-minute trip can be good for seabirds, especially during May/June and August–September. It is also possible for foot passengers to disembark at Tobermory on some crossings from Oban to Coll and Tiree. For details of ferry services contact Caledonian MacBrayne, The Ferry Terminal, Gourock PAI9 IQP (tel: 01475 650100).

There are regular bus services operating between Tobermory and Calgary, Tobermory and Craignure, Craignure and Fionnphort. It is possible to hire cars, mopeds and bicycles on the island—details of these and of bus timetables are available from the Oban or Tobermory tourist information centres. There is a wide variety of bird habitats on the island and space only for a few that typify Mull here.

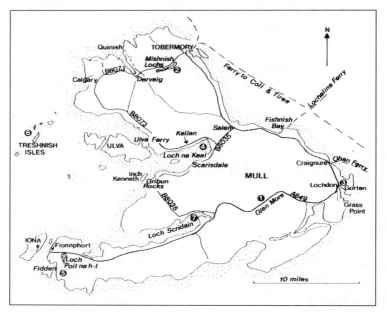

1 GLEN MORE (OS REF: NM 64/32)

Ten miles from Craignure on the A849 towards Fionnphort, Glen More is about 10 miles (16 km) long and rises to c. 200 m. The single-track road through it affords excellent opportunities for observing upland species: Hen Harrier and Short-eared Owl can often be seen hunting over the young plantations; scan the skyline for Buzzard, Golden and White-tailed Eagles, Kestrel and Raven. In the valley floor and on lower hillsides, Curlew, Cuckoo, Whinchat, Stonechat and Wheatear all breed. In winter, Snow Bunting can sometimes beside the road.

2 MISHNISH LOCHS (OS REF: NM 47/52)

Three miles (4.8 km) from Tobermory on the B8073 road towards Dervaig, the Mishnish Lochs are three contiguous lochs stocked with brown trout and popular with anglers. Little Grebe and Grey Heron are present year-round and Red-throated Diver can often be seen April–October. Goosander can sometimes also be seen. Hen Harrier, Buzzard, Golden Eagle and Short-eared Owl all regularly hunt over the surrounding terrain. In winter look for Whooper Swan and Goldeneye. A number of lay-bys on the B8073 afford good views across the lochs.

3 LOCHDON (OS REF: NM 73/32)

Lochdon is a small but complex shallow sea loch 3 miles (4.8 km) south of Craignure on the A849 road to Fionnphort. Rich intertidal silt and mud attract a wealth of passage and wintering waterfowl and waders. Resident birds include Grey Heron, Mute Swan, Eider, Red-breasted Merganser, Hen Harrier, Buzzard and Redshank. Common and Arctic Terns feed in the outer loch during summer, while in winter, Red-throated Diver, Little Grebe and Cormorant are usually seen. Wintering duck numbers build up to a maximum of about 300 Wigeon, 180 Teal and 50 Mallard. A few Goldeneye are generally present. Shelduck return from their moulting grounds in November and the flock usually increases to around 60 birds by March before dispersing to their breeding areas; only a few remain at Lochdon to breed. Passage waders seen annually include small numbers of Grey Plover, Knot, Sanderling, Bar-tailed and Black-tailed Godwits and Whimbrel. Pectoral Sandpiper, Ruff, Spotted Redshank and Green Sandpiper have all been recorded in recent years. Greenshank is regular in late summer/autumn and a few usually overwinter.

The area is best worked on rising or falling tides, ideally about an hour either side of high water. Good views can be obtained from the end of the tarmac road to Gorten, on the north side of the loch; from the main A849 where it runs alongside the inner loch; and from Grass Point, at the end of the road to the south of Lochdon.

4 LOCH NA KEAL (OS REF: NM 50/38)

Three miles (4.8 km) west of Salen on the B8035, Loch na Keal is a large, deep sea loch with varied coastline and several islets and skerries. Shag, Eider, Red-breasted Merganser, Oystercatcher, Curlew and Redshank occur all year. During summer, Common and Arctic Tern frequent Ulva Ferry and Gannet fish in the inner loch. In winter, Loch na Keal is an excellent place for divers, with up to 20 Great Northern, a few Red-throated and the occasional Black-throated regularly present. Common and, very occasionally, Velvet Scoter may be seen, while Razorbill and Black Guillemot are invariably present. Small numbers of Slavonian Grebe winter; peak numbers are usually recorded in April when up to 20 can be present.

The loch can be scanned from both the B8073 Ulva Ferry road and the B8035 around the south shore. Good viewpoints are Kellan, on the northeast shore, Scarisdale on the south and under Gribun Rocks, to the southwest. The last of these overlooks the island of Inch Kenneth and its satellite islets and skerries; this is an area much frequented by Barnacle geese in winter. Otter is relatively easy to observe at Scarisdale and Gribun.

5 FIONNPHORT AND IONA (OS REF: NM 30/23)

Fionnphort is at the end of the A849, some 40 miles (64 km) from Craignure. From here there are frequent ferry crossings to Iona, a mile (1.6 km) across the water. Around Fionnphort there are two main areas of interest:

(a) 1 mile (1.6 km) to the south is Fidden, a diverse mixture of intertidal habitats, coastal farmland and lowland moor. The area is productive for migrant waders and passerines, wintering Greenland White-fronted Goose and occasional raptors.

(b) 1 mile (1.6 km) east of Fionnphort is Loch Poit na h-I, which can be viewed from the main road along the north shore. Little Grebe is present year-round. In winter, White-fronted Goose, Tufted Duck, Pochard and Goldeneye can be seen.

Iona comprises low-lying rocky moorland, fertile hay meadows, sandy bays and exposed sea cliffs. Fulmar, Shag and Kittiwake breed on the southwestern cliffs, and Rock Dove and Jackdaw on many cliffs elsewhere. Linnet, Twite and Yellowhammer are common all year, while Common and Arctic Terns fish in the sound during summer. Iona is the most likely place on Mull to hear a Corncrake (often during the day)— the fields around the abbey and village being the best areas.

6 TRESHNISH ISLES (OS REF: NM 27/41)

An uninhabited, basaltic archipelago between Mull and Tiree. During summer, day trips can be arranged from Ulva Ferry (tel: 01688 400242). Views of the nesting seabirds are best obtained by circumnavigating the islands rather than landing on any particular one. The main island, Lunga, has important breeding populations of Guillemot, Razorbill and Puffin, in addition to more widespread coastal species such as Fulmar, Shag, Kittiwake and other gulls.

Between May and September, Manx Shearwater, Storm Petrel, Gannet and Arctic Skua can be seen on the crossing to the islands. Passage Great and Sooty Shearwaters, Pomarine and Great Skuas are also occasionally sighted. Sealife Surveys, a research organisation operating from Tobermory, offer whale and dolphin watching trips in the waters surrounding the Treshnish Isles, and this is also a useful way to encounter feeding and passage seabirds (tel: 01688 400223 for details).

7 LOCH SCRIDAIN (OS REF: NM 50/27)

This loch is 20 miles (32 km) from Craignure, on the A849 road to Fionnphort. It is best viewed from either the B8035 along the north shore or from various stopping places on the A849 along the south shore. Loch Scridain is similar in dimensions and character to Loch na Keal (see above). The main interest is in winter, when Red-throated, Black-throated and Great Northern Divers can all be seen, the latter being most numerous. Individuals of all three species are occasionally seen in summer. Otter is frequently seen anywhere along the loch shore.

Timing

There is year-round bird interest on Mull. April and May are the optimum months for observing a combination of breeding and migrant bird activity, but late May/July is better for seabirds and August–early October for wader passage. Wintering species, such as Great Northern Diver and various wildfowl, start to build up in October and most linger until at least

April. Midges can be a nuisance from late May until early August. An important consideration when planning an autumn or winter visit is that access to some upland areas may be restricted by stalking activities. Red deer stalking is in progress during September and October—sometimes longer.

Calendar

Resident: Red-throated Diver, Fulmar, Eider, Red-breasted Merganser, Hen Harrier, Sparrowhawk, Buzzard, Golden and White-tailed Eagles, Kestrel, Merlin, Peregrine, Red Grouse, Ptarmigan, Ringed Plover, Snipe, Woodcock, Redshank, Greenshank, Common Gull, Guillemot, Razorbill, Black Guillemot, Rock Dove, Tawny and Short-eared Owls, Great Spotted Woodpecker, Rock Pipit, Grey Wagtail, Dipper, Stonechat, Raven, Siskin, Twite, Redpoll, Crossbill, Yellowhammer.

April–July: Great Northern Diver and Goldeneye often remain in coastal waters until mid-May (the former in superb breeding plumage by this time). Breeders include Manx Shearwater, Golden Plover, Common Sandpiper, Kittiwake, Common and Arctic Terns, Cuckoo, Sand Martin, Tree Pipit, Redstart, Whinchat, Wheatear, Ring Ouzel, Sedge Warbler, Whitethroat and Wood Warbler. Gannet is common offshore from mid-May. Spring passage birds include Pink-footed Goose, Golden Plover, Sanderling, occasional Spotted Redshank and Black-tailed Godwit, Whimbrel, Kittiwake and (in April) White Wagtail.

Whimbrel

August–October: Passage brings Merlin, Golden and Grey Plovers, Knot, Sanderling, Dunlin, Bar-tailed and occasional Black-tailed Godwits, Whimbrel, Redshank and Greenshank. Offshore, Manx and Sooty Shearwaters, Storm and occasional Leach's Petrels, Pomarine, Arctic and Great Skuas, and Kittiwake occur.

November–March: Great Northern is the commonest offshore diver, but small numbers of Black-throated and Red-throated Divers also occur. Other wintering species of interest include Slavonian Grebe, Whooper

Swan, Greenland White-fronted, Greylag and Barnacle Geese, Wigeon, Teal, Pochard, Tufted Duck, Goldeneye, Water Rail, Purple Sandpiper, Turnstone, Iceland and Glaucous Gulls, Fieldfare, Redwing and Snow Bunting. Shelduck numbers build up from late November.

References
Argyll Bird Reports 1980–95 (Argyll Bird Club).
Birds of Mull. M Madders and P Snow. Saker Press (1987).

AB4 ISLE OF ISLAY   OS Landranger 60

Habitat
Islay is a large and varied island 12 miles (19 km) off the Argyll mainland. The most southerly of the Inner Hebrides, it covers about 60,000 ha and measures approximately 25 miles (40 km) from north to south and 20 miles (32 km) east to west. Although lacking the more spectacular mountains of islands such as Mull or Skye, there are quite large areas of upland with several summits in excess of 300 m. Most of these lie in the southeast of the island, where a ridge runs from Port Ellen in the south towards Port Askaig in the east. The northeastern part of Islay is a rugged and remote terrain of summits, small valleys and lochans, bordered by raised beaches and cliffs, while in the west a wide ridge of low moor and farmland, the Rhinns, extends southwestward into the Atlantic.

Two large sea lochs almost separate the Rhinns from the main body of the island: Loch Gruinart to the north and the larger Loch Indaal in the southwest. Of the many magnificent sea cliffs, those of the Oa and Sanaigmore are perhaps the most outstanding. The coastline elsewhere is extremely varied, encompassing rocky and shingle shores, sandy beaches and intertidal mud. Immediately inland from the shore at Ardnave, Killinallan, Laggan Bay and one or two other locations, extensive sand dune systems occur. Loch Gorm is the largest inland waterbody although there are many smaller lochans and areas of marshland. Elsewhere the landscape is characterised by areas of lowland pasture, crofts, peat bog, scrub, coniferous plantation and small deciduous woodlands.

To the birdwatcher, Islay is synonymous with geese and current censuses put the numbers of wintering Barnacle Geese at around 35,000 and Greenland White-fronted Geese at around 15,000. There is much more to Islay than geese however, and the island has important populations of breeding, wintering and migratory species. Over 100 species are present on the island year-round and at least 105 species breed. Recent rarities have included Black Brant, Gyrfalcon and Black-headed Bunting.

Access
Caledonian MacBrayne operate a car and passenger ferry service from Kennacraig, 7 miles (11.3 km) west of Tarbert, to Port Ellen and Port

Askaig on Islay. There are up to three sailings a day, Monday to Saturday, with a single sailing on Sunday. Additional sailings operate during the summer. The trip takes approximately two hours and provides excellent opportunities for seawatching en route.

West Loch Tarbert (see Additional Sites) is very productive for waterfowl (especially divers), gulls and auks in winter, while the waters immediately north of the island of Gigha can hold large numbers of Great Northern Diver from October until April. On Wednesdays, April–October, the ferry departs Kennacraig for Islay, and then continues to Colonsay and Oban, returning via the same route. It is therefore possible to spend several hours ashore on Colonsay before returning to Islay. For details of ferry services, contact Caledonian MacBrayne, The Ferry Terminal, Gourock PA19 1QP (tel: 01475 650100). It is possible to fly to Islay from Glasgow—British Airways Express operates two flights daily from Monday to Friday, with one on Saturday (tel: 01345 222111).

Islay is well endowed with roads, making it possible to view most of the island's bird habitats from a vehicle. This tends to minimise disturbance to the birds and often enables a closer approach (e.g. to feeding geese) than would otherwise be possible. Please be considerate to other road users, and do not obstruct access to gateways or passing places

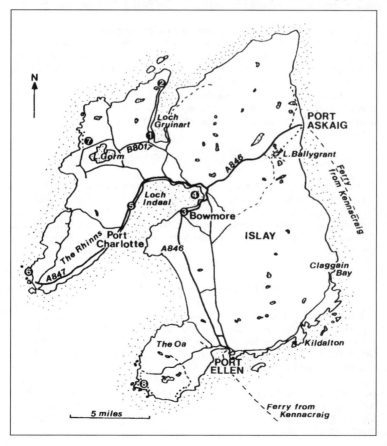

31

when parking. Flocks of feeding Barnacle and White-fronted Geese are readily apparent in roadside fields; areas that can be particularly recommended are Gruinart Flats (see below), the Loch Gorm area, the fields bordering the main A846 Port Askaig–Bridgend road, and beside the lanes south and southeast from Bridgend, as well as the saltmarsh at the head of Loch Indaal.

1 LOCH GRUINART RSPB RESERVE (OS REF: NR 28/67)

This 1667-ha reserve comprises intertidal habitats, saltmarsh, farmland and moorland. It is situated on the south and west sides of Loch Gruinart and can be viewed from the B8017 and the unclassified road that branches north to Ardnave. There is a visitor centre at Aoradh Farm open 10.00 am–5.00 pm seven days a week. Features include panoramic views over the reserve, live closed-circuit television pictures of feeding/nesting birds, displays, videos, information and guided walks. Parking is available at Aoradh Farm. There is also a small hide that overlooks some of the best geese feeding and roosting grounds. This is reached by walking a short distance along the Ardnave road, until the path to the hide is indicated to the right—a second car park is located opposite this path.

Gruinart is particularly important for its wintering Barnacle and Greenland White-fronted Geese. A wide variety of wildfowl and waders breed on the reserve and the area is an excellent place to watch hunting raptors such as Hen Harrier, Golden Eagle, Merlin and Peregrine. Wintering waders are best viewed from the road on the east side of the loch.

Please keep to the public roads during the period when the geese are present. Note also that the reserve is a working farm and that account may need to be taken of farm machinery and animals.

2 ARDNAVE LOCH (OS REF: NR 28/72)

A shallow exposed loch that can be viewed from the end of the minor road north from the Gruinart reserve, on the west side of Loch Gruinart. From October until May it holds a good variety of wildfowl, generally including Mute Swan, Wigeon, Teal, Mallard, Pochard and Tufted Duck. The shoreline of Loch Gruinart, just to the east, is a good place to look for otter.

3 BOWMORE (OS REF: NR 31/6O)

The stone pier at the end of the main street in Bowmore is a good general vantage point for inner Loch Indaal, although the elevated lay-by opposite the hydroelectric generating station 0.5 mile (0.8 km) north of Bowmore is often even better (with room for several cars to park). From October to April a good selection of waterfowl is usually visible, including Red-throated Diver, small numbers of Great Northern Diver and occasional Black-throated Diver, Slavonian Grebe, Scaup (over 1000 sometimes present in midwinter), Eider, occasional Long-tailed Duck, Common Scoter, Goldeneye and Red-breasted Merganser. Dabbling duck and waders occupy the inshore shallows.

The rubbish tip southwest of Bowmore is worth checking for Glaucous and Iceland Gulls, while the shoreline between Raineach Mhor and Gartbreck is a good area for waders on rising and falling tides.

4 HEAD OF LOCH INDAAL (OS REF: NR 32/61)

The extensive intertidal area here is very important for estuarine birds and is one of the principal roost sites for the island's Barnacle Geese. Between November and April Shelduck, Wigeon, Teal, Mallard, Oystercatcher, Ringed Plover, Lapwing, Dunlin, Bar-tailed Godwit, Curlew and Redshank can be seen. Pintail is usually present in the river channel where it opens into the sand flats. Small numbers of Shoveler are usually present, either in the river channel or the freshwater pools at Carnain on the north side of the loch. A visit one hour either side of high tide is best for waders. There are several parking areas around the loch that offer good views. A hide, accessed from a car park 0.5 mile (0.8 km) north of Bridgend on the A847, affords excellent views of the inner loch. This is the best place from which to observe the astonishing spectacle of thousands of Barnacle Geese arriving to roost at dusk. Barn Owl can frequently be seen hunting over the nearby saltmarsh and gorse scrub.

5 BRUICHLADDICH PIER (OS REF: NR 265609)

This is another good vantage point for wintering divers and sea duck (especially Common Scoter which is present year-round: 50–100 in summer and 100–150 in winter) in Loch Indaal. Occurrences of Black-throated Diver have been more frequent here than off Bowmore. The rocks in front of the distillery are one of the best places on Islay for Purple Sandpiper in winter. Also, bottlenose dolphin may be seen in Loch Indaal, and otter frequents the Bruichladdich shoreline.

6 FRENCHMAN'S ROCKS (OS REF: NR 15/53)

The peninsula of Rubha na Faing, opposite these offshore rocks, is the most westerly point on the island and a well-known seawatching location. There can be good passages of seabirds in April–May and August–October, including Manx Shearwater, small numbers of Sooty Shearwater, Fulmar, Gannet, Storm and occasional Leach's Petrels, a few Arctic and Great Skuas, large numbers of Kittiwake and auks, as well as divers and sea duck. Approach the coast from the minor road to Claddach, 0.5 mile (0.8 km) north of Portnahaven. The best time to watch is during the first hour or so after dawn—direct sunlight can be problematical in the evening.

7 SALIGO BAY/SMAULL (RSPB) (OS REF: NR 210663)

A popular coastal walk, with fine views of the Atlantic Ocean to the west and the dramatic cliffs of Cnoc Uamh nam Fear to the north. There is room for the careful parking of a few cars near Saligo Bridge. The area can be productive for passage seabirds, especially from late August to early October. In addition, regular scanning inland is likely to produce views of Buzzard, Golden Eagle, Peregrine, Chough and Raven. Stonechat and Twite are resident, while Whinchat and Wheatear are common in spring and summer. Note that there are no visitor facilities. Further information is available from the RSPB reserve at Loch Gruinart.

8 THE OA (OS REF: NR 26/41)

The sea cliffs at Mull of Oa rise sharply to over 130 m. These are the most impressive cliffs on Islay and a walk from the Mull east towards the even higher (though less vertical) cliffs at Beinn Mhor is a superb experience. If possible, arrange to be picked up at Risabus (NR 315439) and walk the entire cliff-top from Mull of Oa to Imeraval. Allow plenty of time—5–6 hours ideally—to investigate the cliffs and the moors inland. The numerous wild goats are a special feature of these cliffs. Fulmar, Shag, Herring Gull, Guillemot, Razorbill, Black Guillemot and a few Kittiwake breed on the cliffs. Noteworthy species likely to be encountered include Golden Eagle, Peregrine, Chough and Raven. In winter the cliff-tops are a regular haunt of Snow Bunting.

There are many other good birding locations on Islay and this brief list does little justice to such a rich and diverse island. Other places that can be strongly recommended include:

(a) Loch Ballygrant (NR 40/66) for common woodland species and wildfowl.
(b) Port Ellen for gulls and sheltering seafowl.
(c) Claggain Bay (NR 46/53) for Great Northern Divers—present from October until early May.

Timing
One of great attractions of Islay as a birdwatching location is that there is plenty of interest throughout the year, as the island has strong populations of both breeding and wintering birds. For sheer diversity of species, however, September/October and March/April stand out—at these times both breeding and wintering visitors are present and their numbers are further supplemented by passage birds.

Calendar
Resident: Eider, Red-breasted Merganser, Hen Harrier, Buzzard, Golden Eagle, Merlin, Peregrine, Barn Owl, Stonechat, Chough, Raven and Twite.

April–June: Gannet can be seen fishing close inshore during spring. The geese mostly depart in late April, with a few lingering into May; small numbers of passage Brent Goose occur in April/May, Shelduck, Teal, Eider and Red-breasted Merganser all breed. A few Corncrake can be heard at night, though numbers have declined greatly. Spring passage waders include Ringed Plover, Sanderling, Purple Sandpiper, Dunlin and Whimbrel. Common Sandpiper arrives in early April. Breeding seabirds include Fulmar, Shag, Kittiwake, Arctic and a few Common and Little Terns, Guillemot, Razorbill and Black Guillemot. Among passerines that breed are Whinchat, Sedge Warbler, Whitethroat and small numbers of Tree Pipit, Wood Warbler and Spotted Flycatcher. Redpoll, Siskin and (occasionally) Crossbill also breed.

June–July: A moult flock of male Red-breasted Merganser gathers in Loch Indaal and also at Claggain Bay in late June. Common Scoter summers in Loch Indaal. Fledged broods of Short-eared Owl are conspicuous over moorland areas in some years.

August–October: Passage Manx and a few Sooty Shearwaters, Arctic and occasional Great Skuas can be seen from Frenchman's Rocks and from the ferry. The first returning geese usually arrive in mid-September, with the main influx occurring in October. Small numbers of passage Brent and Pink-footed Geese move through. Whooper Swan numbers peak in late October/early November, frequenting stubble fields. Regular passage waders include Ringed and Golden Plovers, Dunlin, Redshank, a few Bar-tailed Godwit and small numbers of Grey Plover, Knot, Sanderling, Black-tailed Godwit and Greenshank. Large thrush movements occur in some years, mostly involving Fieldfare, Redwing and smaller numbers of Blackbird and Song Thrush.

November–March: Great Northern, Red-throated and Black-throated Divers can be seen offshore. Slavonian Grebe, Scaup, Eider, Common Scoter, Goldeneye and Red-breasted Merganser tend to concentrate in Loch Indaal. Whooper Swan is present at several inland waterbodies, especially Loch Gorm, and occasionally around the coast, though most depart by midwinter. Small numbers of Greylag Geese winter, especially near Bridgend, and 1–2 Pink-footed, Snow, Canada and Brent Geese are usually found in the larger flocks of wintering White-fronts and Barnacles. Strong populations of Wigeon, Teal and Tufted Duck winter. Wintering shorebirds such as Oystercatcher, Ringed Plover and Curlew are common, around 200 Bar-tailed Godwit overwinter, and Purple Sandpiper and Turnstone frequent areas of rocky shoreline. Several Glaucous and a few Iceland Gulls are recorded most winters, particularly at Port Ellen and in Loch Indaal. Brambling and Snow Bunting are not uncommon in some years.

Barnacle Geese and Oystercatcher

Note: The Islay Natural History Trust's Wildlife Information Centre, located in the same building as the island's youth hostel, in Port Charlotte, provides up-to-date information on bird sightings, as well as displays and information relating to Islay's natural history. There is an extensive reference library and database of sightings. A laboratory and lecture room may be hired by visiting groups, and educational packages may be arranged on request. Tel: 01496 850288 for opening times.

References

Argyll Bird Reports 1980–95 (Argyll Bird Club).
Birds in Islay. G Booth (1981).
Birds of Islay. R Elliott (1989).
Birds of Islay. M Ogilvie (1992).
Islay Bird and Natural History Report 1988–95. M Ogilvie.

ADDITIONAL SITES

	Site & Grid Reference	Habitat	Main Bird Interest	Peak Season
a	Argyll Forest Park FC OS 56	Vast area of coniferous woods, rugged mountain terrain and some deciduous woodland.	Variety of moorland and woodland species.	All year
		See Argyll Forest Park Guide, available from FC or HMSO bookshops.		
b	Carradale Point SWT Reserve NR 817372 OS 68 or 69	Coastal grassland and low cliffs.	Eider and Red-breasted Merganser.	All year
			Fishing Gannet.	May–Aug
c	Fairy Isles, Loch Sween SWT Reserve NR 766884 Sheet 55	Deciduous woodland, off-shore islands.	Common woodland birds, Grey Heron, Eider, Red-breasted Merganser, gulls and terns.	Apr–Aug
d	Glen Nant NNR NN 020273 OS 50	Oak and open birch woodland with adjacent mature coniferous plantations.	Woodland bird community including Great Spotted Woodpecker, Tree Pipit and Redstart.	Apr–Jul
e	Inverliever Forest FC NM 94/10 OS 55	Artificial lagoon in British Steel works.	Breeding Common Tern and Black-headed Gull.	Jun–Jul
		Mature coniferous forest and oak woodland, open hill ground.	Buzzard, Sparrowhawk, Jay and Crossbill, Hen Harrier and Golden Eagle seen on moors.	All year
f	Knapdale FC NR 82/90 OS 55	Coniferous woodland, hill lochans and open moor.	Buzzard, Sparrowhawk, Hen Harrier and Golden Eagle, Crossbill and Siskin.	All year
g	Ledaig Point NM 902349 OS 49	Peninsula with sand and shingle foreshore.	Passage waders and a few seabirds.	Apr–Jun Aug–Oct
			Inshore Red-throated Diver, terns and Black Guillemot.	Apr–Aug
			Great Northern Diver, Slavonian Grebe and Black Guillemot, Stonechat and Twite.	Oct–Mar
h	Loch Craignish NM 79/01 OS 55	Wide sea loch with many islands; view from B8002 Ardfern road.	Wintering divers and wildfowl.	Oct–Mar

Site & Grid Reference	Habitat	Main Bird Interest	Peak Season
i Loch Feochan NM 84/23 OS 49	Enclosed sea loch with varied foreshore; large intertidal zone at head of loch.	Breeding gulls and terns. Passage and wintering wildfowl and waders.	May–Aug Aug–May
j Loch Gilp NR 85/86 OS 55	Extensive intertidal mud.	Passage and wintering wildfowl and waders.	Aug–Jun
k Machrihanish Seabird Observatory NR 628209 OS 68	Seawatching hide overlooking Machrihanish Bay.	Passage seabirds, including regular rarities.	Spring, autumn
l Oban Harbour NM 85/29 OS 49	Fish quay and sheltered bay.	Mute Swan, Eider, Black Guillemot. White-winged gulls.	All year Oct–Apr
m Taynish NNR NR 73/84 OS 55	Oak woodland, heath, bog and foreshore. Park at reserve entrance just south of Tayvallich.	Typical suite of oak woodland birds including Great Spotted Woodpecker, Redstart and Spotted Flycatcher.	May–Jul
n Ulva Lagoons NR 71/82 OS 55	Small but complex area of tidal basins and pools.	Modest waterfowl numbers including Whooper Swan.	Oct–Mar
o West Loch Tarbert NR 81/62 OS 62	Long, sheltered sea loch with varied shoreline.	Wintering divers, grebes and sea-duck. Dabbling duck frequent head of loch.	Oct–May

Further reading: *Birds of Mid-Argyll*. M Madders, P Snow & J Welstead (1992).

AYRSHIRE & CLYDE

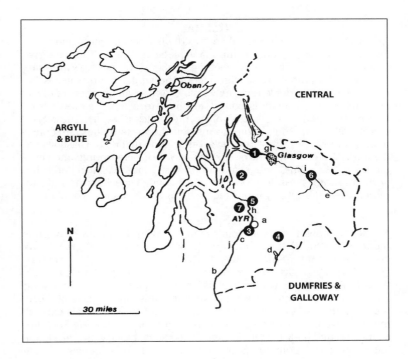

Main sites

AC1 Clyde Estuary
AC2 Lochwinnoch
AC3 Doonfoot
AC4 New Cumnock/Knockshinnock
    Lagoons
AC5 Bogside
AC6 Barons Haugh
AC7 Troon and Barassie

Additional sites

a Ayr Gorge
b Ballantrae
c Culzean Castle and Country Park
d Dalmellington Moss
e Falls of Clyde
f Hunterston
g Possil Marsh
h Shewalton Sandpits
i Strathclyde Country Park
j Turnberry Point

Please note that for convenience, this section includes some sites along the north shore of the Clyde estuary which are located within the administrative area of Argyll and Bute.

AC1 CLYDE ESTUARY OS Landranger 63 & 64

Habitat

Although blighted by industrial and residential development, the Clyde Estuary is an exceptionally important place for birds. The extensive intertidal areas provide rich feeding grounds for passage/wintering waders and wildfowl, while throughout the winter open water is frequented by diving duck, roosting wildfowl and small numbers of divers and grebes. The estuary is considered here to extend seawards from Erskine to Inverkip, a distance of over 18 miles (29 km). The M8/A8 closely follows the south shore, connecting the western dockyard conurbations of Gourock and Greenock with the heartlands of Glasgow. On the north shore, the A92/A814 links the towns of Helensburgh and Dumbarton with Erskine Bridge and northwest Glasgow. In general, the northern shore is less developed than the south, especially around Ardmore, where the estuary is backed by fields and scattered woodland.

Species

Neither wildfowl nor wader totals compare with the numbers of birds recorded on the Firth of Forth or the Solway Firth, yet average peak counts in recent years have exceeded 4000 wildfowl and 13,000 waders. Several diving ducks achieve nationally significant wintering populations. Eider dominate wildfowl totals for the estuary throughout the year; numbers peak in autumn, when over 4000 birds can be present. Maximum numbers of Goldeneye occur in late winter, when totals exceeding 800 have been recorded. Moderate numbers of wintering Pochard, Scaup and Red-breasted Merganser are also seen, along with a few Long-tailed Duck and Common Scoter. Shelduck numbers increase during winter to a maximum of over 500 in February. Up to 100 Mute Swan occur. Dabbling duck include over 300 Wigeon and Mallard, with very small numbers of Pintail.

Other birds using the estuary in winter include small numbers of Red-throated Diver and Slavonian Grebe and up to 80 Great Crested Grebe.

Arctic Terns—adult and juvenile, late summer

Around 200–300 Cormorant and a few Shag can be seen. Gannet occurs regularly in the outer estuary and as far as Ardmore and Loch Long in summer. Wintering waders include over 3000 Oystercatcher, 5000+ Lapwing (peak in November), over 1000 Redshank, moderately large numbers of Dunlin and Curlew (c. 700), with smaller numbers of Ringed Plover and Turnstone. Small numbers of Grey Plover, Knot, Black-tailed Godwit, Spotted Redshank and Greenshank are recorded each winter. Passage waders include Golden Plover, Bar-tailed Godwit, Whimbrel, Greenshank and Ruff.

The estuary also has very large numbers of wintering Black-headed Gull, substantial flocks of Common Gull and smaller numbers of Herring Gull. Small numbers of Common, Arctic and Sandwich Tern occur in July/August, and Black Guillemot may be seen throughout the year.

Access

The vastness of the area and the lack of suitable access points tend to limit the birdwatching potential of the Clyde. The following vantage points can be recommended.

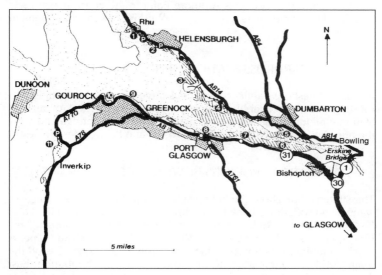

1 RHU (OS REF: NS 27/84)

Two small bays with outflow burns east and west of Rhu Marina attract large numbers of feeding/roosting waders. Moderate tides are best— visit one hour either side of high water. Oystercatcher, Dunlin and Redshank can be seen in the bays; Purple Sandpiper and Turnstone frequent the rocky islet near the marina. Offshore, Eider and a few Goldeneye occur. Black-headed and Herring Gulls feed, bathe and loaf near the outflows.

The area is accessible from the A814 west of Helensburgh. The best vantage points are from the small car park east of the sailing club or from the marina visitors' car park. Please note that there is no vehicular access to the point west of Rhu.

2 HELENSBURGH (OS REF: NS 29/82)

The large seafront car park gives a good overview of the outer estuary. The *Captyanis*, a sugar ship which sank here, has become the venue for a large Cormorant colony. Gannet and Manx Shearwater can be seen off the seafront and up to Ardmore.

3 ARDMORE POINT (OS REF: NS 319786)

This rocky promontory north side of the firth makes an ideal vantage point for wildfowl and waders on the. There are extensive foreshore areas both north and south of the point, attracting large numbers of waders and dabbling duck. In addition, the coastal bramble and gorse scrub here attract Whinchat, Linnet and Yellowhammer. Access the area by taking a minor road along the coast off the A814 Dumbarton–Helensburgh road, 1.5 miles (2.4 km) west of Cardross. A footpath around the edge of the peninsula cuts across the narrow nexus of farm and woodland that connects Ardmore Point to the coast, making a 2-mile (3.2 km) circuit. Passage geese and Whooper Swan can be seen in the area.

4 CARDROSS STATION (OS REF: NS 345773)

Excellent foreshore habitat that attracts large numbers of feeding and roosting waders, and dabbling duck. Turn south off the A814 to Cardross Station, parking in the station car park. Cross the footbridge and view the burn outflow and intertidal areas. Rising and falling tides are best.

5 DUMBARTON ROCK TO BOWLING (OS REF: NS 43/74)

This stretch of foreshore (including Milton Island) holds a good range of waders and waterfowl. Look for Mallard, Wigeon, Teal, Black-tailed and Bar-tailed Godwits, Redshank, Curlew, Curlew Sandpiper, Dunlin, Grey Plover, Greenshank, Red-breasted Merganser, Kingfisher and Snipe. A Terek Sandpiper was observed here in October 1996. Access is off the main A814 at Dumbarton Rock Bowling Green, Dumbarton East Sewage/Gas Works and at Bowling. For views of Milton Island, park at the Little Chef, Milton, walk west on the cycle track and turn left under the railway bridge.

6 WEST FERRY (OS REF: NS 40/73)

This is the most useful of the south-shore access points, giving extensive views of the inner estuary. Leave the M8 westbound from Glasgow at junction 31, the Bishopton exit. Follow the roundabout to a parking space at West Ferry.

7 WOODHALL (OS REF: NS 35/74)

Another good vantage point for the south shore. Exit the A8 at the round-about 5 miles (8 km) east of Port Glasgow.

8 NEWARK CASTLE (OS REF: NS 328746)

A good viewpoint for the middle reaches of the Clyde—large numbers of Eider can usually be seen offshore. Turn off the A8 at the roundabout in Port Glasgow and continue for 0.25 mile (0.4 km) to a car park.

9 WEST GREENOCK (OS REF: NS 26/77)

The esplanade offers ample parking and birdwatching opportunities.

10 GOUROCK BAY (OS REF: NS 24/77)

Reached by taking a no-through road off the A770 Greenock–Gourock road. Limited parking is available at the road end.

11 LUNDERSTON BAY (OS REF: NS 20/74)

The foreshore car park at the north of the bay, part of the Clyde Muir-sheil Country Park, affords excellent views of the outer Firth. A path leads south to the marina at Inverkip.

Timing

Large numbers of birds can be found between October and March. In late summer, small numbers of plunge-diving Gannet at the estuary mouth and fishing terns further upstream can be seen. Passage waders are best looked for in May and again from August until October. Because of the volume of traffic using the roads that surround the estuary, weekday rush-hour periods are best avoided.

AC2 LOCHWINNOCH

OS ref: NS 359581
OS Landranger 63

Habitat

The RSPB's Lochwinnoch Reserve lies approximately 18 miles (29 km) southwest of Glasgow. The A760 Largs–Paisley road divides the reserve into two: the northern part, Aird Meadow, comprises an area of shallow open water and wetland, with willow scrub and some mature woodland; the southern part contains a much more extensive and open water body—Barr Loch. The reserve covers a total of 158 ha plus the shooting rights over another 78 ha of adjoining land. Of great importance for both breeding and wintering wildfowl, it forms part of the Castle Semple and Barr Loch SSSI.

Access

The reserve and nature centre lie off the A760 Largs–Paisley road, 0.5 mile (0.8 km) east of Lochwinnoch village. Access to the reserve is possible daily from 09.00 am to 9.00 pm (or sunset, if earlier) while the opening hours of the nature centre are 09.00 am to 5.00 pm daily. The centre includes an observation tower, which affords comprehensive views of Aird Meadow and the surrounding farmland. There is a modest charge to non-members of the RSPB. Car parking is free. Refreshments are available and there is a gift shop.

The Aird Meadow nature trails lead to three hides which overlook marsh and open-water habitats. The trail and hide west of the meadow have been designed with wheelchair users in mind. Access to a hide overlooking Barr Loch is from a lay-by on the Kilbirnie/Largs road, then by walking along the disused railway line (now resurfaced as a cycle path). Please note that this hide is no longer kept locked, as was once the case.

Lochwinnoch Lochside Station, on the main Glasgow–Ayr railway line, is directly opposite the nature centre. There is an hourly service to and from Glasgow, Monday–Saturday, and a limited Sunday service in summer. There are two buses per hour in each direction between Glasgow and Largs that pass the nature centre, Monday–Saturday. A regular, but reduced, service operates on Sundays throughout the year.

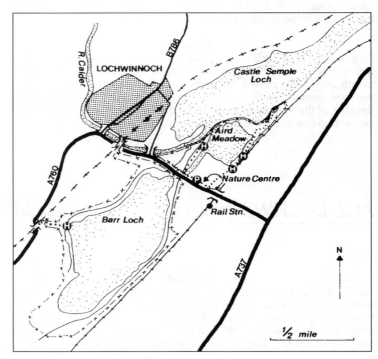

Species

Of the 173 species recorded on the reserve, 66 have bred in recent years. Lochwinnoch is one of the principal Scottish strongholds of Great Crested Grebe, with up to 11 pairs breeding annually. Little Grebe also breeds, as do Teal, Shoveler, Pochard and Tufted Duck. Ruddy Duck bred successfully in 1987, the first breeding record for western Scotland, but the birds are currently absent again. Floating nest rafts have been anchored within view of the hides, enabling breeders such as Great Crested Grebe and Black-headed Gull to be seen. The emergent vegetation surrounding Aird Meadow provides nesting cover for a variety of waterfowl, as well as for a few pairs of visiting Grasshopper Warbler and the commoner Sedge and Willow Warblers. Sparrowhawk, Kestrel and, occasionally, Peregrine hunt over the reserve. Otter is sometimes seen in Aird Meadow.

Timing

There is lively activity for much of the year at Lochwinnoch—visit from April to June for breeders and October to March for wintering wildfowl. Midsummer is probably the least interesting time ornithologically, but botanically the reserve looks superb!

Calendar

March–May: Breeding warblers should have all arrived by late April; wintering wildfowl have dispersed by early May. At any time in April–early June migrant waders may pass through the valley, though there is seldom enough exposed mud on the reserve to attract them. Great Crested Grebe can be seen displaying, while wildfowl and gulls start to nest.

June–July: The breeding season continues; ducks enter eclipse plumage and return wader passage commences in July. Migrant terns occasionally appear.

August–November: Waders such as Whimbrel, Spotted Redshank, Greenshank and Ruff may pause to feed if there is sufficient exposed mud (see comment for March–May). Redwing and Fieldfare pass through in October, often feeding on the hawthorn and rowan next to the nature centre. Wildfowl numbers increase during October, dominated by Mallard but also including moderate numbers of Wigeon, Teal and Tufted Duck, with smaller numbers of Pochard and some Shoveler.

December–February: Moderate numbers of Whooper Swan, Goldeneye and Goosander are generally present throughout the winter; Greylag Geese usually peak at just over 500 individuals. Duck numbers decline slightly from their autumn peak as they disperse to wintering haunts. Colder weather may encourage further immigration into the reserve, providing the waters stay ice-free.

RSPB Site Manager

Lochwinnoch Nature Centre, Largs Road, Lochwinnoch, Renfrewshire (tel: 01505 842663).

Habitat

Doonfoot is located at the mouth of the River Doon, on the southern edge of Ayr. The raised beach here is fringed by a line of sand dunes and there is a short section of low cliff at Greenan. The foreshore includes extensive areas of sand, with small rocky outcrops and mussel beds. Grass fields and marsh border the site to the north of the estuary at Cunning Park. The coastal strip west of the Doon estuary is a designated SSSI.

Timing and Species

The area is primarily of interest in August–May, when up to 1000 duck, 2000 waders and 10,000 gulls can be present. Visits are best timed for two hours before high water or from one hour after, i.e. a rising or falling tide. Calm sea conditions are helpful for looking at the offshore duck. The most numerous wintering duck are Goldeneye (up to 400), which can be seen in November–March. Among gulls, several Glaucous and Iceland are usually seen in late winter, and rarities such as Mediterranean and Ring-billed occasionally occur, with January–March the best period. Waders such as Whimbrel and Sanderling frequent the foreshore on passage in May, and again in July–September. Large numbers (250+) of Snipe and a few Jack Snipe can be found at Cunning Park in December–March.

Access

Doonfoot is accessible at all times and can be reached from Ayr by taking the A719 south, turning right after crossing Doonfoot Bridge onto the road to the shore on the south side of the river. There are three car parks along the south shore.

References

Birds of Ayrshire. A Hogg (1983).
Ayrshire Bird Reports 1976–91. Ed. A Hogg.

Habitat

Situated near the town of New Cumnock, this wetland area has become extremely important for breeding waders and holds many other wetland species, notably Water Rail. Knockshinnock lagoons, owned by the SWT, are the product of land subsidence caused by former coalmining activities in the area. While many of the lagoons have become overgrown in recent years, there are plans to restore the more open areas which formerly attracted many passage waders and wildfowl. To the northwest lie the headwaters of the River Nith and a complex of lochs (Loch o' th' Lowes, Creoch Loch and Black Loch), all of which hold numbers of wildfowl, particularly on passage. The remaining heather moorland and pools nearer to New Cumnock are also worth visiting.

Timing and Species

This site is principally of interest from April to October, although a winter visit can produce Whooper Swan, Hen Harrier and Short-eared Owl. During spring, waders and wildfowl such as Pink-footed Goose, Pintail and Black-tailed Godwit, returning north from the Solway, often pause at the Loch o' th' Lowes. The lagoons are also worth searching for passage species, with a May visit likely to provide displaying Snipe and Redshank in addition to the few pairs of breeding Shoveler. Large numbers of Sedge and Grasshopper Warblers breed here and you are constantly aware of the presence of Water Rail, which become increasingly visible as the season progresses. Uncommon visitors in recent years have included Garganey, Marsh Harrier and Spotted Crake.

Late August to mid-October can be just as exciting, with a build-up of wildfowl (often including the spectacle of migrating Pink-footed and Barnacle Geese in October) and waders, especially Snipe. Less common, but nevertheless regular, are Green Sandpiper, Wood Sandpiper and Ruff in August. The proposed creation of additional open pools may prompt return appearances from Little Stint, Curlew Sandpiper and Spotted Redshank. Rarities at this season have included White-rumped Sandpiper and Wilson's Phalarope.

Access

There is a car park off the B741 New Cumnock–Dalmellington road and an access point and path from Church Lane, New Cumnock (NS 776113).

References

Birds of Ayrshire. A Hogg (1983).
Ayrshire Bird Reports 1976–95. Ed. A Hogg & A Stevenson.

AC5 BOGSIDE FLATS

OS ref: NS 310385
OS Landranger 70

Habitat

Bogside Flats is an area of extensive saltmarsh, lying at the confluence of the rivers Garnock and Irvine. It is bounded to the east by Bogside racecourse (still used occasionally for local meets) and to the west by an ICI industrial complex. In addition to the large area of intertidal mud and saltmarsh pool complex of the Garnock estuary mouth, the area includes a large central area of brackish marsh. Most of the site is privately owned and enjoys limited protection because of its proximity to the ICI explosives facility.

Species and Timing

The site is important primarily as a passage wader feeding area and an increasingly significant wintering wildfowl resort. Wader passage is best observed in autumn—from August to late October large gatherings of Lapwing and Golden Plover occur, numbers of the latter sometimes exceeding 3500. In addition, large flocks of Redshank, Curlew and Dunlin can be present, often accompanied by small parties of Black-tailed Godwit, Ruff, Grey Plover, Curlew Sandpiper and Little Stint. Duck numbers increase as autumn progresses, with Wigeon and Teal regularly peaking at around 700, but start to decline from late February. Mallard is also common and a small numbers of Whooper Swan are usually present. The concentration of such a large number of birds in this relatively small area inevitably attracts wintering predators such as Peregrine, Merlin, Sparrowhawk and Short-eared Owl. A short walk to the mouth of the estuary provides views of the large wintering flocks of Goldeneye and Eider. Rarer visitors are possible—this was the location for Britain's first record of Barrow's Goldeneye, in 1979. Nearby, Irvine Beach Park has a pool which regularly holds Scaup and Tufted Duck during winter, affording the opportunity to study the differences between the females and immatures of these two species.

Access

Bogside is most conveniently reached from Irvine Railway Station or from the town centre in Irvine New Town. Follow the signs marked 'Harbourside' or 'Magnum Sports Centre' to the west. Upon reaching the harbour, the large expanse of mudflat and saltmarsh lies across the River Irvine due north of the harbour car parks. Best viewing times are from approximately two hours before high tide and an hour after high tide. A telescope is advisable. A clear, calm day provides the best viewing conditions, though it is usually possible to find shelter in windy conditions.

The information on Bogside was kindly supplied by Angus Hogg.

References
Ayrshire Bird Reports 1976–91. Ed. A Hogg.
Ayrshire Coastal Survey. SWT.
Birds of Ayrshire. A Hogg (1983).

Habitat

Barons Haugh lies in the Clyde Valley, 1 mile (1.6 km) south of the centre of Motherwell. Despite its proximity to such an industrial area, Barons Haugh is an excellent birdwatching site. The RSPB owns and manages a total of 107 ha of marsh, woodland, scrub, meadows and parkland alongside the River Clyde. Four hides overlook the haugh, two of which are suitable for disabled visitors. In addition there is a one-hour trail around the reserve. People needing access for wheelchairs should contact the warden.

Access

Motherwell can be reached from the M74 by exiting at junction 6 onto the A723 (east) and following signs to the town centre, or from the M8,

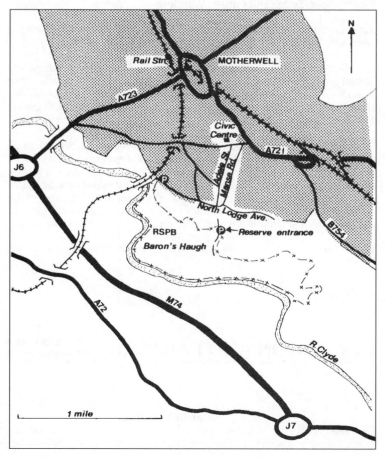

also at junction 6 (south). Once in Motherwell, head for the Civic Centre and take the road opposite (Adele Street). After 0.5 mile (0.8 km), this leads to North Lodge Avenue and the reserve entrance. The nearest railway station is 1.5 miles (2.4 km) to the north, on the Glasgow Central–Edinburgh line.

Timing

The reserve is open at all times. There is year-round bird interest, although midsummer is perhaps the least exciting time to visit. A winter visit is strongly recommended.

Species and Calendar

Resident: Little Grebe, Grey Heron, Mute Swan, Teal, Mallard, Shoveler, Tufted Duck, Water Rail, Moorhen, Coot, Redshank, Grey Wagtail, Kingfisher, Reed Bunting. Willow Tit can also be found here; Baron's Haugh is at the northernmost limit of its range in Britain.

March–May: Breeding visitors arrive, commencing with the Sand Martins which nest in the riverbanks, then Common Sandpiper, Whinchat, Grasshopper, Sedge and Garden Warblers.

June: Ducklings are much in evidence: most adult ducks enter eclipse plumage. Ruddy Duck has been present in recent years.

July–October: Careful control of water levels in muddy areas of the haugh provide optimum conditions for passage waders; 22 species have been recorded, including Ruff, Black-tailed Godwit, Spotted Redshank, Green and Wood Sandpipers and up to 1000 Lapwing. Wintering wildfowl start to increase.

November–February: Wildfowl provide the main interest, with over 50 Whooper Swan sometimes present, as well as numbers of duck such as Wigeon, Teal, Shoveler, Pochard, Tufted Duck and Goldeneye. A feature of the haugh in winter are the upwellings of tepid water around Marsh hide. The water here therefore remains open even when the rest of the haugh freezes over, and concentrations of waterfowl can occur close to the hide. Such situations are also ideal for glimpsing the shy Water Rail.

Further details are available from Lochwinnoch RSPB reserve (tel: 01505 842663).

AC7 TROON AND BARASSIE

OS ref: NS 320314
OS Landranger 70

Habitat

This site is best split into three parts: the Ballast Bank car park and harbour, Barassie Beach and Stinking Rocks. All three have their attractions, with the first having developed as a popular seawatching point. A sandy bay adjacent a convenient car park permits good views of waders and gulls at Barassie Beach. Similar habitat at Stinking Rocks can also be excellent for both sea duck and waders. This site earned its name due to the proximity of several sewage pipes—fortunately now a feature of the past.

Timing and Species

Seawatching off Troon, like at Turnberry Point to the south, is best between late July and October. Thousands of Manx Shearwaters can gather offshore. A strong west or northwest gale in September may provide close views of both Storm and Leach's Petrels, with Mediterranean Shearwater and Sabine's Gull distinct possibilities. All four skuas have been recorded offshore, along with Little Auk in winter. Troon Harbour is also worth a look for Glaucous and Iceland Gulls in winter. Several pairs of Black Guillemot breed here.

Barassie Beach and Stinking Rocks are better for waders and gulls, the latter often reaching five figures in late autumn. Both spring and autumn passage are excellent at Barassie, with visits best timed two hours before and just after high tide. Waders are concentrated into a high-tide roost which is usually viewable from the car park at Barassie Beach. The Stinking Rocks are best two hours before and two hours after high tide, as waders desert the area at high tide itself. Mid-May can provide good numbers of Ringed Plover and Sanderling, with the chance of something less common, like Curlew Sandpiper. August–September are best for numbers and variety, with unusual visitors like Dotterel, White-rumped Sandpiper and Buff-breasted Sandpiper in recent years.

Gulls are worth searching during the August to March, with Mediterranean and Ring-billed Gulls possible. Offshore, it is always worth scanning the wintering sea duck: large numbers of Eider supplemented by Goldeneye and Scaup, with occasional Red-necked and Slavonian Grebes among them.

Access

The Ballast Bank car park is accessed from the road to Troon Marina: leave Troon town centre northwest and turn left just before Troon harbour entrance. Barassie Beach car park can be reached by turning off the A759 in Troon, towards the swimming pool and going right into the car park which lies on the foreshore and is bordered by large clumps of sea buckthorn. Stinking Rocks lie about 1.5 miles to the north, with parking in a housing estate and a short walk to the beach.

References

Birds of Ayrshire. A Hogg (1983).
Ayrshire Bird Reports 1976–95. Ed. A Hogg & A Stevenson.

ADDITIONAL SITES

Site & Grid Reference	Habitat	Main Bird Interest	Peak Season
a Ayr Gorge SWT Reserve NS 457249 OS 70	Oak and birch woodland; steep ravine.	Common woodland birds, Dipper and Grey Wagtail.	All year
b Ballantrae NX 080820 OS 76	Shingle bar and raised beach enclosing saltmarsh, mudflats and brackish lagoons.	Eider, Red-breasted Merganser, Guillemot, Razorbill, Black Guillemot offshore.	All year
		Passage seabirds.	Apr–Sep
		Great Northern, Red-throated and Black-throated Divers.	Autumn Jan–Apr
c Culzean Castle & Country Park NTS NS 234103 OS 70	Shoreline, park, woodlands, streams and ponds.	Woodland birds including Blackcap and Garden Warbler.	May–Jul
		Winter shorebirds and offshore divers/sea-duck.	Nov–Mar
	Visitor Centre and ranger service.		
d Dalmellington Moss SWT Reserve NS 460060 OS 70	Extensive wet moss and willow scrub.	Water Rail and Willow Tit. Sedge, Grasshopper, Garden Warblers. Fieldfare, Redwing and Brambling. Whooper Swan.	All year May–Jun Oct–Nov Jan–Feb
e Falls of Clyde SWT Reserve NS 88242 OS 71	Mixed woodland, gorge and waterfalls.	Common woodland birds, including Willow Tit, Dipper and Grey Wagtail.	All year
	Visitor centre and ranger service.		
f Hunterston NS 20/53 OS 63	Extensive sand and mudflats, now partially reclaimed.	Wildfowl, including up to 200 Shelduck and 300 Wigeon.	Jan–Mar
g Possil Marsh SWT Reserve NS 585700 OS 64	Shallow loch, marsh and surrounding scrub.	Breeding waterfowl, passage wildfowl, waders and passerines	All year
h Shewalton Sand-pits SWT Reserve NS 327371 OS 70	Pools and lagoons, dune grassland, scrub and riverbank.	Passage waders and wintering wildfowl.	Aug–Oct Oct–Mar

Site & Grid Reference	Habitat	Main Bird Interest	Peak Season
i Strathclyde Country Park NS 72/57 OS 64	Loch and nature reserve with trails and visitor centre.	Wintering wildfowl including Wigeon, Mallard, Pochard, Tufted Duck, Goldeneye, Goosander and regular Smew.	Oct–Mar
j Turnberry Point NS 19/07 OS 70	Peninsula at north end of open bay; sandy foreshore with rock outcrop.	Eider and Red-breasted Merganser.	Aug–Sep
		Passage seabirds.	Aug–Oct
		Late winter divers.	Mar–Apr

BORDERS & LOTHIANS

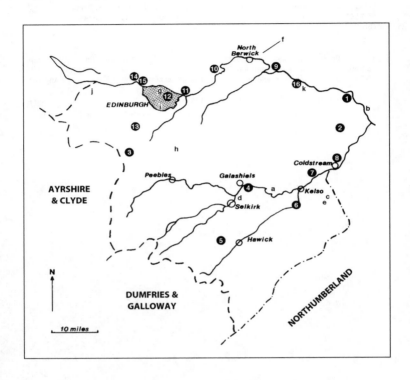

Main sites

BL1 St Abbs Head
BL2 Duns Castle
BL3 West Water Reservoir
BL4 Gunknowe Loch and Park
BL5 Alemoor Reservoir
BL6 River Teviot Haughlands
BL7 River Tweed, between Kelso and
     Coldstream
BL8 The Hirsel
BL9 Tyninghame/John Muir Country
     Park
BL10 Aberlady Bay
BL11 Musselburgh
BL12 Duddingston Loch
BL13 Threipmuir Reservoir
BL14 Hound Point
BL15 Dalmeny
BL16 Barns Ness

Additional sites

a Bemersyde Moss
b Burnmouth
c Hoselaw Loch
d Lindean Reservoir
e Yetholm Loch
f Bass Rock
g Botanic Gardens Edinburgh
h Gladhouse Reservoir
i Hermitage of Braid
j Linlithgow Loch
k Skateraw

Habitat

St Abbs Head is a rocky headland situated some 13 miles (21 km) north of Berwick-upon-Tweed. The sheer cliffs, up to 100 m high, plunge dramatically into the North Sea and provide nest sites for around 60,000 seabirds. Inland of the cliffs, the habitat is largely grazed grassland with a man-made freshwater loch and trees/scrub in a sheltered valley. The NTS and the SWT jointly manage 81 ha of the cliffs and inland habitats, which are a designated NNR.

Species

Around 350 pairs of Fulmar and 320 pairs of Shag nest on the cliffs; both species can be seen virtually all year. The cliffs also hold an impressive total of around 16,000 pairs of Kittiwake, 26,000 Guillemot, 1500 Razorbill and 20 or so pairs of Puffin. Herring Gull, Rock Pipit, Wheatear and Raven also breed.

Shags—breeding plumage

The trees and scrub surrounding Mire Loch attract migrant passerines such as the commoner chats, flycatchers and warblers, as well as the occasional rarity. Spectacular numbers of passage thrushes are sometimes witnessed, while the area is probably the most reliable in Scotland for passage Firecrest.

Offshore, passage seabirds can be seen in April/May and especially in September/October (see Calendar). Small numbers of wildfowl occupy the loch in winter, including up to 30 Goldeneye and a few Wigeon. Divers, particularly Red-throated, can be seen at sea. Good waterfowl passage is often a feature of seawatches.

Quail are annual visitors to the roadside fields north of Coldingham.

Access

Turn off the A1 onto the A1107 at either Burnmouth (from the south) or Cockburnspath (north) and continue until Coldingham is reached.

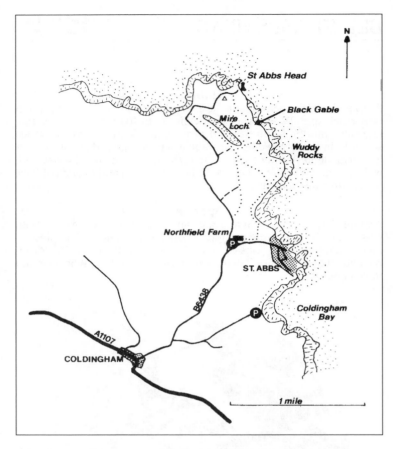

Here, take the B6438 to St Abbs. There is free parking at Northfield Farm Steading, as well as a visitor centre and coffee shop. A path leads east for 300 m, then north around the cliffs towards the lighthouse. It is possible to return inland to the visitor centre via footpaths, making a 3-mile (4.8 km) circuit. There are many good vantage points along the cliff-top; the best seawatching point is from Black Gable, the lowest point on the cliffs between Kirk and Lighthouse Hills and level with the dam end of Mire Loch. The trees near the dam may hold migrant passerines. South of St Abbs, the scrub at Coldingham Bay is well worth checking in spring and autumn—rarities such as Pallas's Warbler and Olive-backed Pipit have been found here in recent years. Buses to Coldingham run from Berwick and Edinburgh.

Timing

The reserve is an interesting location at any time of year. For nesting seabirds, visit between April and July. Migrants are most likely in April/May and again from August to October—easterly winds combined with poor visibility provide the ideal conditions for passerines, north to east winds for sea passage. Winter wildfowl and coastal seafowl should be present from October through to March/April.

Calendar

Resident: Little Grebe, Fulmar, Gannet, Shag, Mute Swan, Tufted Duck, Yellowhammer and Linnet.

March–May: Seabirds arrive back at nest sites. Migrants include Wheatear, Whinchat, Redstart and common warblers. Turtle Dove, Wryneck, Black Redstart, Bluethroat and Red-backed Shrike are annual while Night Heron, King Eider, Hoopoe, Water Pipit, Rose-coloured Starling, Golden Oriole, Great Reed, Subalpine, Marmora's and Dartford Warblers, Red-breasted Flycatcher and Rustic Bunting have been recorded.

June–July: Nesting seabirds, breeding Wheatear, common warblers (including Lesser Whitethroat). Shearwater passage starts.

August–November: Frequent Manx Shearwater, Great and Arctic Skuas, Common Scoter and divers, with smaller numbers of Sooty Shearwater, Little Gull, Black Tern and Pomarine Skua. Cory's, Balearic and Great Shearwaters, Long-tailed Skua and Mediterranean Gull have also been recorded. Return passage of passerines usually includes excellent, sometimes spectacular, numbers of Goldcrest, common warblers, thrushes, Redstart and flycatchers. Water Rail, Siberian Chiffchaff, Yellow-browed and Reed Warblers, Red-breasted Flycatcher, Firecrest, Wryneck and Red-backed Shrike are annual, while rarities include Honey Buzzard, Richard's Pipit, Greenish, Pallas's, Dusky, Radde's, Aquatic and Icterine Warblers, Siberian Stonechat and Little Bunting.

December–February: Wigeon and Goldeneye on Mire Loch; Scaup, Long-tailed Duck and Smew are occasional. Red-throated and occasional Great Northern and Black-throated Divers, Eider and small numbers of Common Scoter can be seen offshore. Sparrowhawk, Kestrel, Merlin and Peregrine are frequently seen hunting over the reserve.

Warden

Ranger's Cottage, Northfield, St Abbs, Berwickshire TD14 5QF (tel: 01890 771443).

References

Borders Bird Report 1985, pp. 53–7. Ed. R Murray.
The Seabirds of Berwickshire. SRD da Prato and ES da Prato. *Scottish Birds*, vol. 11 (1980).

BL2 DUNS CASTLE

OS ref: NT 778544
OS Landranger 67/74

Habitat

Both the shallow loch of Hen Poo and nearby Mill Dam (sometimes known as Oxendean Pond) were created in the 18th century, as part of the landscaping works undertaken on the Duns Castle estate. The SWT currently manages 77 ha of the estate, including the two lochs and the surrounding mixed-policy woodland.

Access
The reserve is well signposted from the main square in Duns, which is some 15 miles (24 km) west of Berwick-upon-Tweed on the A6105. Several tracks and rides lead through the estate and there is a bird hide on the west bank of Hen Poo. Access from the north is off the B6365, 0.6 mile (1 km) before it joins the A6112. There is a car park, but the entrance is difficult to spot.

Species
Emergent vegetation around the loch fringe provides nesting cover for Mute Swan and Mallard, but the loch is more important as a wintering site than for breeding. Overwintering duck include Pochard and Goosander. In the woods, Great Spotted and Green Woodpecker, Jay, Redstart, Lesser Whitethroat, Garden Warbler, Blackcap and Chiffchaff all breed. Five species of tit have been recorded, including Marsh Tit. Pied Flycatcher have been encouraged to breed by the provision of nest boxes.

Timing
The grounds are open all year but the area is best visited during either the spring, when the woodland breeding species are of interest, or in winter for wildfowl on the lochs.

BL3 WEST WATER RESERVOIR

OS ref: NT 117525
OS Landranger 72/65

Habitat
West Water Reservoir lies 320 m above sea level in the Pentland Hills, 2 miles (3.2 km) west from West Linton. The site is very exposed and is surrounded by wet peatland, marsh grassland, rough pasture and heathland, principally used for sheep grazing and as grouse moor. Variations in the level of water in the reservoir can produce extensive areas of exposed mud in autumn, with smaller areas of sand and shingle.

The reservoir covers 51 ha, including a main island and two others exposed at low water levels. It is a designated SSSI, being of regional significance for breeding wildfowl, gulls and waders, as well as an important location for wintering wildfowl.

Species
Since the reservoir was formed in the 1960s, 120 species have been recorded. Several pairs of Mallard, Teal (up to ten broods) and Tufted

Duck breed and these can be seen throughout the year at the reservoir. Mallard and Teal usually number about 300 each in late autumn/early winter, while peak counts of Tufted Duck can exceed 50 in early winter.

Up to five pairs of Ringed Plover, ten or so pairs of Lapwing, five pairs of Dunlin and small numbers of Snipe nest along the shoreline and in adjoining areas, together with Curlew and Redshank (10+ pairs each) and at least six pairs of Common Sandpiper. Grey Heron, Kestrel, Red Grouse, Black-headed, Common and Great Black-backed Gulls can be seen all year. Dipper frequents the reservoir outflow.

Wader passage can be very good in the autumn, if there is sufficient exposed mud: Oystercatcher, Ringed Plover and Knot are frequent, while Little Stint, Dunlin, Ruff, Greenshank, Green Sandpiper and Turnstone may occur in small numbers, but are not recorded annually. The best areas of mud for these are in the southwestern bay. Up to 20,000 Common Gull roost at the reservoir in spring and autumn.

West Water is a major Pink-footed Goose roost site and birds are present from mid-September until early May; 10,000 are regularly recorded, with peak counts in recent years of over 25,000. Up to 100 Greylag Geese can occur and small flocks of Barnacle Geese have been recorded on passage and in winter. White-fronted, Brent and Snow Geese have also been reported. Ten or so Goldeneye and a maximum of 20 Goosander are present in winter.

Timing

The area is worth a visit at any time of year. We do not advise a dawn or dusk visit to see roosting geese: this would involve a relatively long walk in the darkness and could well result in disturbance to the roost. Resting geese can generally be seen on a daytime visit in September–October, or again in April. We must stress, however, that regardless of the time of day, any geese present must on no account be disturbed.

Access

West Linton is situated on the A702, 15 miles (24 km) from Edinburgh. Turn off towards Baddinsgill at the south end of the bridge over Lyne Water and park at the entrance to West Linton Golf Course, 0.5 mile (0.8 km) later. From here, walk along the road which crosses the golf course for 1 mile (1.6 km) to the waterkeeper's cottage, then on to the reservoir. There is a regular bus service from Edinburgh.

Access to the dam is restricted and visitors are not encouraged to walk around the reservoir. It is advisable to contact the waterkeeper before proceeding to the reservoir. The hillside adjacent to either end of the dam is probably the best vantage point. Care must be taken not to disturb geese at dawn and dusk—do not stand above the skyline on the hillside or go near to the shoreline. The geese roost right up to the dam, so extra caution is needed if approaching at dawn. This is currently one of the least disturbed goose roosts in the area, with only a limited amount of fishing and shooting activity. Please therefore take into account any access notices that may be erected. The site is managed by East of Scotland Water (tel: 0131 445 4141), and is open in daylight hours.

References

Based upon information kindly supplied by AW Brown.

BL4 GUNKNOWE LOCH AND PARK

OS ref: NT 52351
OS Landranger 73

Habitat
This area is situated beside the River Tweed near Galashiels and is at the junction of four river systems: the upper and lower Tweed Valley, the Gala Water Valley and the Ellwyn Water Valley. It is a housing and industrial development area, but retains a large area of parkland, scrub, developing and established woodland, and riverbank. The dismantled railway now carries part of the Southern Upland Way. The parkland is managed by the Borders Council

Species
Gunknowe Loch attracts a small wintering flock of Mute Swan, plus occasional Whoopers. Passage Wigeon, Mallard, Tufted Duck, Pochard and Goldeneye occur.

The area holds a variety of woodland species, including Great Spotted and Green Woodpeckers, Wood Warbler, Blackcap, Marsh Tit, Redpoll and Siskin. Sand Martin breeds, Sedge and Grasshopper Warblers can be found in scrubland areas, while Whinchat and Wheatear occur on passage. Grey (and occasionally Yellow) Wagtail frequents the riversides, and Dipper and sometimes Kingfisher can be seen. The River Tweed holds Little Grebe, Goosander and Moorhen.

Large nocturnal movements can occur in spring and autumn, principally of waders, geese and thrushes, the birds presumably using the valley systems for navigation. In winter, Redwing, Fieldfare and Brambling may be seen.

Access
Access to the area is possible from the main A6091 road, 2 miles (3.2 km) from Galashiels. There is a car park at Gunknowe Loch. Several paths and tracks lead into the area.

Timing
The area is worth a brief visit at any time of year, though spring and autumn are likely to be the most productive times.

BL5 ALEMOOR RESERVOIR

OS ref: NT 397148
OS Landranger 79

Habitat
This upland reservoir lies at c. 300 m altitude, some 8 miles (13 km) west of Hawick. It covers just under 6 ha and is divided by the B711, with a

60

narrow channel linking the two halves. The East Loch is surrounded by conifers, which eventually open out onto moorland, while the West Loch is only partially enclosed by conifers and includes an area of scrub and heather, again giving way to open moorland. The site is owned by the Water and Drainage Department of The Borders Council.

Species

Great Crested Grebe, Mute Swan, Teal, Mallard, Tufted Duck and Coot have bred at Alemoor. Both Whooper Swan and Goldeneye have lingered late or oversummered in recent years. The reservoir is an important assembly site for the Ettrick Forest Wigeon breeding population, which assembles here in April with most dispersing to neighbouring lochs to breed soon afterwards. From late June fledged broods arrive to augment the males and failed breeders, and up to 50 can be seen in summer.

The surrounding coniferous plantations hold Short-eared Owl, Siskin and Crossbill, while Redstart and Grasshopper Warbler have bred in recent years.

Common Sandpiper

In winter, dabbling duck numbers vary according to water level; the peak count of Teal is 230, but other species are much less numerous. The East Loch is generally better for diving duck, including Tufted Duck, Pochard, Goldeneye and Goosander. Whooper Swan is a regular visitor.

Passage waders are recorded in only small numbers, but have included Golden Plover, Knot, Sanderling, Little Stint, Curlew Sandpiper, Ruff, Spotted Redshank, Greenshank, Green and Wood Sandpipers, and Turnstone.

Timing

Wintering wildfowl provide the main interest and a visit between October and March is recommended. Passage waders occur during spring and late summer/autumn.

Access

The reservoir can be reached by taking the A7 from Hawick towards Carlisle, turning right after c. 2 miles (3.2 km) onto the B711 to Roberton. Park and view the lochs from the road 2.5 miles (4 km) beyond the village. The West Loch is generally the most productive for birds.

References
Borders Bird Report 1982, pp. 32–4. Ed. R Murray.

BL6 RIVER TEVIOT
HAUGHLANDS

OS ref: NT 675255–709275
OS Landranger 74

Habitat and Access
This area comprises arable and pastureland bordering the River Teviot between Nisbet Village and Kalemouth, northeast of Jedburgh. Most of the area can be seen from the A698 Jedburgh–Kelso road and the B6400 Crailing–Nisbet road. The period October to April is the best time to visit.

Species
The haughlands are productive for Mute, Whooper (up to 250 have been recorded) and occasionally Bewick's Swans in winter. Pink-footed and Greylag Geese are also numerous, with a total of up to 1500 present on occasion, while Barnacle Geese are sometimes seen. Wintering duck include up to 700 Mallard (usually in severe winters), 150 Goldeneye and lesser numbers of Wigeon, Tufted Duck and Goosander.

The area is a good place in which to observe the spring migration of Oystercatcher, while movements of Lapwing, Golden Plover, thrushes and finches can be conspicuous in spring and autumn.

Breeders include Mute Swan, Mallard, Goosander, Ringed Plover, large numbers of Sand Martin and several pairs of Yellow Wagtail.

BL7 RIVER TWEED,
BETWEEN KELSO
AND COLDSTREAM

OS ref:
NT 724343–849401
OS Landranger 74

Habitat and Access
An area with similar characteristics to the Teviot Haughlands, the interest again being wintering wildfowl and passage birds. There are several good vantage points along the two roads that traverse the area—the A698 Kelso to Coldstream road on the north bank of the Tweed and the B6350 Kelso to Cornhill road on the south bank. A circular tour can be devised using these roads, taking in the Hirsel (B8) at the same time. Birgham Haugh (NT 790380), viewed from the south side, is a good site

for a variety of species representative of the area. Access to the north bank of the river at NT 795391 is from Birgham village—walk west and rejoin the main road via the anglers' footpath west of Birgham.

Species
As many as 350 Whooper Swan and up to 50 Mute Swan winter in the Wark/Coldstream area. Goose numbers usually reach about 2000 (maximum 4000), mostly composed of Greylag, but with some Pink-footed. The river and adjacent haughland are used by dabbling duck such as Teal, up to 250 Wigeon and 1400 Mallard. The peak counts are generally during cold winters. Tufted Duck, up to 300 Goldeneye and 150 Goosander have been recorded. This is one of the few sites in the Borders that receive regular visits from Smew. Miscellaneous wintering species include inland-feeding Cormorant and small numbers of Golden Plover, Lapwing and Redshank.

Breeders include those species listed for the Teviot Haughlands with Yellow Wagtail a particular speciality of Birgham/Springhall Haughs, where there is a population of 5–10 pairs, including breeding birds of the *flava* form. The riverside and adjacent fields at Birgham are the best area; Ringed Plover and Sand Martin also breed here, while passage waders such as Greenshank, Ruff and Green Sandpiper are a possibility in July/August.

BL8 THE HIRSEL

OS ref: NT 827403
OS Landranger 74

Habitat
The Hirsel is a 1214-ha private estate located 1 mile (1.6 km) north and east of Coldstream. It is of outstanding importance for both waterfowl and woodland species. The main attraction is Hirsel Lake, a shallow freshwater loch (depth averaging less than 1.5 m) that occupies about 17 ha, fringed by reeds along its north shore and wooded to the south. The lake was created from a damp hollow in 1786 and with the exception of Yetholm and Hoselaw Lochs in the Cheviots, Hirsel Lake is the largest inland, lowland open waterbody in the Borders.

The adjacent policy woodlands at Dundock Wood were planted in the late 18th century and comprise mostly oak, ash and pine, with a dense understorey of azalea and rhododendron which provides excellent warbler habitat. Selective thinning and replanting have formed a mixed and structured woodland, with good canopy, understorey and shrub layers. The strips of woodland south of the lake probably date from the later 19th century. Leet Water, a small tributary of the Tweed, meanders through wet pastureland to the east, bordered by more deciduous woodland.

Despite its man-made origins, the variety of high-quality habitats at the Hirsel mean that it supports one of the highest breeding bird diversities in southeast Scotland. The lake is of regional, if not national, importance for passage and wintering wildfowl (especially Whooper Swan, Mallard, Shoveler and Goosander). The area is a designated SSSI.

Species

Nearly 150 species have been recorded at the Hirsel. Mallard and Coot are the dominant species on the lake, while Little Grebe, Grey Heron, Mute Swan, Canada Goose, Shoveler, Tufted Duck, Pochard and Moorhen have all bred in recent years; Ruddy Duck is usually present in summer. Sedge Warbler and Reed Bunting nest in the reedbeds.

Because of the proximity of the River Tweed, many waterfowl use Hirsel Lake as a roost, especially if the river is in spate or disturbed by anglers. Peak counts are usually recorded in late autumn and early winter. Waders are scarce due to the absence of extensive mud around the edges of the lake. Water Rail is present throughout the year and may possibly breed, but is more numerous in winter.

Dundock Wood holds breeding Great Spotted Woodpecker, Redstart, Garden Warbler, Blackcap, Pied and Spotted Flycatchers, together with two species which have become something of a speciality at the Hirsel: Marsh Tit and Hawfinch. The Leet has breeding Common Sandpiper, Grey Wagtail, Dipper and Kingfisher. Goosander, Sand Martin and passage Yellow Wagtails occur. Grassland areas along the Leet are used by hunting raptors. The adjacent mixed woodland with many over-mature

Great Spotted Woodpecker

trees is ideal passerine habitat; Green Woodpecker and Jay can be seen here, Pied Flycatcher breeds and Nuthatch has been recorded (bred in 1989). The fruit trees that grow between the stable block and the house are especially attractive to Hawfinch. Swifts annually occupy nest boxes sited below the windows of the mansion.

Access

The main entrance to the Hirsel is signposted off the A698 Kelso–Coldstream road at the southeast Lodge (NT 837934), on the outskirts of Coldstream. There is a car park near a stable block (NT 827401), which is now a visitor centre, c. 1 mile (1.6 km) from the road. From here, signed paths lead around the estate. Route leaflets and bird lists are available. A second car park is situated on the A697 Coldstream–Edinburgh road, next to Dundock Wood (NT 820395). Several paths are

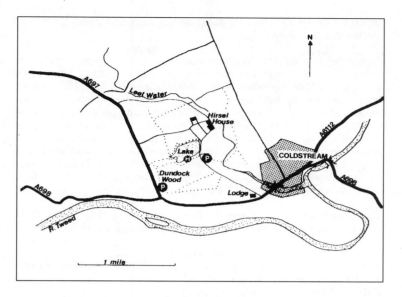

open to the public and provide good views of most of the best bird areas. It is possible to walk around the lake (0.75 mile or 1.2 km), although the height of the reeds reduces visibility around much of the shore. A recently constructed hide, the result of work by the Borders SOC branch, has overcome this problem to an extent and the dam shore also provides some good vantage points. Another path (1.25 miles or 2 km) leads between the main house and the old stable block to Leet Water. This crosses the River Leet and heads south, re-crossing the river and returning back the visitor centre car park. There is a bus service connecting Coldstream with Kelso, Berwick-upon-Tweed and Edinburgh.

Timing

Bird interest at the Hirsel is sustained throughout the year. Both the lake and the woods have considerable populations of breeding species and a spring or early summer visit is therefore very rewarding. Waterfowl numbers increase after the end of the breeding season as passage birds move through, and large numbers use the lake as a roost during autumn and winter. Access is possible virtually all year, except at Christmas and New Year.

Calendar

April–June: Breeding bird activity on the lake and in the woods dominates the interest. Mid-June is the best time for Shoveler and Pochard ducklings. Dundock Wood is very colourful at this time due to the flowering rhododendron and azaleas.

July: Duck enter eclipse plumage. Midsummer is perhaps the least exciting time to visit.

August–October: Waterfowl numbers start to increase; Mallard and Coot are the most numerous species, but peak counts have included 165 Mute Swan, 400 Wigeon and 300 Goosander. Shoveler numbers usually reach c. 100 by October. Passage Green and Wood Sandpipers have been recorded along the Leet

November–December: Large numbers of Whooper Swan (maximum count 120) sometimes join the overwintering waterfowl. Up to 1000 Greylag and 400 Pink-footed Geese, 4000 Mallard, 150 Teal, 100+ Wigeon and c. 90 Shoveler have been recorded. Diving ducks, especially Goldeneye, tend not to increase until late winter/early spring: counts of 100 Pochard and 350 Goosander have been made. Coot numbers have exceeded 300 on occasion, but have declined greatly in recent years. Scaup, Smew and Pintail are seen annually, while Slavonian and Black-necked Grebes, Canada Goose, Mandarin, Gadwall, Red-crested Pochard and American Wigeon have occurred. March is the best month in which to see Marsh Tit and Hawfinch.

For further information contact: The Estate Office, The Hirsel, Coldstream TD12 4LF (tel: 01890 882834), or visit the information centre.

References
Birdwatching at the Hirsel. R Murray. *Scottish Bird News* (December 1987).
Borders Bird Report 1986, pp. 54–6. Ed. R Murray.
Birds of the Borders. RD Murray (1986).

BL9 TYNINGHAME/JOHN MUIR COUNTRY PARK
OS ref: NT 64/78
OS Landranger 67

Habitat
Tyninghame, or the John Muir Country Park, lies west of Dunbar in East Lothian. The 704-ha park is dominated by the estuary of the River Tyne, with its extensive intertidal mudflats and saltmarsh habitats. Sandy substrates underlie the northern part of the estuary, which is bounded by the rocky headland of St Baldred's Cradle. Southeast of the river mouth the sand shores are backed by the dunes of Spike Island with the rocky shoreline of Dunbar further east. A long narrow spit, Sandy Hirst, extends into the Tyne estuary from the north shore. An extensive plantation of Scots pine is located to the north of the Linkfield car park. The area is otherwise vegetated by grassland and scrub. The park has been accorded SSSI status in recognition of its biological and geological importance.

Species
Over 225 species have been recorded in the Tyninghame area, reflecting the rich diversity of habitat here. Small numbers of Eider, Shelduck and Ringed Plover attempt to nest in the dunes and along the shoreline, but breeding success for all these species is low. Over 200 pairs of Kitti-

wake nest on the cliffs at Dunbar Harbour. The Tyninghame Estate woodlands hold breeding Green and Great Spotted Woodpeckers and the commoner species of tit, warbler and finch. Hawfinch may possibly breed.

It is the large numbers of passage and wintering birds, however, that make this area so important. Up to 250 Mallard roost on the sea at the mouth of the Tyne in winter, with over 600 Wigeon and around 70 Teal frequenting the estuary. Shelduck numbers usually peak at well over 100 in March. Up to 100 Common and a few Velvet Scoters winter offshore and small numbers of Eider are invariably present. Goldeneye regularly feed at the mouth of Biel Water and a total of over 50 use the area in midwinter. Long-tailed Duck and Red-breasted Merganser are often present; in late summer a moult flock of around 80 Goosander are usually present. Between 20 and 30 Mute Swan can be seen year-round in the fields adjacent to the embankment at the west end of the estuary and in winter these are joined by up to 25 Whooper Swan and the occasional Bewick's Swan. Up to 500 Greylag and small flocks of Pink-footed Geese feed in these fields in winter and occasionally roost on the mudflats at night, but shooting disturbance probably prevents larger goose roosts from forming. Wintering waders include over 700 Oystercatcher, a minimum 40 Ringed and 100 Grey Plovers, 250 Lapwing (late winter), 500–1000 Dunlin, over 80 Bar-tailed Godwit, c. 200 Curlew and c. 300 Redshank. Two or three Greenshank usually linger through the winter. Turnstone and Purple Sandpiper frequent the rocky shoreline below the cliffs at Dunbar and between 700 and 1000 Knot occur on the rocks around St Baldred's Cradle or at the mouth of Biel Water. Small flocks of Golden Plover occasionally occur on the golf course at Winterfield. Birds of prey that regularly visit the estuary include Sparrowhawk, Merlin and Peregrine; Hen Harrier and Short-eared Owl are less regular.

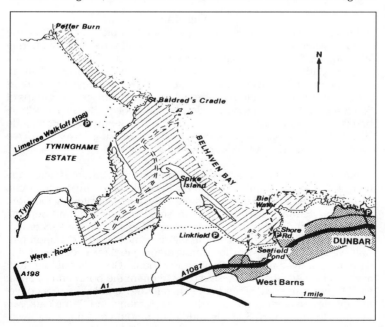

Small numbers of Shore Lark are likely throughout winter, especially on the Spike Island saltmarsh. Snow Bunting and Twite also occur; Lapland Bunting is occasional. A returning Water Pipit has been a feature in recent winters.

Access

The country park is reached by turning off the A1 onto the A1087 1 mile (1.6 km) west of Dunbar. Turn left 0.25 mile (0.4 km) later and follow this minor road to the Linkfield car park. Alternatively, continue on the A1087 through West Barns and into Dunbar, turning left to Shore Road car park. A coastal path links the two car parks and there are information boards giving details about the park. It is also feasible to continue west from the Linkfield car park along the south side of the estuary towards Ware Road. Parking at the west end of Ware road, just off the A198, is not recommended. There are regular bus and train services to Dunbar. Tyninghame Estate, to the northwest, is privately owned and access is possible only along certain paths. Park at Tyninghame Links car park at the end of Limetree Walk (off the A198, 1 mile (1.6 km) north of the bridge over the River Tyne). See map for details.

Timing

The park is open at all times and can be interesting at any time of year. The prime time for bird activity, however, is from September through to May. An ebbing or flowing tide is best for watching waders—the inner estuary and Spike Island areas in particular are best visited two hours either side of high water. The high-tide roosts are rather variable and depend to a large extent on the degree of human disturbance—the main ones are at the north and south ends of Spike Island ('spring' tides) and during neap tides, on the north side of the inner estuary.

Calendar

April–July: Some 400–500 Eider are present either offshore or within the estuary, while around 140 Shelduck can usually be seen. Wintering Wigeon and Teal have mostly dispersed by mid-April, but passage duck such as Gadwall, Shoveler, Pintail or even Garganey may put in an appearance at the river mouth or Seafield Pond. Large numbers of Ringed Plover and Dunlin pass through, together with smaller groups of Sanderling (May), Common Sandpiper and Spotted Redshank. Whimbrel is occasionally seen in April–early June. Passerine migrants include White Wagtail, Wheatear, Whinchat, Redstart and Ring Ouzel, with Tree Pipit, Siskin and Crossbill occurring in the woods.

August–October: Large numbers of Gannet occur offshore in late summer, with passage Manx Shearwater, Kittiwake and Great and Arctic Skuas also present. St Baldred's Cradle is the best seawatching location. Brent and Barnacle Geese occur in small numbers during September/October and a few passage Pintail and Shoveler are also recorded. Goosander is sometimes present in the river mouth. Less common passage waders regularly recorded during autumn include Greenshank, Little Stint, Curlew Sandpiper, Spotted Redshank, Green Sandpiper, Ruff and Black-tailed Godwit. These mostly frequent the north end of Spike Island until disturbed, when they generally move onto the less conveniently viewed northern saltmarsh. Snow Bunting and Shore Lark can often be found around Spike Island in late autumn and linger into winter. Short-eared Owl can sometimes be seen hunting over the dunes, both in autumn and winter. Several hundred gulls gather in late autumn to feed, bathe and roost at the mouths of Peffer Burn and Biel Water. Little Gull and Black Tern are occasional visitors to the estuary. Around 100 Shag and 25 Cormorant fish the outer estuary and can be seen loafing on the rocks at the mouth of the Tyne.

November–March: Wintering wildfowl and waders provide the main interest. Shelduck numbers reach a peak of over 100 in late February/early March. Offshore, modest numbers of Red-throated Diver and occasional Black-throated and Great Northern Divers occur. Recent rarities have included Brunnich's Guillemot and Kentish Plover.

Adjacent Site

SEAFIELD POND (OS REF: NT 659784)

This old clay pit between West Barns and Dunbar has been flooded to form a freshwater pond. Willow, alder and hawthorn have been established around its edge, providing nesting habitat for Willow and Sedge Warblers and Reed Bunting. The site is easily accessible from the Shore Road car park (see above). Mute Swan, Mallard, Coot and Moorhen are resident, while Little Grebe, Pochard and Tufted Duck are present throughout the winter. Regular winter visitors include Whooper Swan, Pink-footed Goose, Shoveler, Scaup, Long-tailed Duck, Goosander and Kingfisher. Dipper frequents nearby Biel Water in winter.

References

Birdwatching Sites in the Lothians. Ed. IJ Andrews (Lothian Branch of SOC).
John Muir Country Park, East Lothian. Fact sheet by R Anderson.
Lothian Bird Reports 1987–90. Ed. IJ Andrews/O McGarry. SOC.

BL10 ABERLADY BAY
OS ref: NT 64/81
OS Landranger 66

Habitat

Aberlady Bay lies on the south shore of the Firth of Forth, some 16 miles (26 km) east of the centre of Edinburgh. Extensive intertidal mud- and sand flats provide rich feeding for wildfowl and waders, while a diverse mixture of saltmarsh, sand dunes, grasslands, open fresh water, scrub and mixed woodland habitat support a wide range of migrant and breeding species. Aberlady is a LNR, covering 582 ha (only 119 ha lie above the high-water mark, however), managed by East Lothian District Council, although most of the land is in fact privately owned. The area is a SSSI and is notable not only for birds but also for its outcrops of limestone and sandstone, and for its examples of dune and saltmarsh succession.

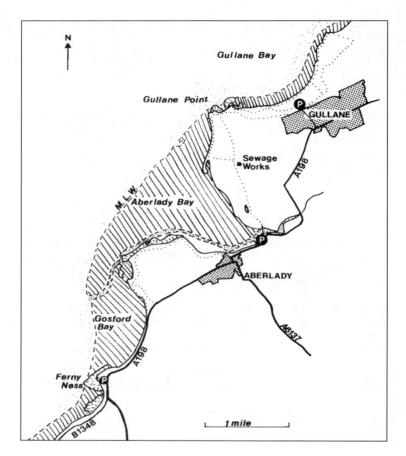

Access

Aberlady Bay is reached via the A198 Musselburgh–North Berwick road and can be viewed from the roadside immediately east of Aberlady village. There is a car park 0.5 mile (0.8 km) beyond the village. From here a track crosses the footbridge and heads north to Gullane Point, with a left branch, just beyond the sewage works, which goes to the coast. The point is an excellent place for seawatching. Please keep to the main paths, especially during the breeding season. Access to the saltmarsh is tolerated except from April to June. Dogs must be kept on a lead and are not permitted between April and July. Other locations to try are as follows.

GOSFORD BAY (OS REF: NT 44/78)

This can be viewed from the B1348, east of Port Seton, and the A198, which it joins immediately before Ferny Ness. There is a parking space at Ferny Ness, which makes a good vantage point. A footpath leaves the A198 at the north end of Gosford Bay and follows the headland into Aberlady Bay. The key to the hide midway along this path is available from the Aberlady warden. This is probably the best site in Britain for grebes. In August, up to 50 adult Red-necked Grebes in full summer plumage are regular (double figures are guaranteed!). In winter, up to 160 Slavonian Grebe can be present. Surf Scoter was a feature of March–April every year between 1983 and 1990 inclusive.

GULLANE BAY (OS REF: NT 47/83)

Gullane Bay lies immediately northeast of Aberlady Bay LNR and can be viewed from Gullane Point (see Aberlady access details) or approached more directly from a large car park north of Gullane itself, reached by turning left off the A198 along Sandy Loan. There are buses from Edinburgh to Aberlady car park and Gullane. The nearest train stations are 3 miles (4.8 km) away at Longniddry and Drem.

Timing

The area is interesting throughout the year, although from September to March is probably the optimum time to visit for birds. The area is best viewed from the A198 at low tide, but the saltmarsh on the east side of the bay is better at high tide. Strong sunlight can be a problem on afternoon high tides. Relatively calm sea conditions are essential for viewing seafowl; a north/northeasterly wind is best for seabirds such as skuas and Little Auk.

Species

Around 250 species have been recorded at Aberlady, reflecting both the importance of the site and the high level of coverage given to the area by birdwatchers. Breeders include Little Grebe, c. 40 pairs of Shelduck, at least 200 pairs of Eider, as well as Partridge, Moorhen, Coot, over 30 pairs of Ringed Plover, Lapwing, Snipe and Redshank. Common breeding passerines include Skylark, Meadow Pipit, Dunnock, Sedge and Willow Warblers and Reed Bunting. Around five pairs of Lesser Whitethroat and a few pairs of Garden Warbler, Blackcap and Spotted Flycatcher oversummer.

Sparrowhawk and Kestrel are seen regularly throughout the year; Merlin, Peregrine and Short-eared Owl are chiefly seen in autumn and winter. Long-eared Owl sometimes breed and are joined by winter visitors. Summering birds include Knot, Sanderling, up to 150 Lesser Black-backed Gull and (especially in late summer) large numbers of Sandwich Tern. Guillemot and Razorbill can be seen offshore year-round, but Black Guillemot and Puffin are uncommon summer visitors. Fulmar and Gannet can be seen throughout much of the year, but are commonest in April–September; small numbers of Manx Shearwater are recorded March–October. Common and Velvet Scoters can be seen year-round, although the latter is much scarcer than the former. Populations of both peak in spring and autumn. Surf Scoter is almost annual in its occurrence on this coast.

Common passage and wintering waders include Oystercatcher, Ringed, Golden and Grey Plovers, Knot, Sanderling, Snipe, Bar-tailed Godwit, Curlew, Redshank and Common Sandpiper. Migrant waders recorded less frequently are Little Stint, Curlew Sandpiper, Ruff, Black-tailed Godwit, Whimbrel, Spotted Redshank, Greenshank, and Green and Wood Sandpipers. Rare waders recorded in recent years have included Avo-

Shelducks

cet, Little Ringed, Kentish, Caspian and Greater Sand Plovers, American Golden Plover, White-rumped, Sharp-tailed and Broad-billed Sandpipers, and Wilson's Phalarope. Passage Herring Gull and Kittiwake occur in great numbers during spring and autumn.

Red-throated Diver is common offshore in winter, while Black-throated and Great Northern Divers are seen occasionally. Great Crested, Red-necked and Slavonian Grebes are common passage and winter visitors, but Black-necked Grebe is rare. A flock of Whooper Swan, usually less than 40-strong but on occasion comprising over 100, roosts on the reserve from November until March, sometimes joined by a few Bewick's Swan, although in recent winters these have tended to roost inland. Large numbers of Pink-footed Geese overwinter and small parties of Greylag Geese occur, especially in severe weather and on spring passage. Canada and Barnacle Geese are rare in winter but are seen regularly on passage, especially in September/October. Brent Geese are seen occasionally on passage or may linger in winter. Moderate numbers of dabbling duck overwinter. Gadwall is very occasionally seen; Pintail and Shoveler are scarce visitors in spring and autumn. Visiting diving duck include occasional Pochard and Tufted Duck, Scaup and Goosander. About 100 Long-tailed Duck usually winter, with smaller numbers of Goldeneye. Black-headed, Common and Great Black-backed Gulls winter in large numbers, and Glaucous Gull is seen annually. Water Rail, Jack Snipe and occasionally Greenshank also winter.

Calendar

March–May: Red-necked Grebe is usually present in Gullane Bay during April/May. Small numbers of Shoveler may be seen, while Marsh Harrier are almost annual May visitors and Montagu's Harrier has been recorded. Wood Sandpiper is a regular, if scarce, spring migrant. Among various passerine migrants passing through the reserve, Yellow Wagtail is particularly notable—up to nine have been seen around the pools at the edge of the saltmarsh, including individuals of the Blue and Grey-headed races. White Wagtail also occurs.

June–July: Small numbers of Bar-tailed Godwit, Knot and Grey Plover oversummer. A large influx of Sandwich Tern in late summer augments the summer populations of Common, Arctic and Little Terns.

August–November: As many as 150 Red-throated Diver congregate in Gullane Bay from September to April, with small numbers of other divers. Red-necked Grebe assembles off Ferny Ness in late summer/early autumn (a maximum of 68 have been recorded), where up to 154 Slavonian Grebe are present in October–March. Up to 120 Cormorant roost on the sand spit in late summer. Pink-footed Goose numbers peak in October/November—over 17,500 have been recorded at dawn and dusk, when they move between their roost on the mudflats and their feeding areas in the fields around Drem. Numbers of Wigeon, Teal and Mallard increase from September; a moulting flock of Eider at Gullane Bay has reached nearly 7000 in some years, with up to 6000 Common and 600 Velvet Scoters, while a smaller concentration of Red-breasted Merganser occurs in early autumn. Shelduck return from their moulting grounds in November. Large numbers of passage waders move through: Whimbrel, Spotted Redshank, Greenshank, and Green and Wood Sandpipers are regular, and Little Stint and occasional Curlew Sandpiper are also seen. Arctic, Great and, more rarely, Pomarine Skuas harass the gulls and terns offshore. Little Gull and Black Tern are annual in late summer/early autumn. Thrushes, including large flocks of Fieldfare and Redwing and occasional Ring Ouzel, move through in October.

December–February: Wintering species still present; Shelduck numbers peak, with up to 200 present. Purple Sandpiper and Turnstone occupy areas of rocky foreshore. There are usually several Short-eared Owl hunting over the reserve during winter (calm, sunny afternoons are best). Flocks of up to 200 Tree Sparrow, 200 Greenfinch and 1200 Linnet are present on the saltmarsh and nearby stubble, with smaller numbers of Redpoll, Twite, Brambling and Snow Bunting. Shore Lark and up to 70 Lapland Bunting have been recorded in some winters.

References
A Checklist of the Birds of Aberlady Bay Local Nature Reserve. PR Gordon in *Lothian Bird Report 1987*. Ed. IJ Andrews (Lothian branch of the SOC).

SNH Warden
Laundry House, Dalkeith Country Park, Dalkeith, Midlothian EH22 2NA (tel: 0131 654 2466).

Habitat

Musselburgh lies on the eastern outskirts of Edinburgh, at the mouth of the River Esk. The coast here has been subjected to much industrial development, but although not a particularly scenic place Musselburgh is justly famed for its birdlife. In the past, the flooded lagoons on the east bank of the Esk were renowned for attracting migrant waders. However, they have now been filled with ash from nearby Cockenzie Power Station, landscaped and large numbers of mainly broadleaf trees planted. A ranger is employed to manage the site. A wader scrape, consisting of six shallow pools lined with clay, was created in 1993 to compensate for the loss of the freshwater pools.

Species

The area is exceptionally productive for birds, with large numbers of waterfowl offshore in winter, important populations of passage and wintering wildfowl and waders, huge numbers of roosting gulls and considerable seabird traffic in the firth. Offshore wintering sea duck include nearly 1000 Eider, over 500 Goldeneye, around 100 each of Long-tailed Duck and Red-breasted Merganser, up to 250 Common Scoter, around 50 Velvet Scoter and small numbers of Scaup (formerly very numerous). Modest numbers of Red-throated and occasional Black-throated Divers are generally present in winter and, in addition, up to 200 Great Crested Grebe, small numbers of Slavonian Grebe, occasional Red-necked and even Black-necked Grebes can be seen. Wintering Oystercatcher numbers sometimes exceed 2000, while between 1000 and 3000 Knot, up to 1000 Bar-tailed Godwit, 300–400 Dunlin, 200–300 Curlew, over 150 Redshank, 100 each of Ringed Plover and Turnstone and small numbers of Grey Plover and Lapwing are not unusual.

Passage waders include large numbers of Golden Plover, Lapwing, Redshank and Turnstone, with smaller numbers of Sanderling, Ruff, Black-tailed Godwit, Whimbrel, Greenshank and Common Sandpiper. Little Stint and Curlew Sandpiper are recorded regularly, but Spotted Redshank, and Green and Wood Sandpipers are scarce.

Common and Velvet Scoters

Very large numbers of gulls bathe and loaf in the mouth of the Esk, including up to 5000 each of Black-headed and Common Gulls, 8000 Herring Gull, smaller numbers of Great Black-backed Gull and occasional Glaucous, Iceland, Ring-billed and Mediterranean Gulls (especially in spring).

Seawatching in July–October can produce Fulmar, Manx Shearwater (late summer), Gannet (main passage in September) and Kittiwake. Arctic Skua is seen regularly in August–October, with small numbers of Great and occasional Pomarine and Long-tailed Skuas also recorded. Sandwich Tern can be seen between April and October, with a peak of around 1000 present in August. Smaller numbers of Common Tern are recorded and one or two Black Terns occur each autumn.

The long list of rarities that has been recorded at Musselburgh is as much a testament to the efforts of local observers as to the richness of the site; it includes Surf Scoter, Red-crested Pochard, Pectoral, Buff-breasted and White-rumped Sandpipers, Franklin's Gull, Forster's and Lesser Crested Terns, Citrine Wagtail and Red-throated Pipit.

Access

Offshore waterfowl can be viewed from a number of points along the A199 Leith–Musselburgh road. To reach the outflow of the Esk, turn left off the main road east from Musselburgh (signed to the racecourse), then right to park at the north end of Balcarres Road and walk east to the river on the track. The seawall along the east side of the river is a good vantage point, especially at low tide, when most bird activity will be at the river mouth. Continue further along the seawall as far as the sewage outfall (a distance of just over a mile), scanning offshore. The land around the lagoons is mostly owned by Scottish Power and access on foot is permitted except to the active lagoons. Access to the west end is from the Prestonpans road west of the racecourse. Follow signs into Levenhall Links Leisure Park, then follow the road and bumpy track west and north to park at the sailing loch, near the bird reserve and wader scrape.

Timing

The timing of a visit is crucial in order to savour the full range of species to be found at Musselburgh. The optimum time to visit is about 2.5–3 hours before high water (on spring tides, around an hour or so later on neaps). The waders feeding at the river mouth should then be gradually driven closer before they fly to the lagoons to roost. Offshore waterfowl will usually be closer inshore at high water—relatively calm sea conditions are important. Strong afternoon sunlight can be problematic when birding at the river mouth in winter. Birdwatching at Musselburgh can be exciting at any season, although September–March is the period of most activity.

Calendar

March–June: Goldeneye and Long-tailed Duck can be seen displaying prior to their departure north. Large numbers of Turnstone and Ringed Plover move through in late April/early May. Lesser Black-backed Gull return in mid-March and there is a marked Common Gull passage. Mediterranean and Ring-billed Gulls have been recorded at this time. Regular spring migrants include Sandwich and Common Terns, Common Sandpiper, hirundines, White Wagtail and Wheatear.

July–October: Return passage of waders such as Curlew, Golden Plover, Knot and Bar-tailed Godwit commences in early July. Small numbers of Grey Plover and occasional Ruff, Whimbrel and Spotted Redshank also occur. Little Stint and Curlew Sandpiper are likely following easterly winds. Very large numbers of Sandwich Tern can be seen in August, with smaller numbers of Common and occasional Black Terns in August/September. A few Little Gulls pass through in October/early November. By late autumn a moulting flock of c. 400 Red-breasted Merganser has generally built up in the river mouth. Passage duck include Wigeon and Teal, with occasional Pintail and Shoveler. Great Crested Grebe numbers peak in September, but Red-necked Grebe does not usually arrive until October. Offshore, Manx Shearwater and a few Great and Arctic Skua are sometimes present, though Musselburgh is not particularly well situated for seawatching.

November–February: Wintering divers, grebes, sea duck, waders and gulls provide the main interest (see above). In addition, modest numbers of Guillemot and other auks occur offshore with regular Black Guillemot and Little Auk in recent years. Skylark and Linnet frequent rough ground surrounding the lagoons and Twite, Snow and Lapland Buntings are common along foreshore habitats in some winters. Peregrine, Merlin and Short-eared Owl are seen regularly.

References

Birdwatching Sites in the Lothians. Ed. IJ Andrews. (Lothian branch of SOC).
A Checklist of the Birds of Musselburgh Lagoons. IJ Andrews.
Lothian Bird Reports 1987–90. Ed. IJ Andrews/O McGarry. SOC.
Scottish Bird News 43 (September 1996).

BL12 DUDDINGSTON LOCH

OS ref: NT 284725
OS Landranger 66

Habitat

This excellent birding site lies at the southern edge of Holyrood Park, just below Arthur's Seat and only a short distance from the centre of Edinburgh. Both the loch and Bawsinch, a triangular piece of ground now supporting scrub, mixed woodland, grassland and freshwater ponds, are managed by the SWT. Marshland, reedbeds and willow and poplar woodland surround some of the shoreline. The reserve covers a total of 26 ha and is a designated SSSI. One of the most important and long-term projects at the reserve is the reintroduction of indigenous Scottish broadleaf trees such as aspen, birch, ash, alder, cherry and hazel.

Species

Breeders include Little and Great Crested Grebes, Grey Heron, Mute Swan, feral Greylag Goose, Mallard and Tufted Duck. Sparrowhawk breeds in the woodland and Sedge Warbler occur in the reedbeds. Cormorant, Teal and Pochard are seen regularly and a colony of a dozen or so Grey Herons nest in the reedbeds. One or two Bitterns have been regular in recent winters and escaped Night Herons (often unringed) from the free-flying colony at Edinburgh Zoo are frequently noted. A visit to Holyrood Park can be strongly recommended. Fulmar now breeds regularly on Salisbury Crags, with up to 30 adults present in spring and summer. Meadow Pipit, Skylark and Linnet breed, while Wheatear and Ring Ouzel occur on passage.

Timing

The visitor centre at Holyrood Park is open daily from 10.00 am to 5.45 pm between June and September; weekends only, 10.00 am to 4.00 pm, in April–May and October–December.

Access

Duddingston Loch is between Holyrood Park and Craigmillar and can be reached from the A1 along Old Church Lane, off Duddingston Road West. There is a car park at the loch. Part of the northern shore, beside the public road through the Royal Park, is open to the public. A permit and key to the hide on the southeast shore are available from the visitor centre at Holyrood Park. A deposit is payable. The car park by Holyrood Palace is a good base for exploring the park from the north side.

BL13 THREIPMUIR RESERVOIR

OS ref: NT 16/63
OS Landranger 65/66

Habitat

Threipmuir Reservoir and the adjoining Harlaw Reservoir are situated at the foot of the Pentland Hills, approximately 10 miles (16 km) from the centre of Edinburgh, and lie within the Pentland Hills Regional Park. Between them, the reservoirs cover c. 100 ha, plus surrounding marshland, reedbed, scrub woodland, plantations, arable land and improved pasture. Red Moss, a 23-ha reserve managed by the SWT, is immediately north of Bavelaw Marsh, at the western end of Threipmuir, while the marsh itself is managed as a reserve by the City of Edinburgh Council. This locality is one of the most important areas in the Lothians for breeding and wintering waterfowl and yet it has so far received only limited attention from birders. The species information given below is based on regular visits over the last five years by Allan Brown, former SOC recorder for Midlothian.

Species

More than ten pairs of Little and five pairs of Great Crested Grebe attempt to breed in most years, mostly on Bavelaw Marsh. Feral Greylag Geese breed and Mallard is quite numerous. Summering duck in recent years have included Wigeon, Shoveler and Pochard. A moult flock of over 100 Tufted Duck use the main reservoir in July/August. Ruddy Duck are increasingly regular in spring/summer.

Red Grouse occur on Black Hill, to the southeast, while Grey Partridge is widely distributed in the surrounding farmland. Moorhen and Coot both breed on Bavelaw and Water Rail sometimes nest. Breeding waders include Golden Plover on Black Hill and Common Sandpiper in the eastern part of the reservoir. Over 2000 pairs of Black-headed Gull usually breed at Bavelaw—the most important colony in the Lothians. A few pairs of Spotted Flycatcher also breed in the area; small numbers of Tree Pipit and Redpoll can be found in the birch wood at Red Moss, while Bavelaw Marsh holds 25–30 pairs of Sedge Warbler and around 20 pairs of Reed Bunting in spring.

Regular spring passage waders include Oystercatcher, Curlew, Red-shank and Golden Plover (best late April). Whinchat and Wheatear are occasionally numerous at East Threipmuir, while Chiffchaff, Whitethroat, Blackcap and Garden Warbler are occasional. Small flocks of Siskin occur in both spring and autumn. Low water levels in the autumn often attract Ringed Plover and Dunlin or scarcer waders such as Ruff, Whimbrel, Spotted Redshank and Greenshank. Flocks of several hundred Common Gull are a feature of both spring and autumn passage and Lesser Black-backed Gull may linger into November.

Redwing and Fieldfare are often abundant in autumn, while mixed flocks of finches and buntings, sometimes including Brambling and occasional Snow Buntings, exploit the autumn stubble fields. Small

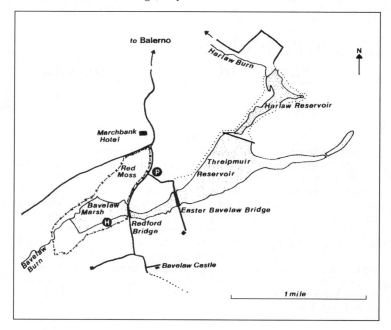

numbers of Whooper Swan visit in winter, while up to 600 Greylag Geese feed/roost at the main reservoir. Smew is occasionally recorded. Hen Harrier and Short-eared Owl are frequently seen hunting over Red Moss and Sparrowhawk, Kestrel, Merlin and Peregrine may occur.

Access

From the A70 Edinburgh–Lanark road, turn south to Balerno and then left immediately after crossing the Water of Leith. This road leads to a car park near Red Moss some 2 miles (3.2 km) further on (see map), past the former Marchbank Hotel. From the car park, walk to Redford Bridge, which is one of the best general vantage points for birding. A hide overlooks Bavelaw Marsh, but the key must be obtained in advance from the Pentland Hills Ranger Service at Hillend Park, Biggar Road, Edinburgh EH10 7DU (tel: 0131 445 3383). Access to the marsh itself is not permitted. It is also possible to walk to the north end of Easter Bavelaw Bridge from the car park—from here an extensive view of the main reservoir can be obtained. A path leads along the north shore and circuits Harlaw Reservoir. In view of the relative paucity of coverage by birdwatchers at this site, records of bird observations would be very useful—there is a log book in the hide, but please also submit sightings to the Lothian recorder.

Timing

The area is of year-round importance. Breeding waterfowl and a variety of passerines provide the interest between April and July, passage waders move through in April/May and August to October, while wintering waterfowl, thrushes and finches can be numerous from October to March.

References

Threipmuir Reservoir. AW Brown (1988). Unpublished.

BL14 HOUND POINT

OS ref: NT 158796
OS Landranger 65

Habitat and Access

Hound Point extends into the Firth of Forth from its south shore just east of the Forth Bridge. It is an excellent, if rather unusual, seawatching vantage point and can be reached by walking east along the coast from South Queensferry (a distance of c. 2 miles or 3.2 km). Birds can approach from almost any direction (some seem to suddenly appear overhead!), but it is in the north and east quarters that effort should be concentrated, scanning the horizon frequently to find distant birds, which can then be followed. Small numbers of seabirds may possibly continue into the Forth Valley and cross to the Clyde in the west, although to what extent this occurs is not entirely clear.

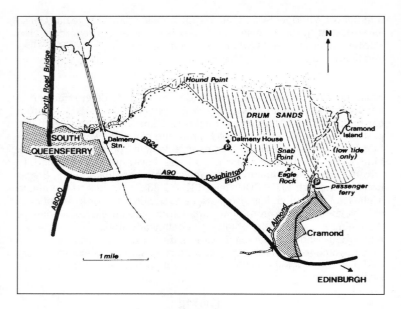

Species

A wide variety of seabirds can be seen at Hound Point, including Fulmar, Manx Shearwater, Gannet, Kittiwake and Guillemot, as well as divers and the other auks. The area is particularly good for skuas—Arctic Skua is seen regularly from late July until November, both on passage and harassing terns for prey; in the right conditions (see Timing), very large movements of Pomarine and Long-tailed Skuas can occur in autumn. There is generally a regular passage of the former in late autumn (October–November). Small numbers of Great Skua can also be seen, though this has been the rarest of the four skuas in recent years. Passage birds tend to gain height as they pass up the Forth and fly (often in flocks) west over the Forth bridges. Large numbers of Sandwich Tern are present in August and very small numbers of Little Gull and Black Tern occur annually in autumn. In addition, occasional records of Leach's Petrel, Cory's Shearwater, Osprey, phalaropes, Sabine's, Mediterranean and Glaucous Gulls, and Caspian Tern have been a feature of recent years.

Small parties of Brent, Barnacle and Pink-footed Geese pass through in September–October. Large numbers of Cormorant can be seen around Inch Garvie, to the west, in winter, while Shag tends to loaf on The Buchans, to the east. In some years, Little Auk is seen in early winter.

Timing

The best time to visit Hound Point is August–October, though spring passage can be productive and there may be considerable movements of birds in winter during gales. Light winds from the northwest through north and east to southeast produce the best seawatching here, with few birds in southerly or westerly winds. Onshore winds with clear weather and broken cloud, such as occurs after the passage of a front, are often productive, while a sudden clearing in sea mist that may have been present for a few days also appears to stimulate activity.

References

Birdwatching Sites in the Lothians. Ed. IJ Andrews (Lothian branch of SOC).

BL15 DALMENY

OS ref:
NT 137784–190770
OS Landranger 65

Habitat and Access

The shore path to Hound Point from South Queensferry (see L6 above) continues around the coast, following the perimeter of the woods and farmland of the Rosebery Estate to the River Almond, some 3 miles (4.8 km) beyond Hound Point. A passenger ferry across the river connects the walk with Cramond, where there is a large car park. The best vantage points for waders and wildfowl are at Eagle Rock, Snab Point and near Dolphinton Burn. Ideally, walk the entire length of coast from Cramond to South Queensferry either by arranging to be picked up at the far end or by using the bus services that connect the two access points with Edinburgh. Alternatively, the shore path can be joined by visiting Dalmeny House/gardens, open daily except Fridays and Saturdays from May to September, 2.00 pm to 5.30 pm.

Species

Modest numbers of Shelduck and Eider breed in the area and their young can be seen on the water in late June/early July. Small numbers of Mallard are present in spring, but passage and wintering birds increase the population to over 200 individuals. Wigeon, Teal and small numbers of Pintail and Shoveler occur in autumn. Eider, Goldeneye and Red-breasted Merganser overwinter and Tufted Duck and Pochard are sometimes recorded in severe weather, when their inland haunts freeze over.

Drum Sands support very large numbers of passage and wintering waders, most of which roost on Cramond and other islands. Over 2000

Red-breasted Mergansers and male Wigeon

Oystercatcher and Dunlin, up to 700 Curlew and 400–500 Redshank can be found in autumn and winter; smaller numbers of Bar-tailed Godwit, Turnstone, Whimbrel, Greenshank and Black-tailed Godwit occur on passage in autumn, while Little Stint and Curlew Sandpiper are occasional.

Woodland breeders include Green and Great Spotted Woodpeckers, Jay and the commoner warblers and tits.

Timing

The passenger ferry across the Almond operates daily (except Fridays) between 09.00 am and 7.00 pm, April–September, and 10.00 am and 4.00 pm, October–March. There is a very modest charge. Note: check that the ferry is running before committing yourself to a walk from South Queensferry to Cramond. Many waders roost on Cramond Island, so the best time to watch birds here is 2–3 hours before high water (depending on tide height) when the waders will be gradually pushed off by the incoming tide. Any offshore duck will also tend to come closer.

References

Birdwatching Sites in the Lothians. Ed. IJ Andrews (Lothian branch of SOC).
Lothian Bird Reports 1987–90. Ed. IJ Andrews/O McGarry. SOC.

BL16 BARNS NESS
OS ref: NT 723773
OS Landranger 67

Habitat and Access

Barns Ness is one of the more accessible of the southeast coast migration watchpoints. It can be reached by turning off the A1 Dunbar–Berwick road 5 miles (8 km) east of Dunbar at Torness Power Station and proceeding (via Skateraw) to the car park at the beach. The previous access from the A1 via the cement works may be blocked. There is a lighthouse near the end of the promontory and the area just north of it is the best seawatching vantage point, except in especially stormy conditions when the higher ground near the wire dump (see map) is preferable. The campsite south of the road is backed by a small plantation and has buckthorn hedges and sycamore trees near its entrance, all of which can be good for migrant passerines. Please note that exploration of the campsite is possible only in October–March, when it is closed. Other good places for migrants are the wire dump and the lighthouse garden.

Calendar

March–May: Early-spring migrants such as White Wagtail, Black Redstart, Wheatear and Chiffchaff usually first appear at the start of April, with passage of Meadow Pipit, hirundines, Robin, Wheatear, Blackbird, Willow Warbler, Goldcrest and various finches starting later and continuing

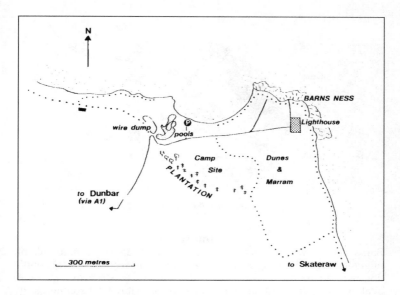

until late May. Small numbers of Tree Pipit pass through and a few Yellow Wagtail are regular. Less usual spring passage migrants include Wryneck, Bluethroat, Lesser Whitethroat, Pied Flycatcher and Red-backed Shrike. Offshore, Fulmar, Manx Shearwater, Gannet, Kittiwake, a few skuas, terns and auks are likely.

June–July: Breeding species at Barns Ness include Shelduck, Ringed Plover, Sedge Warbler and Linnet. Yellow Wagtail usually oversummer.

August–November: Wigeon, Teal and Goldeneye move past Barns Ness in numbers, especially in westerly winds, with smaller numbers of scoters and Red-breasted Merganser. Moderate numbers of waders appear along the coast in August/early September, but few linger. Little Stint, Curlew Sandpiper, Ruff, Whimbrel, Spotted Redshank, Greenshank and Green Sandpiper are generally recorded at this time. A large flock of Golden Plover is regular on the rocks. Strong northeasterly winds can produce large movements of Manx Shearwater, Arctic Skua and Kittiwake, with smaller numbers of Great Skua and occasional sightings of Sooty Shearwater and (in October–November) Pomarine Skua. Black Tern is occasionally seen in August and Little Gull is possible later in autumn. Regular passerine migrants include Dunnock, Robin, Redstart, Whinchat, Blackbird, Whitethroat, Garden Warbler, Blackcap, Chiffchaff, Pied and Spotted Flycatchers and Goldcrest. Up to 40 Tree Sparrow pass through in August. Rarer species occasionally recorded in autumn include Richard's Pipit, Icterine, Barred, Pallas's, Radde's and Yellow-browed Warblers, Firecrest, Red-breasted Flycatcher, Great Grey Shrike, Common Rosefinch and Little Bunting. Redwing and Fieldfare are generally first seen in late September and continue to arrive throughout October. Small numbers of Brambling are likely at this time.

December–February: Purple Sandpiper and Turnstone frequent the rocky shoreline in winter.

Female Red-backed Shrike

Timing

Barns Ness is worth a visit at any time of year, although large falls of migrants or good passages of seabirds obviously require special conditions and do not occur often. April–June and August–November are the peak months. The best fall conditions are probably light southeasterly winds with attendant drizzle, especially if clear conditions prevail on the continent. For seawatching, strong northeasterly winds are best and in winter, northerly and easterly gales may bring divers close inshore, or produce a Glaucous Gull or perhaps a Little Auk. (See also Skateraw, Additional Sites below)

References

Birdwatching Sites in the Lothians. Ed. IJ Andrews (Lothian branch of SOC).
Lothian Bird Reports 1987–90. Ed. IJ Andrews/O McGarry. SOC.

ADDITIONAL SITES

	Site & Grid Reference	Habitat	Main Bird Interest	Peak Season
a	Bemersyde Moss SWT Reserve NT 616339 OS 74	Shallow ponds and marsh with surrounding emergent vegetation and willow carr.	Over 10,000 pairs Black-headed Gull breed; also 10–12 pairs Tufted Duck and Grasshopper Warbler.	Jun–Aug
			Water Rail, Shoveler, Pochard, Moorhen.	All year
			Wintering wildfowl, including Greylag Goose and Whooper Swan.	Oct–Mar

Permit required—contact David Grieve, Forleys Park, Goslawdales, Selkirk TD7 4FP. There is an observation hide at this site.

	Site & Grid Reference	Habitat	Main Bird Interest	Peak Season
b	Burnmouth NT 959610 OS 67	Coastal migration point in east-southeast-facing cleft: two steep gullies and coastal slopes with gardens and dense scrub.	Passage warblers, Robin, thrushes, etc., occasional rare passerine migrants, and passage seabirds.	Mar–May, Aug–Nov
		Cliffs to north.	Breeding seabirds including Fulmar, Kittiwake, Guillemot and Razorbill.	May–Jul

	Site & Grid Reference	Habitat	Main Bird Interest	Peak Season
c	Hoselaw Loch SWT Reserve NT 808318 OS 74	Freshwater loch, peat bog and surrounding farmland.	Wintering wildfowl including large numbers of roosting Greylag Goose.	Oct–Mar
			Large assemblies of male Goosander.	May

Permit required—contact Keith Robeson, 12 Albert Place, Kelso, Roxburghshire TD5 7JL.

	Site & Grid Reference	Habitat	Main Bird Interest	Peak Season
d	Lindean Reservoir Borders RC NT 502292 OS 73	Small inland waterbody with sanctuary area and hide. Path around edge.	Common waterfowl: Little and Great Crested Grebes, Tufted Duck, Whinchat, Sedge Warbler.	Apr–Aug
			Wigeon, Teal, Pochard, Goldeneye, Goosander and Whooper Swan.	Oct–Mar

	Site & Grid Reference	Habitat	Main Bird Interest	Peak Season
e	Yetholm Loch SWT Reserve NT 803279 OS 74	Shallow loch and fen.	Feeding waterfowl including Great Crested Grebe, Shoveler and Pochard.	May–Jun
			Wintering wildfowl including Whooper Swan, Pink-footed Goose and Teal.	Oct–Mar

	Site & Grid Reference	Habitat	Main Bird Interest	Peak Season
f	Bass Rock NT 602873 OS 67	Spectacular volcanic rock island.	About 20,000 pairs Gannet, plus other breeding seabirds.	May–Jun

Contact Fred Marr (tel: North Berwick 01620 2838) for details of boat trips.

Site & Grid Reference	Habitat	Main Bird Interest	Peak Season
g Botanic Gardens Edinburgh NT 244753 OS 66	Area of exotic shrubs and trees close to city centre.	Hawfinch is a speciality.	Apr–May
h Gladhouse Reservoir NT 29/53 OS 66	Large reservoir in the Moorfoot Hills; can be viewed from the road along the north shore.	Wintering wildfowl including Wigeon, Teal, Mallard, Tufted Duck, Goldeneye and Goosander. Pink-footed Goose roost autumn.	Oct–Mar
i Hermitage of Braid NT 244703 OS 66	Ancient semi-natural woodland in the valley of the Braid Burn.	Woodland and scrub species including Wood Warbler, Lesser Whitethroat, Green and Great Spotted Woodpeckers.	Apr–Jun
j Linlithgow Loch NT 010770 OS 65	Small inland loch adjacent to M9.	Wintering wildfowl. Displaying Great Crested Grebe.	Oct–Mar Spring
k Skateraw NT 730759 OS 67	Streamside with scrub and trees.	Passage migrants.	Apr–Jun Aug–Oct

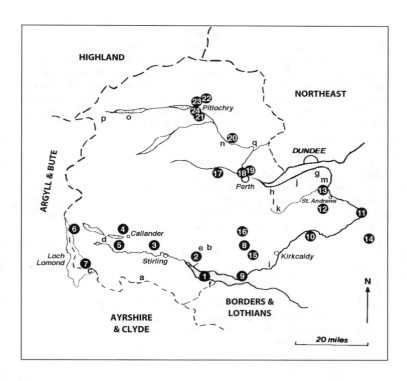

Main sites

C1 Forth Estuary
C2 Gartmorn Dam Country Park
C3 Doune Ponds
C4 Pass of Leny
C5 Lake of Menteith
C6 Inversnaid RSPB Reserve
C7 Inchcailloch
C8 Lochore Meadows Country Park
C9 North Queensferry and Inverkeithing
C10 Largo Bay
C11 Fife Ness
C12 Cameron Reservoir
C13 Eden Estuary
C14 Isle of May
C15 Loch Gelly
C16 Loch Leven
C17 Strathearn
C18 River Tay at Perth
C19 Scone Den
C20 Loch of the Lowes
C21 Loch Faskally
C22 Ben Vrackie
C23 Killiecrankie
C24 Linn of Tummel

Additional sites

a Carron Valley Reservoir
b Dollar Glen
c Endrick Mouth
d Queen Elizabeth Forest Park
e Tillicoultry Glen
f Blackness Castle
g Morton Lochs
h Newburgh
i Pettycur Bay
j Moonzie
k Rossie Bay
l Lindores Loch
m Tentsmuir Point
n The Hermitage
o Rannoch Forest
p Rannoch Moor
q Stormont Loch

Habitat

This is the section of the Forth extending from Stirling east to the road bridge at Queensferry. The area is largely an industrial domain and the riverbanks are lined with various factories, chemical plants and power stations. Grangemouth Docks lie on the south shore of the middle reaches of the estuary. Although aesthetically uninspiring, the area is of major importance for passage and wintering birds, especially ducks and waders. Large areas of invertebrate-rich intertidal mud are available for feeding birds.

Timing

The estuary is at its most productive for birds during autumn and winter; August/September and December–February are probably the optimum periods at most of the sites detailed below. A visit to the sites around Grangemouth, however, is likely to be rewarding at any time of year. Ideally, visits should be within three hours of high water.

Access

1 CAMBUSKENNETH (OS REF: NS 808939)

This section of river is tidal more by virtue of the water 'backing up' at high tide, rather than by saline water reaching this far upstream. It is not a particularly rich feeding area, but does attract winter wildfowl such as Pochard, Tufted Duck, Goldeneye and Goosander, especially when

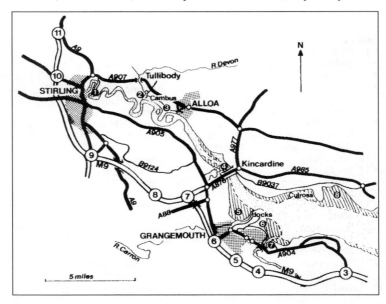

freshwater bodies begin to freeze over. Cambuskenneth is easily reached on foot from central Stirling, by way of a footbridge across the river
or by car along a minor road to the abbey, off the A907 road between
Stirling and Alloa. Cornton, immediately west of the Auld Brig near the
town centre, is another good location.

2 CAMBUS POOL (OS REF: NS 847936)

This is a flood pool of the River Forth, trapped behind the embankment,
and is controlled by the SWT as a wildlife management area. The water
is slightly brackish and tends to dry out at the margins in late summer.
Recent conservation work has established a shingle spit, areas of reeds
and screening trees and shrubs. It is of particular interest during spring
and autumn and now has a fairly impressive bird list. Access is gained
from the A907 Alloa–Stirling road: turn south onto an unclassified road
to the distillery, signed 'Cambus', just west of the turning to Tullibody.
Cross the disused railway line, turn right at the junction ahead, then bear
left over the bridge across the River Devon—there is room for a few cars
to park on the roadside, near the road end. From here, follow the (often
muddy) right of way along the right-hand bank of the River Devon, until
it joins the River Forth. Dipper and Grey Wagtail often frequent this area
in winter. A track alongside the River Forth leads to Cambus Pool. There
is a bus service to the Cambus turn-off from Stirling and Alloa. The optimum times to visit are probably mid-April to late May and again from
late June to early September. Wader migration should be at its peak during these periods. The pool is best watched at high tide, if possible in the
early morning before disturbance by local dog walkers and shooters
(September–January) occurs.

Grey Heron, Cormorant, Kestrel, Sparrowhawk and Black-headed Gull
are resident. Small numbers of Mallard, Coot, Moorhen and Lapwing
breed; up to three pairs of Sedge Warbler and 1–2 pairs of Reed Bunting
nest in the scrub and emergent vegetation. Gadwall, Teal, Shoveler and
Red-breasted Merganser (spring) occur on passage. The area is most
notable for migrant waders, however, including occasional rarities. Ringed Plover, Dunlin, Ruff, Black-tailed Godwit, Whimbrel, Spotted Redshank, Greenshank, and Green, Wood and Common Sandpipers are all
regular on passage. The pool is also excellent for watching hirundines
in late summer. In winter, Little Grebe, Whooper Swan, Tufted Duck,
Goldeneye, Goosander, Peregrine, Water Rail, Jack Snipe, various gulls,
Guillemot, Short-eared Owl and Kingfisher (up to three) are regular.

3 TULLIBODY AND ALLOA INCHES
(OS REF: NS 86/92 AND 87/91)

This section of river lies between Cambus and Alloa and holds large
concentrations of wildfowl and a variety of waders in winter. The site is
particularly important for wildfowl during severe winter weather. Tullibody Inch can be viewed by walking east along the north bank of the
Forth from the village of Cambus: take the turn off the A907 mentioned
above for Cambus Pool but turn left, then right, in Cambus village, along
Forth Street. There is room for one or two cars to park at the end of the
lane. A track beyond the locked red gate leads to the riverbank. The

small pool upstream, at the mouth of the River Devon, sometimes holds passage waders.

Access is also possible from Alloa, by taking a right turn off the A907 immediately after the cricket ground when travelling into the town, then the second right afterwards. Continue until the road degenerates into a rough track, then park and walk on a right of way to the shore at Long-carse Farm. The surrounding farmland has good numbers of Grey Partridge. Where the dismantled railway crosses the River Forth there is a large Cormorant roost of approximately 100 birds. The area also has a resident population of 50–70 Shelduck. Several hundred Pink-footed Geese sometimes frequent the area in March/April.

4 KINCARDINE BRIDGE (OS REF: NS 92/87)

This comparatively undeveloped part of the estuary can hold moderate numbers of wildfowl and waders. If approaching from Kincardine, turn left off the A876 immediately before the bridge and park after 0.25 mile (0.4 km) under the bridge. A small pier on the other side of the railway makes a good vantage point, or walk west along the seawall. Access to the south bank is possible by crossing the bridge and taking the first turning on the right. Keep right at the corner ahead, cross over Pow Burn after 0.5 mile (0.8 km) and park on the right; a public path leads to the Forth foreshore. Waders roost on the salting below Pow Burn.

5 SKINFLATS (OS REF: NS 92/83)

The intertidal and foreshore areas at Skinflats, situated on the south shore of the estuary between Kincardine and Grangemouth Docks, are some of the most important on the entire Forth estuary. Over 140 species have been recorded at Skinflats and it is of great significance for wintering duck and waders: almost all of the Forth's Pintail winter here and very large numbers of Shelduck occur. Peak wader counts include over 2000 Knot, 1200 Redshank, 5000 Dunlin and 2000 Golden Plover. Passage birds include a wide variety of species, among which hundreds of Grey and Ringed Plovers are significant. Raptors that regularly hunt the area include Sparrowhawk, Kestrel, Merlin, Peregrine and Short-eared Owl. Black Tern is possible in spring and autumn. Twite and Snow Bunting sometimes frequent the seaward side of the embankment in winter, and this is a reliable site for small numbers of Lapland Bunting.

The RSPB lease 413 ha here from the Crown Estate Commissioners and a private landowner. The reserve was established primarily to underline the importance of the area and to help ward off threats of reclamation for industry, rather than as a public site with viewing facilities. Feeding birds tend to be very distant, and at roost they are easily disturbed. Inland of the reserve at its southern end is an area of subsidence pools and farmland known as Skinflats Pools, which is currently under local authority ownership. These saline lagoons have produced several outstanding waders in the past, while the bushes around the lagoons can be good for migrant passerines such as Whinchat, Redstart and various warblers.

At present, however, the future of the pools is uncertain and problems of access along the north bank of the River Carron and of disturbance both here and on the saltmarsh mean that the only access to Skinflats that can be recommended is to view the area from Grangemouth Docks, looking west across the River Carron. This is reached by taking the A904 into Grangemouth and then West Docks Road from the roundabout at the west end of town. There are several vantage points along this road, where parking is possible, and it is feasible to obtain good views of the large flocks of Shelduck, Pintail, Knot, Redshank and Dunlin.

6 GRANGEBURN (OS REF: NS 95/82–3)

This burn mouth discharges into the Forth southeast of Grangemouth Docks and is approached along East Docks Road. (A permit is required from the Forth Port Authorities.) It should be worked on a rising tide, when any waders will be pushed into the burn and may roost on the adjacent reclaimed land. This is one of the more reliable sites for Curlew Sandpiper in early autumn. Up to 1000 Teal are among a number of duck species that can be found on the open pools here, while the reed-fringed pool within the docks may have Pintail, Shoveler and Snipe. Black-tailed Godwit and Ruff are fairly regular in autumn and the god-wits can often be seen in winter. Arctic, Great and occasionally Poma-rine Skuas occur in September and October; other seabirds include Gannet, Kittiwake and auks in late summer.

7 KINNEIL (OS REF: NS 96/81)

The mudflats and reclaimed land at Kinneil lie between Grangemouth Docks and Bo'ness. Take the A904 east from Grangemouth, turning left onto a small road to the sewage works, signed 'Kinneil Kerse', 1.5 miles (2.4 km) from the industrial area. Park on the road verge c. 0.5 mile (0.8 km) further, from where it is possible to walk along a rough track to the seawall, about 300 m distant. This is an excellent vantage point at high tide, though care should be taken to avoid the sludge on some parts of the embankment. Large numbers of Great Crested Grebe are present in autumn and late winter, while Shelduck can be seen year-round—flocks of over 2000 moulting birds gather in August and September, although they tend to congregate well offshore. Many of these remain throughout the winter. Scaup is sometimes also present. The sewage-settling tank immediately east of the Avon mouth is now largely overgrown and attracts few waders, although it is a good place for pipits and wagtails. Many of the waders now use the large lagoon behind the seawall; their composition varies through the year, but Knot, Dunlin and Redshank numbers are usually high and Black-tailed Godwit is regular in autumn and winter, while the surrounding marshy ground is good for Jack Snipe. In autumn, over 20 species of wader can be seen in this area and it is probably the best place in Scotland for Little Stint. The best time to visit is on a rising tide; beware of disturbing the roosting/feeding waders here at high tide. Up to 20 Pintail occur in the lagoon and offshore; 1000 Teal (the same as those at Grangeburn) are sometimes present in the estuary. Sparrowhawk, Kestrel, Merlin, Peregrine and Short-eared Owl often hunt the area.

The Falkirk Council tip attracts many gulls, including Glaucous. Large flocks of Linnet and lesser numbers of Twite are not uncommon in winter. The seawall sometimes harbours migrant passerines, e.g. Whinchat and Wheatear, while Sedge Warbler migrates through the area in autumn. Several vagrants have also been recorded here. Small numbers of Rock Pipit overwinter.

8 TORRY BAY (OS REF: NT 01/85)

This bay, situated on the north shore of the estuary 5 miles (8 km) west of Dunfermline, actually lies within Fife but is included here for the sake of completeness. It is approached via the B9037 road to Culross; a track along the northern perimeter of the bay affords excellent views of the varied foreshore. The area holds important numbers of wintering Mallard, Wigeon, Red-breasted Merganser, Knot, Dunlin, Black-tailed and Bar-tailed Godwits, Curlew and Redshank. Passage Brent Geese sometimes occur in small numbers.

Between Torry Bay and Kincardine Bridge lie two major wader roosts, located on the ash-settling pans of Kincardine and Longannet Power Stations. However, access to both of these sites is possible only by permit. Telescope viewing is possible from the railway bridge at NS 965857, a short walk from Culross Road. On very high tides, these sites can hold several thousand waders; Longannet also boasts a regular autumn roost of over 1000 Sandwich Tern and is a good location at which to see Little and Glaucous Gulls.

Calendar

April–May: Passage waders can be good; Curlew Sandpiper and Spotted Redshank have been a feature of recent years; Pectoral Sandpiper has also been recorded. White Wagtail passage in late April.

June–July: In common with most estuarine areas, the Forth has a relatively restricted breeding-bird community: Shelduck and c. 50 pairs of Common Tern breed, but there is little else to detain the birder in summer. Return passage of waders, especially small numbers of Whimbrel and Greenshank, generally starts in July.

August/October: Large numbers of terns and skuas sometimes enter the estuary in late summer and early autumn. Other seabirds also occur, especially during easterly gales, the species most frequently involved being Manx Shearwater, Gannet and Kittiwake. Passage waders such as Ruff, Black-tailed Godwit, Whimbrel and Spotted Redshank may occur in August, but the prime month for migrant shorebirds is September, when many thousands of birds occur. Wildfowl numbers also increase at this time, although the huge moulting flock of Shelduck will already be complete.

November–March: The very large numbers of overwintering waterfowl and waders dominate the interest, although birds of prey and flocks of finches and buntings in the vegetation are also important. White-winged gulls can usually be found at Kinneil and Culross/Torry Bay.

References

Birdwatching on the Forth estuary. DM Bryant. *Scottish Birds*, vol. 11, no. 3 (1980).

C2 GARTMORN DAM COUNTRY PARK

OS ref: NS 920943
OS Landranger 58

Habitat

Gartmorn Dam was constructed in 1713 and is one of the oldest man-made reservoirs in Scotland. It is a shallow, rich waterbody with a great diversity of aquatic plant and invertebrate animal life. As a consequence, Gartmorn is extremely attractive to wildfowl. The 75-ha country park includes not only the freshwater reservoir but also a small area of woodland and unimproved grassland. It incorporates land designated as a SSSI and a LNR. Clackmannan Council manages the site and employs a full-time Ranger Service.

Timing

The country park is open from dawn to dusk throughout the year. There is a visitor centre near the park entrance, open daily between April and September and only at weekends in October–March. The birdlife is of interest all year, although peak activity is during the breeding season and in winter.

Access

From Alloa, take the A908 to Sauchie—the country park is clearly sign-posted thereafter. There are three car parks near the entrance. A bus service from Alloa passes within 0.25 mile (0.4 km) of the park. A 3-mile (4.8 km) footpath circuits the reservoir and two bird observation hides provide excellent views over the LNR.

Species

Two or three pairs of Great Crested Grebe, about ten pairs of Little Grebe, three or four pairs of Tufted Duck and a couple of pairs of Grey Heron breed at Gartmorn Dam. Passage visitors have included Red-necked and Slavonian Grebes, various wildfowl and waders and occasional Osprey. In winter up to 80 Whooper Swan occur, while 1200–1600 Wigeon, around 600 Teal, 2000 Mallard, 60 Pochard, 200–300 Tufted Duck and 40 Goldeneye can be present. Pintail, Shoveler, American Wigeon, Scaup, Smew, Goosander and Red-crested Pochard are all occasional winter visitors.

Calendar

March–April: Wintering waterfowl disperse, leaving residents such as Little and Great Crested Grebes, Mute Swan, Mallard, Tufted Duck, Coot and Moorhen. Reed Buntings take up territory in scrub areas.

May–June: Breeding season—waterside birds as above. Seven species of warbler breed in the surrounding woodland and scrub; Woodcock can be seen roding at dusk; Great Spotted Woodpecker and a variety of other woodland species breed.

July–September: Wildfowl enter eclipse plumage and are at their least impressive during July and August. Possibility of passage waders.

October–March: Large numbers of overwintering wildfowl (see above). Grey Heron, Snipe and Water Rail can be seen; Waxwing (occasional), Brambling, Redwing and Fieldfare use the surrounding area.

Senior Countryside Ranger
Clackmannan Council, Gartmorn Dam Country Park, Alloa (tel: 01259 214319).

C3 DOUNE PONDS

OS ref: NN 726019
OS Landranger 57

Habitat
Doune Ponds is a recently created reserve managed by Stirling Council and located immediately northwest of the village of Doune, on the Stirling–Callander road. Although not, as yet, a particularly notable birding location, on-going conservation work is helping to establish a varied and interesting mixture of habitats, and the area has the potential to become a wildlife site of considerable local importance. A series of pools occupy what was once a sand and gravel pit, closed in the mid-1970s. The largest of these is only 1.5 m deep, although this may deepen in winter. This is linked, in the west, to a small silt pond which is now surrounded by a prolific growth of emergent vegetation. To the north, a small scrape has been constructed for waders. A plantation of Scots pine, larch and beech was established along the western edge during the early 1970s to screen the site. Willow and birch have colonised much of the reserve, while mixed plantations surround a recently formed marshy pool.

Access
Doune Ponds are reached by taking the A820 Dunblane road east from its junction with the A84 Callander–Stirling road. Turn left onto Moray Street immediately before Doune church, and then take the second left to a car park beside the ponds. There is an information board at the reserve entrance. There is a bus service to Doune from Stirling and Callander; the ponds are within easy walking distance. The reserve is open at all times. A nature trail, slightly over 0.5 mile (0.8 km) long, links the principal areas of interest. Please keep to this trail and note that dogs must be kept on a lead. Hides overlook the central and west ponds—keys can be obtained from the 'Spar' shop, 36 Main Street, Doune. The eastern hide is accessible to wheelchair users. Please note that access around the north pond is not permitted. A leaflet describing the reserve is available from local tourist information offices.

Species
Resident: Grey Heron, Mute Swan, Tufted Duck, Buzzard, Coot, Moorhen, Snipe, Coal Tit, Goldcrest, Siskin. Hawfinch has been recorded in the

Spotted Flycatcher

area. In spring and summer the reserve holds Oystercatcher, Common Sandpiper, Whitethroat, Sedge Warbler and Reed Bunting. Over 90 species have been recorded since 1980. This is a developing reserve that will hopefully attract more birds and birdwatchers in the future. Records from the reserve are therefore of importance and should be entered in the log book in the east hide or forwarded to the Stirling Council Countryside Ranger Service, Beechwood House, St Ninian's Road, Stirling FK8 2AD (tel: 01786 442875).

C4 PASS OF LENY

OS ref: NN 595089
OS Landranger 57

Habitat

The Pass of Leny is the narrow gorge containing the fast-flowing outflow from Loch Lubnaig, east of Ben Ledi. It lies mostly within the extended boundary of the Queen Elizabeth Forest Park (see Additional Sites) and is one of the better sites within the park for birds. Oak woodland adorns the valley sides, with some alder growing nearer to the river and conifer plantations on the higher slopes.

Species

Resident woodland birds include Buzzard, Sparrowhawk, Great Spotted Woodpecker, Siskin and Redpoll. Crossbill can usually be found at the west end of the glen. Dipper and Grey Wagtail frequent the river. In spring and summer, Tree Pipit, Redstart, Wood Warbler, Garden Warbler, Whinchat, Spotted Flycatcher and Cuckoo are present. Goosander and Common Sandpiper breed along watercourses. Redwing and Fieldfare are common during October and November; a winter visit should produce the resident species, large numbers of tits, Redpoll and Bullfinch. From Coireachrombie, at the northwest end of the glen, it is possible to ascend Ben Ledi (879 m). Capercaillie is occasionally glimpsed on the lower section of this path (especially early in the morning), but is very scarce here. Above the treeline, Wheatear, Ring Ouzel and Raven can be found in spring, with occasional Snow Bunting in winter. A few Ptarmigan occur near the summit. (Please note that adequate clothing and footwear are essential for this climb.)

Access

The best way to approach Pass of Leny is to take the cycleway and footpath which runs south of the river between Kilmahog and Coireachrombie: the oakwoods midway along this track are particularly good. Kilmahog lies 1 mile (1.6 km) west of Callander on the A84. There are car parks at both Kilmahog and Coireachrombie. A steeper climb through oak woodland and conifer plantation, following FC trails, is possible from the Falls of Leny car park, located on the A84, 1 mile (1.6 km) west of Kilmahog. However, this area is less interesting for birds. A bus service connects Callander/Kilmahog with Stirling. The Stirling Council Countryside Ranger Service operates the cycleway and organises guided walks in the area—contact Beechwood House, St Ninian's Road, Stirling FK8 2AD for details.

C5 LAKE OF MENTEITH

OS ref: NN 57/00
OS Landranger 57

Habitat

A large, low-lying waterbody situated at the foot of a ridge of hills that runs from Aberfoyle to Callander. A narrow belt of emergent vegetation fringes the lake, which is surrounded by arable ground, a small area of lowland heath to the west, with deciduous and coniferous woodland to the south. A wooded peninsula extends into the lake from the south shore, with a small wooded island, Inchmahome, just off its northwest tip. The lake is heavily fished and the disturbance caused by the small outboard-engine boats probably explains the scarcity of breeding waterfowl.

Species

Three or four pairs of Great Crested Grebe are usually present on the lake in April–September; they attempt to nest most years, but their breeding success is poor. Lake of Menteith is primarily of interest during winter, when around 50–100 Mallard (exceptionally up to 500), small numbers of Tufted Duck and Pochard, 15–20 Goosander (midwinter) and up to 50 Goldeneye (late winter) can be present. The lake is an important roost site for Pink-footed Geese, with up to 2000–3000 having been recorded, plus small numbers of Greylag Geese. In early spring the lake attracts good numbers of hirundines.

Access

Lake of Menteith is reached via the A873 Stirling–Aberfoyle road, which passes along its northern shore. There are three useful vantage points from which to scan the lake:

PORT OF MENTEITH CAR PARK (OS REF: NN 583009)

The jetty here affords the most comprehensive views. Weather permitting, there is a boat service to the priory on Inchmahome between April and September.

NORTH SHORE (OS REF: NN 568010)

There is room for a few cars to park on the A873 roadside, 1 mile (1.6 km) west of Port of Menteith. A stile gives access to the shore. This is a useful viewpoint for the western part of the lake.

EAST SHORE (OS REF: NN 588003)

This lay-by and public access point is a good vantage point for the southeast corner of the lake. There is a bus service connecting Port of Menteith with Stirling and Aberfoyle.

C6 INVERSNAID RSPB RESERVE

OS ref: NN 337088
OS Landranger 56

Habitat

The RSPB reserve at Inversnaid is situated on the east shore of Loch Lomond, 4 miles (6.4 km) south of its apex. Deciduous woodland on the steep hillside above the loch leads to a ridge of crags with moorland beyond. Part of the 374-ha reserve is classified as a SSSI.

Access

Inversnaid is reached by taking the B829 west from Aberfoyle. Turn left at the junction with an unclassified road after c. 12 miles (19 km)—this road terminates at Inversnaid Hotel car park after 4 miles (6.4 km). An alternative approach that may be feasible in summer is to take the pedestrian ferry across Loch Lomond from Inveruglas on the west bank. Contact Inversnaid Hotel for details (tel: 01877 386223). From the northwest corner of the hotel car park, the reserve is reached by walking north along the West Highland Way, which closely follows the loch shore for 600 m. Just beyond the boathouse a trail branches to the right.

At first it climbs through an area of open birch wood, before passing into denser oak woodland. The trail emerges onto open hills and, after crossing a small burn, reaches a viewpoint affording a superb vista of Loch Lomond and the surrounding mountains. The trail then descends to another burn followed by a second viewpoint. From here the path leads steeply downhill through more open woodland to rejoin the West Highland Way at the loch shore. Turn left to return to the car park. Please note that Inversnaid Lodge and grounds are private. There is a daily post-bus and newspaper bus service from Aberfoyle.

Timing
Inversnaid is accessible at all times and a warden is usually present from May to July. Resident woodland birds make a visit worthwhile at any season, but the reserve is best visited in May–July, when summer migrants make the place exceptionally interesting. Migrant wildfowl and waders use Loch Lomond during spring and autumn.

Calendar
Resident: Goosander, Buzzard, Black Grouse, Woodcock, Great Spotted Woodpecker, Grey Wagtail, Dipper, Raven and Siskin. Golden Eagle can sometimes be seen over the ridge east of the reserve. Signs of pine marten are frequently encountered on the trails, but these animals are rarely seen.

May–July: Red-breasted Merganser, Common Sandpiper, Tree Pipit, Redstart, Whinchat, Wood Warbler and Spotted Flycatcher. The provision of nest boxes has led to an increase in the breeding population of Pied Flycatcher, with 46 pairs nesting in 1988.

October–March: Resident woodland species are joined by Fieldfare and Redwing; Goldeneye is present on the loch.

Warden
c/o RSPB Scottish Headquarters, Dunedin House, 25 Ravelston Terrace, Edinburgh EH4 3TP.

Wood Warbler

Habitat

The 56-ha island of Inchcailloch is situated in the southeastern part of Loch Lomond and is part of a much larger NNR that includes four other islands and an area of mainland at Endrick Mouth. Though quite small, Inchcailloch is a hilly island, rising to a maximum of 85 m. It is largely covered with oak woodland that was mostly planted in the early 19th century, but alder grows around the shore and in wetter areas, while there are stands of Scots pine and larch on the higher ground. Greater woodrush forms a dense carpet on the woodland floor in places.

Access

At its nearest point, the island lies only 200 m offshore and can be reached via Balmaha, on the B837, 3 miles (4.8 km) from Drymen. A ferry service and boat hire is operated by McFarlane & Son, Balmaha Boat Yard. There are no access restrictions, except that groups of 12 or more persons are requested to contact SNH, tel: 01786 450362. There is a 2.5-mile (4 km) nature trail around the island. Dogs must be kept on a lead.

Timing

Inchcailloch is best visited between May and July, when breeding woodland birds provide the main interest. A midwinter trip to the island as part of a day's general exploration of the area can also be recommended.

Species

Buzzard, Great Spotted Woodpecker and Jay can be seen year-round at Inchcailloch. During summer the woods hold strong breeding populations of Tree Pipit, Wood Warbler, Garden Warbler and Spotted Flycatcher. Small numbers of Redstart and Blackcap are also present. On Loch Lomond, Mallard and small numbers of Teal, Wigeon, Shoveler, Tufted Duck and Red-breasted Merganser occur at any season. Shelduck can be seen in spring and summer. In winter, Greylag and Greenland White-fronted Geese visit the area; these roost at Endrick Mouth (see Additional Sites) to the southeast. Other regular wintering wildfowl include Pochard and Goldeneye.

References

Inchcailloch. Leaflet published by SNH South West Region.

C8 LOCHORE MEADOWS COUNTRY PARK

OS ref: NT 16/95
OS Landranger 58

Male Siskin

Habitat and Access

Lochore Meadows Country Park covers an area of about 400 ha, including the 105-ha Loch Ore. It lies at the centre of a reclamation scheme that has transformed a former coalmining wasteland into a landscaped area of open grassland and young woodland. The park incorporates a nature reserve at the western end, which can be reached by exiting the M90 at junction 4 and driving east past Kelty on the A909; turn left onto the B996 Cowdenbeath–Kinross road after 1 mile (1.6 km) and then take the first right to a car park. There is a bus service to Kelty from Cowdenbeath/Dunfermline. Alternatively, approach from the south via the A92 and Lochgelly town. From the car park, a track leads to the meadows—take a left turn at the junction c. 0.25 mile (500 m) later to reach Kon Lipphardt hide. Both the track and the hide have been constructed to enable wheelchair access. The other tracks form a circuit that circumnavigates the main waterbody (the total distance of this walk is about 3.5 miles or 5.6 km).

Species

Birds present in or just adjacent to the park in the breeding season include Little and Great Crested Grebes, Mute Swan, Pintail, Wigeon, Tufted Duck, Pochard, Moorhen, Coot, Snipe, Green Woodpecker, Grasshopper, Wood and Sedge Warblers, Whitethroat, Whinchat and Reed Bunting. Common Sandpiper, Redshank and Curlew can also be seen and the loch attracts many hirundines in late summer. Wildfowl numbers are swelled in winter by visiting Whooper Swan, Mallard, Pintail, Wigeon, Teal and Pochard. Other notable wintering species include Redwing, Fieldfare, Redpoll, Siskin and Goldfinch. This is a relatively new birdwatching location and consequently any records from visitors would be much appreciated by the Fife Ranger Service. Recent additions to the bird list include Night Heron, American Wigeon, Ruddy Duck, Red-crested Pochard and Smew. For more information contact: Fife Ranger Service, Lochore Meadows Country Park, Crosshill, Lochgelly, Fife (tel: 01592 860086).

C9 NORTH QUEENSFERRY AND INVERKEITHING

Habitat

On the north shore of the Firth of Forth, immediately east of the Forth Bridge, there is a number of good but relatively little-known birding locations. At Inverkeithing, a sheltered bay provides good feeding for both waders and wildfowl, while the more open coastline at Port Laing and St Davids Harbour is important for wintering divers/grebes and for fishing terns in summer.

Access and Species

INNER BAY (OS REF: NT 28/22)

Wildfowl numbers are generally at their highest at Inverkeithing when birds are forced from their inland haunts. Several hundred Tufted Duck, over 100 Goldeneye and Pochard, and good numbers of Shelduck, Teal and Eider occur. In addition, small numbers of Red-throated Diver, Great Crested Grebe, Cormorant, Scaup, Long-tailed Duck, and Common and Velvet Scoters are often present. Other species take refuge in the bay during and following strong easterly winds: Great Northern Diver, Red-necked Grebe, Little Gull and even Little Auk have been recorded. Moderate numbers of wintering waders also frequent the area, including small numbers of Ruff in recent years. The best vantage points over the inner bay at Inverkeithing are West Ness, at the southern entrance to the bay, or from near the wooden pier.

PORT LAING (OS REF: NT 134813)

Common, Arctic, Sandwich and occasional Roseate Terns can be seen fishing inshore during summer and early autumn. Two White-winged Black Terns were recently recorded off North Queensferry. Fulmar and Kittiwake are present further offshore. From late summer, Arctic Skua may be observed harassing the terns; Great and Pomarine Skuas are usually recorded later in autumn. Large passages of Kittiwake, with smaller numbers of skuas, sometimes occur in autumn and these may move across country to the Firth of Clyde. Seawatching is best from the high ground above the old pier around Port Laing, reached from Carlingnose. In recent years, passage skua numbers have been very good and have included up to 50 Long-tailed Skua off Inverkeithing Bay. Red-throated, Great Northern and occasional Black-throated Divers are recorded offshore in winter, along with five species of grebe and many auks. Inverkeithing is accessible by bus and rail from Edinburgh, Dunfermline and Kirkcaldy.

References

Coastal Birdwatching in West Fife. JS Nadin. *Fife and Kinross Bird Report 1986*. Ed. DE Dickson.

C10 LARGO BAY

Habitat

Largo Bay is situated on the south Fife coast, immediately east of Leven. It is approximately 3.5 miles (5.6 km) wide and consists of a fairly deep tidal bay, backed by extensive sand dunes. The intertidal substrate is largely sand and mud, although a rocky area exists near the central bay at Lower Largo and there is a muddy shingle area at the east end where Cocklemill Burn runs into the sea. Inland of the dunes is rough grassland and improved pasture. Just under a mile (1.6 km) inland from Elie, east of Largo Bay, is Kilconquhar Loch, a 55-ha shallow freshwater body surrounded by trees and gardens.

Species

Largo Bay is notable for its wintering waterfowl, which include Red-throated, Black-throated and (occasionally) Great Northern Divers, wintering grebes, particularly Slavonian and Red-necked, Scaup (up to 300 present at Leven), Eider, Long-tailed Duck (up to 300 regularly recorded off Methil Docks, adjacent to Levenmouth), Common and Velvet Scoters, Goldeneye and Red-breasted Merganser. Very large numbers of Eider and both scoters use the bay as a moult site. Surf Scoter is annually recorded—February to May is probably the best period for these birds. The bay does not attract particularly large numbers of either passage or wintering waders, although moderate numbers of Grey Plover and Purple Sandpiper occur and several hundred Knot and smaller numbers of Sanderling can be seen. Levenmouth is an excellent location for Glaucous and Iceland Gulls; Mediterranean Gull has occurred and Little Gull sometimes on passage. Little Auk can be numerous in the outer bay during some winters. Kilconquhar Loch holds a variety of breeding waterfowl, including Little and Great Crested Grebes, Gadwall and Shoveler.

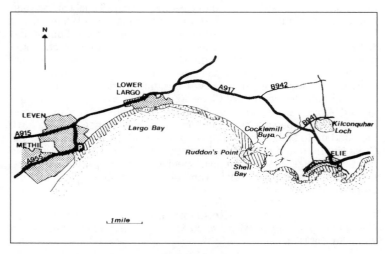

Access

The bay is easily accessible on foot from car parks at Levenmouth (oppo-site Methil Power Station) or Lower Largo. The free car park at the east end of Lower Largo affords a particularly good view of the Bay. Alterna-tively take the A917 east from Lower Largo to a turn-off to Shell Bay Car-avan Park, 1 mile (1.6 km) before Elie. From here, follow the minor road through the caravan site to Ruddon's Point (c. 2 miles or 3 km). Please note that inn October–March the entrance gate to the caravan site is closed from 4.00 pm to 09.00 am daily. By following shore paths and the beach, it is possible to walk the 4 miles (6.4 km) from Leven to Ruddon's Point, although Cocklemill Burn is difficult to cross at high tide. There is a bus service from Leven to Lower Largo and Elie. Kilconquhar Loch can be viewed from the churchyard in Kilconquhar village, reached by taking the B941 turn-off from the A917 Elie–Leven road.

Timing

The best time to visit is from October until April, although congregations of terns and sea duck can be seen in late summer. High tide is best for seeing sea duck and for waders at Ruddon's Point, low tide for white-winged gulls at Levenmouth.

Calendar

October–April: Offshore divers, grebes, sea duck, wintering gulls (includ-ing occasional Little Gull in late winter). White-billed Diver has been recorded in recent years.

May–June: Breeding wildfowl on Kilconquhar Loch; late wintering Gold-eneye sometimes also present.

July–September: Variable numbers of Little Gull gather at Kilconquhar Loch during late July/August in some years. At sea, passage terns include Sandwich, Common and Arctic, together with the occasional Roseate.

References

The Birds of Fife. AM Smout (1986).
Fife and Kinross Bird Reports 1981–. Eds. M Ware & DE Dickson.

C11 FIFE NESS

OS ref: NO 638098
OS Landranger 59

Habitat

Fife Ness lies at the eastern extremity of the Fife peninsula and is renowned for its migrant birds. The area is characterised by farmland, a golf course, coastal scrub and a few copses of sycamore-dominated woodland. Small areas of gorse and bramble are strewn along the coast, interspersed with sporadic pines. The shoreline is mostly rocky, with the exception of a sandy beach to the north. Inland, 1 mile (1.6 km) to the southwest is a disused airfield, now largely given over to cereal or root crops. The SWT manages just over 0.5 mile (0.8 km) of coast to the southwest at Kilminning and also a small, enclosed area of gorse, shrubs and trees immediately inland of the tip of the peninsula, called Fife Ness Muir. This contains several artificial pools created by Dr Jim Cobb and is probably the best place for passerine migrants.

Access

1 FIFE NESS MUIR (OS REF: NO 638098)

Take the minor road east of Crail (a continuation of the main street) and follow it to the car park at Balcomie Golf Course, which is reached in 1.5 miles (2.4 km). From here, walk through the gate to the right of the road and then immediately left, towards the sea. Fife Ness Muir is on the hill to the right and can be reached only from the east by the cottage on the shore.

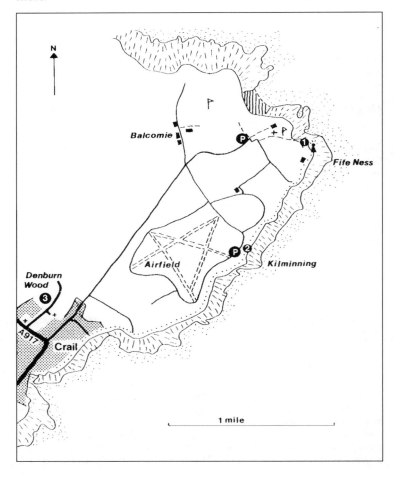

2 KILMINNING COAST (OS REF: NO 63/08)

Turn right off the golf course road, 1 mile (1.6 km) out of Crail, parking at the far end of the track. The Fife long-distance coastal footpath, slightly overgrown in places, affords access in both directions along the coast. This path can also be joined at Crail or Fife Ness. There is a bus service from Leven to Crail.

Most areas of vegetation offer suitable cover for migrant birds in spring and autumn. In addition to the above sites, Crail Airfield is worth checking for waders, pipits, larks and buntings, while the quarry immediately below the golf clubhouse may hold passerine migrants.

In the past, there has been some animosity shown towards birders by one or two local people, who have felt that their privacy has not been properly respected. In order that this tension is not exacerbated, it is very important that visitors behave responsibly; in particular, permission should be sought before entering the land around Balcomie Farm; Craighead Farm is an even more sensitive area and is probably best avoided altogether.

3 DENBURN WOOD (OS REF: NO 614080)

A mature copse bordering the churchyard; the wood has a variety of different shrubs and trees, a stream and some grassy areas at the top of the wood, which has produced some very good passage migrants in recent years, including Yellow-browed, Pallas's and Barred Warblers, Golden Oriole, a northern-race Treecreeper and Rose-coloured Starling. It is well worth visiting, especially after the birds have filtered through from Fife Ness.

Timing

Fife Ness is primarily of interest for its migrants and both spring and autumn are excellent times to visit. Offshore waterfowl provide some midwinter interest; but southeast, east or northeast winds are best for migrants.

Species

Offshore, Gannet, Cormorant, Shag, auks and several species of commoner waders can be seen year-round. Sandwich, Common, Arctic and sometimes Little Terns occur in spring and autumn. Small numbers of passage waders frequent the shore and tidal pool adjacent to the 16th tee. Sedge Warbler, Corn Bunting and, very occasionally, Stonechat breed. An impressive number and variety of passerine migrants make landfall at Fife Ness (see Calendar) during spring and autumn.

Calendar

March–May: Common and scarce migrants that are fairly regularly recorded include Long-eared Owl, Wryneck, Bluethroat, Black Redstart, Ring Ouzel, occasional Firecrest and Red-backed Shrike. Rarer visitors have included Nightingale, Common Rosefinch, Ortolan Bunting and Subalpine Warbler. Offshore, passage seabirds such as shearwaters, skuas and terns occur in April and May. This is also a good time for divers.

Yellow-browed Warbler and Firecrest

June–July: Quiet, although Gannet, large numbers of Eider, Kittiwake, terns and auks can usually be seen offshore. A few marauding skuas may occur in July. Local breeding species include Corn Bunting and (rarely nowadays) Stonechat.

August–October: Offshore, Manx and Sooty Shearwaters, Arctic, Great and Pomarine Skua, terns and auks may be visible. Small numbers of Little Gull are often present; Little and Black Terns are recorded annually and Sabine's Gull has been seen. A few divers are usually present, mostly Red-throated. Groups of Barnacle and occasional Brent Geese may be seen in late September–October, en route to their wintering grounds. Migrant chats, thrushes, warblers and flycatchers can be abundant, especially during easterly winds. Yellow-browed Warbler is seen annually, while Icterine, Barred, Pallas's and Radde's have been recorded. Red-breasted Flycatcher and Isabelline Shrike have been reported.

November–February: Red-throated, occasional Black-throated and Great Northern Divers, Shag, Cormorant, occasional skuas, white-winged gulls and auks can be present inshore. Little Auk is occasionally seen, especially after persistent northerly winds. Purple Sandpiper and Turnstone frequent the rocky shoreline. Geese, Hen Harrier, Golden Plover, various finches, Lapland and Snow Bunting are all possible.

References

The Birds of Fife. AM Smout (1986).
Fife and Kinross Bird Reports 1981–. Eds. M Ware & DE Dickson.
Seawatching at Fife Ness. J Steele in *Fife and Kinross Bird Report 1986*. Ed. DE Dickson.

Habitat

Cameron Reservoir is a waterbody of approximately 40 ha lying 150 m above sea level, 4 miles (6.4 km) southwest of St Andrews. The north bank is now largely grassland, following the felling of conifers there in the 1950s. To the east is the stone dam, while the south shore is still mainly forested with spruce, larch and Scots pine. Sallows form a thick cover at many points along the water's edge. There is another stone and concrete containing wall to the west, with marshland beyond. The surrounding upland farmland is given over to sheep pasture, with some tillage. The reservoir, owned by East of Scotland Water, is a designated SSSI.

Species

Little and Great Crested Grebes, Mute Swan, Mallard, Tufted Duck, Moorhen and Coot are present all year at Cameron Reservoir, but it is in late autumn/early winter that the area becomes especially important for birds. Around 6000 Pink-footed Geese (and up to 13,000 on occasion) roost on the reservoir in October–November; these are easily watched as they arrive at sunset, from the hide on the north shore without fear of disturbance. Occasional White-fronted and Snow Goose can often be seen among the Pink-feet. A few hundred Greylag Geese are also generally present and the reservoir has good populations of a variety of wintering wildfowl, including Whooper Swan, Wigeon, Teal, Pochard, occasional Gadwall and even Smew. Ruddy Duck is a regular autumn visitor. Short-eared Owl often hunts the grassland area on the north bank. Recent records show this to be without doubt one of the best passage wader sites in Fife. Though obviously dependent upon water levels, Greenshank and Spotted Redshank are regular spring and autumn migrants; Wood, Green and Common Sandpiper numbers fluctuate annually, and Little Ringed Plover has also been recorded. A Crane was seen here in the mid-1980s. Small numbers of Shoveler occur in spring/summer. The emergent and scrub vegetation around the edge of the reservoir has breeding Sedge Warbler and Reed Bunting.

Timing

The reservoir is worth visiting throughout much of the year, though July is probably the least inspiring month. An autumn or winter visit is strongly recommended: the best time for watching the geese fly in is from one hour before sunset until dark, using the hide as a vantage point (see below). Calm conditions are preferable for identifying waterfowl; in strong sunlight the south bank will afford better views.

Access

From the A915 St Andrews–Leven road, turn west along the track to Cameron Kirk and drive beyond it to a left turn to the car park at the reservoir keeper's house. There is a bus service along the A915 from St Andrews. It is possible to walk the entire perimeter of the reservoir (c. 2.5 miles or 4 km), but the south bank is very marshy. Elsewhere, the tracks are good. The east and west dams, the hide on the north shore and various locations along the south shore all provide good vantage points. Please note that dogs are not permitted except on a lead. (Note: the hide, dedicated to John Wiffen, belongs to the SWT and is kept locked: the key is available only to SWT/SOC members—contact Ian Cummings, St Andrews (tel: 01334 473773). For membership details of both of these organisations, see Useful Addresses.)

References
Based upon information kindly supplied by Chris Smout and the late John Wiffen.
The Birds of Fife. AM Smout (1986).
Fife and Kinross Bird Reports 1980–. Ed. DE Dickson.

C13 EDEN ESTUARY

OS ref: NO 485195
OS Landranger 59

Habitat
This 891-ha LNR lies immediately north of St Andrews. The habitat mainly comprises intertidal mudflats and sandbanks, with extensive mussel and cockle beds. There is a small area of saltmarsh on the south shore. To the east, a series of low sand dunes extend north from St Andrews, sheltering the estuary. The area is a SSSI and is managed by Fife Council. There is a visitor centre in Guardbridge, behind the Post Office (see map). In addition, the Fife Bird Club have built a hide at the Edenside Stables, halfway between Guardbridge and Coble Shore.

Species
The Eden estuary is a relatively small area, yet it is of outstanding importance for passage and wintering wildfowl and waders. Shelduck and Red-breasted Merganser are sometimes present in internationally important numbers while Scaup, Common and Velvet Scoters, Eider and Long-tailed Duck achieve nationally significant levels on occasion. The most numerous winter waders are Oystercatcher, Knot, Dunlin, Bar-tailed Godwit and Redshank. Two specialities of the area are Grey Plover (500+) and Black-tailed Godwit (100+), the latter favouring the Edenside area of the south shore. Sanderling can be numerous around the estuary mouth and flocks of Golden Plover, Lapwing and Curlew are common. In autumn the estuary can host an array of passage waders, regularly including Little Stint, Curlew Sandpiper, Ruff and Spotted Redshank. A Wilson's Phalarope was recorded in recent years.
Red-throated Diver is regular offshore in wintering, while Black-throated and Great Northern are occasionally seen. Small numbers of Great Crested Grebe are present on passage and during winter, but Red-necked and Slavonian Grebes are scarce. Passage and wintering Merlin, Peregrine and Short-eared Owl frequently hunt the area.

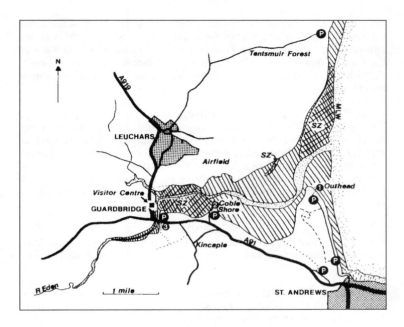

Access

Please note that access is not allowed to the north shore without a permit and that sanctuary zones (see map) must not be disturbed. These zones have been designated to minimise disturbance to the principal wildfowl and wader roosts. Outside the sanctuaries, wildfowling takes place between 1 September and 20 February. It is recommended that visitors contact the Fife Ranger Service (address below) for information about the estuary and for the key to the hide in Balgove Bay. There are three publicly accessible vantage points that enable most of the estuary to be worked.

1 OUTHEAD (OS REF: NO 495198)

This lies at the end of the sandy peninsula that extends into the estuary mouth from the south shore. Take the shore road north from St Andrews, signposted for West Sands. There is a car park at the end of this and it is only a short walk to Outhead. There are also tracks from this road to Balgove Bay.

2 COBLE SHORE (OS REF: NO 468194)

Turn off the main A91 St Andrews–Cupar road 3.5 miles (5.6 km) east of Guardbridge. There is a parking area at the end of the short track.

3 GUARDBRIDGE (OS REF: NO 455189)

There is an extensive lay-by adjacent to the LNR notice board immediately east of the bridge on the A91; this gives good views of the inner estuary. On the opposite side of the A91 a footpath to Kincaple Den provides a good vantage point for the tidal reaches of the River Eden above the road bridge. This is a likely location for Black-tailed Godwit, Greenshank and Goosander in winter. There are regular buses between Cupar and St Andrews.

Timing
The vantage points detailed above are accessible all year; there are relatively few breeding birds here, however, and the main interest is in passage and wintering species. A visit during August to May is recommended. A rising or falling tide is best for seeing most birds. Duck numbers are often much higher following strong easterly winds and both wildfowl and wader populations can increase dramatically in severe weather.

Calendar
April–May: A large Ringed Plover passage can be observed during May, mainly at Balgove Bay. Other spring passage waders may also be present.

June–August: Gannet is sometimes seen in the outer estuary. Large flocks of Red-breasted Merganser congregate at Edenmouth in July–August, joined by Sandwich, Common and Arctic Terns, which often attract marauding Arctic Skua. Early passage waders, such as Whimbrel, pass through.

September–October: Wader passage continues. Small numbers of Barnacle Geese pass through.

November–March: Whooper Swan is a regular, if unpredictable, visitor. Several hundred Greylag Geese roost on the estuary. Wigeon, Teal, Mallard, Goldeneye, Red-breasted Merganser and Goosander are common overwintering species. Pintail, Shoveler and Tufted Duck are regular visitors. Sea duck, including spectacular numbers of Common and Velvet Scoters, gather at Edenmouth—in recent years these have occasionally included a Surf Scoter. Very large numbers of waders feed and roost. Shelduck numbers peak in February/early March and some remain to breed. Snow Bunting is frequently seen, while large numbers of Reed Bunting have roosted at Guardbridge in previous winters.

Fife Ranger Service
Craigtoun Country Park, by St Andrews, Fife KY16 8NX (tel: 01334 473666).

References
The Birds of Fife. AM Smout (1986).

C14 ISLE OF MAY

Habitat

The Isle of May is situated at the mouth of the Firth of Forth, some 5 miles (8 km) southeast of the Fife coast. The 57-ha island consists of hard volcanic rock, rising to 55 m on the west side, which is largely vertical sea cliff and sloping gradually to sea level to the east. Vegetation is sparse and the trapping areas of the Bird Observatory, established in 1934, offer the best cover for migrants. It has been designated a NNR by SNH, who have recently purchased the island from the Northern Lighthouse Board.

Timing

Migrants are the primary attraction of the Isle of May and therefore April–May and August–October are the optimum periods to visit. However, breeding seabirds also provide much interest between May and July.

Access

During summer it is possible to arrange a day trip to the island from Anstruther, depending on tides and weather (tel: 01333 310103 for details). All who wish to stay at the Observatory must complete an application form, obtainable from the bookings secretary, Mike Martin (tel: 0131 331547 evenings only). Details of the boat crossing from Anstruther are supplied when the booking has been confirmed. Visitors must take their own sheets or sleeping bag and sufficient food for the duration of their stay—this can be obtained in Crail or Anstruther, except on Sundays. The cost of accommodation is modest and a maximum of six people can stay at one time. The usual period of stay is one week, starting and finishing on a Saturday, although bad weather can delay plans.

Species

Large numbers of seabirds breed: over 1000 pairs of Shag, several thousand pairs each of Kittiwake and Guillemot, about 1000 pairs of Razorbill and an estimated 10,000 occupied Puffin burrows have been counted. There is an increasing number of Fulmar and large populations of Herring and Lesser Black-backed Gulls. Other breeding species of interest include Eider (c. 500 pairs), Oystercatcher, a few Common and Arctic Terns, Rock Pipit and Wheatear.

Over 240 species have been recorded on the Isle of May, an impressive total partially due to the fact that the island has been studied during migration periods for more than 50 years. Large falls of migrants are most likely when strong east or southeasterly winds coincide with poor visibility. In autumn, spectacular numbers of relatively common birds can occur en route to their winter quarters; thrushes are probably the most usual of these, but other species are sometimes involved, for instance 15,000 Goldcrests were once recorded and over 1000 Brambling appeared on another occasion. Scarcer species are regularly seen and Wryneck, Bluethroat, Icterine, Barred and Yellow-browed Warblers, Red-breasted Flycatcher, Great Grey and Red-backed Shrikes, Common Rosefinch, Lapland and Ortolan Buntings are all almost annually record-

Light phase Arctic Skua and Common Gulls, autumn

ed. Rarities such as Spoonbill, Red-footed Falcon, Pallas's Sandgrouse, Siberian Thrush, Daurian Redstart, Pied Wheatear, Paddyfield, Olivaceous, Melodious, Subalpine and Pallas's Warblers have all occurred at least once, as have Red-throated and Olive-backed Pipits, Thrush Nightingale, Pine Grosbeak, and Yellow-breasted and Rustic Buntings.

Seawatching can be worthwhile—divers, sea duck, shearwaters, petrels and skuas can all be seen at various times (see Calendar).

Calendar

April–May: Passerine migrants likely, including possible rarities. Breeding seabirds return to nest sites; Manx Shearwater, and Great and Arctic Skuas usually visible offshore.

June–July: Fledged seabirds start to disperse in July. Common and Arctic Terns breed, and are occasionally joined by Sandwich Tern.

August–October: Peak migration period; large falls of migrants possible especially during easterly winds. Offshore, passage seabirds include Manx and Sooty Shearwaters, Storm Petrel, and Great, Arctic and Pomarine Skuas.

November–March: Offshore, divers, Black Guillemot and Little Auk are regular; and Merlin and Peregrine, Long-eared and Short-eared Owls are frequently seen during this period. Woodcock pass through, while Purple Sandpiper and Turnstone frequent the rocky shoreline.

References

The Isle of May: a Scottish Nature Reserve. WJ Eggeling (1960, reprinted 1985).
One Man's Island. K Brockie (1984).

Habitat and Access

A freshwater loch bordered by mixed woodland, *Phragmites* swamp, willow carr and grassland. The National Coal Board owns the northern shore of this 79-ha site, while the south shore belongs to Wemyss Estate. Fife Skiing Club leases Loch Gelly. Access to the loch is only from the A92 Cowdenbeath–Kirkcaldy road at the Lochgelly East Link Road interchange. At this junction take the road signed to Auchtertool and park on a small, metalled track 20 m along on your right. Steps lead from here to a path on the north side of the loch. It is possible to walk around the loch if you are prepared to negotiate long grass and mud in places.

Species

Over 108 species have been recorded. Loch Gelly attracts very good numbers of duck and waders (when the water level is low), especially in autumn. Breeders include Little Grebe, Mute Swan, Greylag Goose, Shelduck, Pochard, Shoveler, Teal and Grasshopper Warbler. Five species of grebe, three species of swan and 18 species of duck have been recorded. Ruddy Duck is a regular visitor, and Garganey, Pintail and Ring-necked Duck have all been noted. Passage waders include Wood, Green and Common Sandpipers, Ruff, Greenshank and Spotted Redshank. Others seen at Loch Gelly include Spoonbill, Corncrake, Black Tern and Little Gull. Hundreds of hirundines can be present in autumn, while Swift may be present in thousands in July.

The site is also important botanically; species of particular interest include water sedge, tea-leaved willow, ivy duckweed, yellow loosestrife, horned pondweed and yellow water lily.

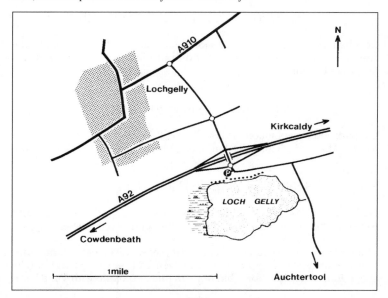

Habitat and Species

Loch Leven is a NNR managed by SNH. The 1597-ha loch and surrounding fertile farmland is internationally important as both a breeding and wintering wildfowl site. The loch is mostly shallow and contains seven islands including St Serf's Island, where over 1000 pairs of duck nest each year. These include Shelduck, Wigeon, Gadwall and Shoveler, although Mallard and Tufted Duck are by far the most numerous. The island is also harbours a large Black-headed Gull colony and a smaller one of Common Tern. Around the loch, Oystercatcher, Lapwing, Snipe, Curlew and Redshank nest in the few remaining wetland areas, while Ringed Plover and Common Sandpiper breed near the shore.

Loch Leven is especially significant as a winter feeding and roost area for Pink-footed Geese and is one of the major arrival points in Britain for these birds in autumn. Many of these subsequently disperse to wintering grounds elsewhere, but several thousand remain and move onto the surrounding farmland to feed, using the loch to roost throughout the winter. Between 1000 and 5000 Greylag Geese also winter here and varying numbers of Whooper Swan are often recorded. A few Canada, Barnacle, Brent and White-fronted Geese are sometimes found among the goose flocks. Up to ten species of duck winter on the loch, including Wigeon, Gadwall, Shoveler, Pochard and Tufted Duck.

Access

Apart from the RSPB reserve at Vane Farm, there are three vantage points around the shore of the loch to which access is permitted.

1 BURLEIGH SANDS (OS REF: NO 134040)

Reached via the unclassified road which turns east off the main Kinross–Milnathort road immediately north of Kinross. Park 1.5 miles (2.4 km) after this turn.

2 FINDATIE (OS REF: NT 171993)

Car park and viewpoint on the B9097 road, 2.5 miles (4 km) from junction 5 of the M90 and 0.5 mile (0.8 km) east of the RSPB reserve at Vane Farm.

3 KIRKGATE PARK (OS REF: NO 128018)

Half a mile (0.8 km) out of Kinross, along Burns-Begg Street; from April to September boats leave the jetty here for Loch Leven Castle.

There are information boards at all three places. Given calm conditions, many of the species found on Loch Leven can be viewed with a telescope from these locations, but none of them compare with Vane Farm

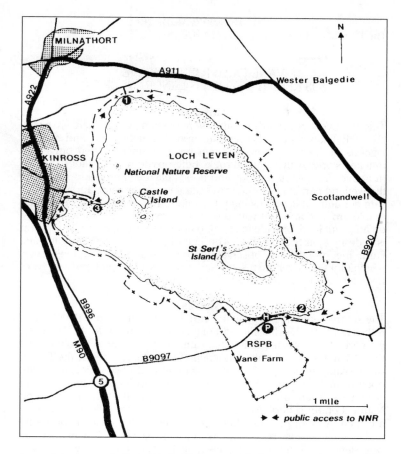

for variety or proximity to birds. Please note that access to the rest of the shore and islands is not permitted without prior consent of SNH, which issue permits only to people engaged in scientific research. Small escorted groups can be arranged.

Calendar

Resident: Great Crested Grebe, Fulmar, Cormorant, Grey Heron, Mute Swan, Wigeon, Gadwall, Teal, Mallard, Shoveler, Pochard, Tufted Duck, Ruddy Duck, Sparrowhawk, Moorhen, Coot, Lapwing, Snipe, Curlew, Black-headed and Lesser Black-backed Gulls, Jackdaw, Rook.

Breeding visitors: Shelduck, Common Sandpiper, Common Tern.

Regular migrants: Slavonian and Black-necked Grebes, Ruff, Black-tailed Godwit, Spotted Redshank, Greenshank, Green and Wood Sandpipers, Sand Martin.

Winter visitors: Whooper Swan, Pink-footed Goose, Greylag Goose, Pintail, Goldeneye, Goosander, Short-eared Owl, Fieldfare, Redwing.

115

SNH Reserve Manager
The Pier, Loch Leven, Kinross KY13 7UF (tel: 01577 864439).

VANE FARM RSPB RESERVE
(OS REF: NT 160991, OS LANDRANGER 58)

Habitat
This 231-ha reserve is on the south shore of Loch Leven. There are a variety of habitats within the reserve, from the marshland and shallow lagoons of the loch shore, through mixed farmland, then birch and bracken slopes with scattered rocky outcrops, to heather moorland 150 m above. A series of lagoons and floods has been created to diversify the wetland part of the reserve; this attracts nesting duck and waders in summer and wildfowl in winter. Gleanings from the reserve's two main arable crops, combined with the close-grazed sward created by cattle on adjacent land, provide ideal conditions for visiting geese. Vane Farm is a designated SSSI by SNH. The Loch Leven Nature Centre at Vane Farm incorporates an observation room with mounted telescopes, which looks out over the reserve and provides a comprehensive view of Loch Leven. There are also gift and coffee shops.

Access
The reserve entrance is located on the south side of the B9097 Glenrothes road, 2 miles (3.2 km) east of junction 5 of the M90. Access to the car park and the nature trail to the summit of the Vane is possible at all times. The hides and trails are reached via a tunnel below the B9097, overlooking the scrape. The nature centre and observation room are open from 10.00 am to 5.00 pm daily, only closing for Christmas and New Year. There are resident field teaching staff at the Loch Leven Nature Centre; school parties are welcome, but please book well in advance. A ramp permits wheelchair access to the observation room, and a picnic area is also accessible to wheelchair users. The nearest railway station is 5 miles (8 km) away at Lochgelly, on the Edinburgh–Dundee line, though Cowdenbeath is probably more convenient.

Timing
The most spectacular time to visit is October–March, when the geese are present. However, passage and breeding birds provide alternative interest and the educational displays and activities at the nature centre continue throughout the year.

Species
Over 130 species have been recorded on the reserve, c. 70 of which are winter visitors. The observation room at Vane Farm is a good place from which to see the large flocks of Pink-footed and Greylag Geese that use Loch Leven area in winter. Likewise, Whooper Swans are also often visible on the loch; up to 200 have been recorded but their appearances are rather unpredictable. Bewick's Swan is becoming a common winter visitor. As many as ten species of duck occur in winter and Wigeon, Teal, Mallard, Shoveler, Pochard and Tufted Duck may be seen year-round. Sparrowhawk, Buzzard and Kestrel are regularly seen over the reserve, as is Peregrine. A permanent sluice has been constructed to reverse previous agricultural drainage, and the reinstated wetland has

resulted in an increased in the numbers of breeding Lapwings.

The birch woods have a rather limited bird community, but Tree Pipit, Whinchat and Spotted Flycatcher are present in spring and Long-tailed Tit, Redpoll and Siskin throughout autumn and winter. See Loch Leven section for general species list.

Calendar

March–May: Pink-footed Goose numbers peak in March, as birds from more southerly wintering haunts move into the area. During April and early May, skeins of departing geese can be seen, leaving just a few individuals by mid-May.

June: Perhaps the quietest month, but Great Crested Grebe, Shelduck, Gadwall and Redshank may all be present.

July–October: Passage waders that may appear at the scrapes include Knot, Black-tailed Godwit, Greenshank, and Green and Wood Sandpipers. The main influx of wintering geese occurs late in September and during early October; Pink-foot numbers can reach almost 15,000 before they begin to disperse to their winter haunts. Smaller numbers of Greylag Goose and Whooper Swan also appear, though the latter can be very unpredictable.

December–February: By midwinter, goose numbers have declined and stabilised. Whooper Swan is present in varying numbers, sometimes joined by Bewick's Swan. Dabbling ducks generally include Wigeon, Gadwall, Shoveler and the occasional Pintail; diving duck such as Tufted Duck, Goldeneye and Goosander are usually present. At dusk, large numbers of Woodpigeon cross the reserve to their roost site. Chaffinch, Greenfinch, Yellowhammer and occasionally Brambling can be seen around the car park.

RSPB Warden

Loch Leven Nature Centre, Vane Farm, by Loch Leven, Kinross KY13 9LX (tel: 01577 862355).

Pink-footed Geese

Strathearn is a well-known area for wintering geese and has been covered extensively in earlier guides. However, a number of factors have persuaded us not to wholeheartedly recommend the area as a birdwatching site. Numbers of Greylag are much lower than they were 10–20 years ago, probably reflecting the change to winter cereals and the resultant hostility of farmers towards the geese. After a large peak in early autumn, Pink-footed Goose numbers are also low throughout winter. Access is very problematical—all of the land is private and visitors are generally unwelcome. In a nutshell, there are better places in which to see geese in Central Scotland such as Stormont Loch, Loch of Kinnordy, Loch Leven and Montrose Basin, where access is less problematic and is less likely to cause friction between landowners and birdwatchers. Roadside views of feeding geese are possible at Tibbermore (NO 050237), best in late September and early October, and Kinkell Bridge (NN 932168), from November to March. Parking is awkward at both places and care should be taken not to obstruct access.

C18 RIVER TAY AT PERTH
OS ref: NO 120245
OS Landranger 53

Habitat
This 2.5-mile (4 km) section of the Tay upstream from Perth Bridge as far as its confluence with the River Almond is an interesting and easily accessible area for riparian birdlife. The west bank is largely short-turf grassland with scattered mature trees. At Woody Islands there is deciduous woodland, a small conifer plantation and areas of hawthorn/blackthorn scrub. On the east bank, large houses with extensive gardens occupy the southern part of the riverbank, with the parkland of Scone Palace further north.

Species
In recent years, one of the great attractions of this section of river has been the small feral population of Mandarin Duck, which bred in nest boxes in Upper Springland and adjacent gardens. However, this population now appears to be extinct. There are usually several 'winged' Pink-footed and Greylag Geese present but these have not been known to breed. Red-breasted Merganser, occasional Kingfisher, Dipper and Grey Wagtail all frequent the river throughout the year. Tawny Owl and Great Spotted Woodpecker are present in the woodland and garden habitats, and Jackdaw nest in the stonework of Perth Bridge (which is also a year-round Starling roost). Other residents include Herring and Great Black-backed Gulls, Rook, Carrion Crow and Goldfinch.

In summer, Oystercatcher, Ringed Plover, Lapwing, Common Sand-piper, Common Tern, Skylark, Grey Wagtail, Sedge and Garden Warblers, Whitethroat, Blackcap and Spotted Flycatcher occur. Sand Martins nest in drainage holes in the retaining wall of Tay Street.

Lesser Black-backed Gull, hirundines, Whinchat and Wheatear occur on passage in spring, while Oystercatcher, Lapwing and Curlew move through in autumn. Over 500 Pied Wagtail roost in the *Salix* scrub on an island against the pier at the east end of Perth Bridge during late summer.

Up to 500 Greylag Geese roost on the river below Scone Palace from November to March/April. Other wintering wildfowl include Mute Swan, Wigeon, Tufted Duck and Goosander, though numbers depend largely on the severity of the weather, with more birds moving onto the river when nearby open-water habitats freeze. Little Grebe, Cormorant (over 100 have been recorded at a tree roost here) and Coot are all generally present in winter. Fieldfare, Redwing, Siskin and Redpoll utilise adjacent habitats. Birds recorded only occasionally include Black-throated Diver, Great Crested Grebe, Whooper Swan, Canada Goose, Teal, Pochard, Golden Plover and Greenshank. It is also worthwhile checking the gulls for any less common species that may occur from time to time.

Note: many of the Mallard on the River Tay here are of the 'Cayuga' strain, with variations from glossy black with a white breast to almost pure Mallard. The Scottish Council for Spastics' Upper Springland complex has a wildfowl collection, elements of which wander onto the river and can be the cause of considerable confusion for the unwary!

Access
Access is feasible to the west bank only. Metered parking is possible in Perth city. There is a surfaced path, suitable for wheelchair users, over most of the route from Perth Bridge to the Almond confluence. Good views are also afforded by the bridges in Perth and from Tay Street.

Timing
The river is worth a look at any time of year. It is an interesting, convenient and brilliant place to go birding!

C19 SCONE DEN

OS ref: NO 136258
OS Landranger 53

Scone Den is a narrow valley nearly 1 mile (1.6 km) long with mature deciduous woodland, scrub and gardens. Den Road runs alongside the burn and gives access to an old quarry surrounded by ash trees and hawthorn growing on its floor. Access is off the A94 in Scone. Park at Cross Street or Burnside, on the outskirts of the town of Scone and c. 0.25 mile (0.4 km) south of Den Road. The road is unsurfaced, but negotiable by wheelchair users.

The residents are largely woodland/scrub species and include Great Spotted Woodpecker, Jay, Tawny Owl and Hawfinch. The latter is most commonly seen in November–April, often in the vicinity of the old quarry—much of the quarry floor scrub has recently been cleared for house construction, so this may affect the attraction of the site to Hawfinch. Dipper can be seen along the burn throughout the year. In summer, breeding visitors include Grey and Pied Wagtails, Whitethroat, Garden and Willow Warblers, Blackcap and Spotted Flycatcher. In addition, Kingfisher, Green Woodpecker and Chiffchaff are occasional.

C20 LOCH OF THE LOWES

OS ref: NO 050440
OS Landranger 52 or 53

Habitat

This SWT reserve comprises the shallow, reed-fringed and interconnected Loch of Lowes and Loch of Craiglush. Both lochs are bordered by mixed woodland, which includes Scots pine, juniper, oak, bird cherry and ash. The reserve covers 135 ha and is a designated SSSI. It is famed for its nesting Ospreys, a new pair of which took up residence in 1991 after an absence of eight years.

Species

During spring and summer the Ospreys are a major attraction, and excellent views of the nest can be obtained from the SWT hide on the loch shore. The reserve is also of interest for many other species. Little and Great Crested Grebes breed in the reeds at the west end of the loch; Teal, Mallard and Tufted Duck are resident, except when the loch freezes in winter. Common Sandpiper, Sedge Warbler and Reed Bunting also breed. Over 1000 Greylag Geese use the loch as a roost in autumn; Canada Geese breed and are seen regularly.

The surrounding woodland holds Woodcock, Green and Great Spotted Woodpeckers, Treecreeper, Siskin and Redpoll. Breeding visitors include Tree Pipit, Redstart and Garden Warbler.

Access

Access to the reserve and visitor centre is from the unmarked road off the A923 Dunkeld–Blairgowrie road c. 1.5 miles (2.4 km) east of Dunkeld. The hide is equipped with optics during the visitor centre opening hours and is accessible to wheelchair users. Further along the road to the car park, a number of lay-bys allow the southern shore of the loch to be scanned, but the observation hide is by far the best vantage point. The visitor centre contains displays explaining the conservation importance of the reserve; audio-visual programmes are shown on request. Ranger staff and volunteers are on hand to answer questions relating to the SWT reserve. A limited amount of foreign language information is available.

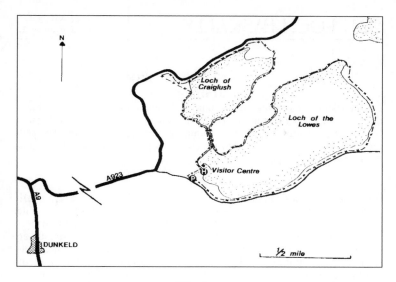

Timing

Loch of the Lowes is important for breeding birds and wintering wild-fowl: visits are therefore recommended between April and June or October and March. The observation hide is open at all times and a visitor centre is open daily 10.00 am to 5.00 pm April–September, except mid-July to mid-August when it is open 10.00 am to 6.00 pm.

Calendar

April–June: Osprey usually arrive in late March or early April; Great Crested Grebe can be seen displaying in April. Woodland migrants, such as Willow Warbler, start to arrive in mid-April, although species such as Sedge Warbler and Spotted Flycatcher are not usually seen until late May.

October–March: Wintering wildfowl include Goosander, Greylag Geese, Wigeon, Pochard and Goldeneye.

Reserve Ranger

Loch of Lowes Visitor Centre, Dunkeld (tel: 01350 727337, April–September).

References

Loch of Lowes. Compiled by VM Thom. Revised by AH Barclay (1990).

C21 LOCH FASKALLY

OS ref: NM 930584
OS Landranger 52

Habitat

Loch Faskally was created in the late 1940s when the River Tummel was dammed at Pitlochry for hydroelectric power generation. The loch is bordered by mature woodland, dominated by oak and beech. The policy woodlands near Faskally House are a diverse and rich songbird habitat, currently managed by the FC.

Species

Buzzard, Green and Great Spotted Woodpeckers, Siskin and Redpoll are present all year in the woodlands. Crossbill is sometimes seen, while strong populations of Wood and Garden Warblers, and small numbers of Tree Pipit and Chiffchaff, occur in summer. Red-breasted Merganser, Common Sandpiper, Grey Wagtail and Dipper frequent the loch and its shore during summer. Kingfisher is seen most autumns. In winter, locally important concentrations of wildfowl occur, including Little Grebe, Greylag Goose, Wigeon, Teal, Mallard, Pochard, Tufted Duck, Goldeneye and occasionally Smew. A few Cormorant overwinter.

Access

There are car parks at the following points:

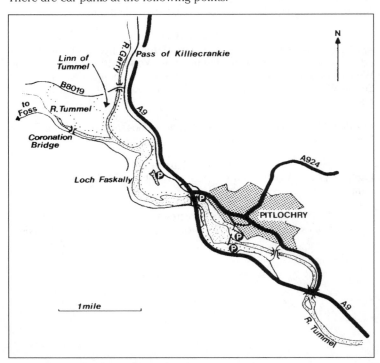

(1) South of the dam at Pitlochry, next to the fish ladder (NN 935577).
(2) North of the dam, signposted from the town centre (NN 936579).
(3) Near the boating station beyond the Green Park Hotel, north of the town centre (NN 928587).

Lochside paths lead from all of these car parks. In summer, it is probably better to park at the FC visitor centre off the old A9, north of Pitlochry (NN 922592), where a number of marked paths give access to the policy woodlands and the loch side. A circular walk around the loch can be made from any of these car parks by making use of the paths and the minor road to Foss. The River Tummel should be crossed at Coronation Bridge (a footbridge) and the River Garry at the old bridge at the foot of the Pass of Killiecrankie. This route takes in the Linn of Tummel (see separate entry). Alternatively, the south basin of the loch (south of the A9 bridge) can be easily circuited on paths.

C22 BEN VRACKIE

OS ref: NN 951633
OS Landranger 43 and 52

A reasonably accessible mountain summit approached through mainly coniferous woodland and managed heather moorland. Although the area is not exceptional for birds, it has a range of species typical of upland east-central Scotland. Sparrowhawk and Buzzard occur in the woodland with Kestrel, Red Grouse and Short-eared Owl on the moors. Few birds are found at the summit, though Ring Ouzel and Twite are possible, and there are fine views of the surrounding terrain. From the centre of Pitlochry, take the A924 Braemar road, turn left in Moulin (behind the Moulin Inn) and follow this road for c. 0.25 mile (0.4 km), without deviation, to a small car park (NN 945598, OS 52). Allow c. 1.5 hours for the ascent to the summit of Ben Vrackie.

Wheatears, spring

C23 KILLIECRANKIE

OS ref: NN 906628
OS Landranger 43

Wren

Habitat

The Killiecrankie RSPB reserve comprises 465 ha of oak-dominated woodland, pastureland and birch woodland, rising from the gorge of the River Garry to the crag and heather moorland 300 m above. The area is a designated SSSI. The oak woods, which also contain ash, Wych elm and alder, are of considerable botanical interest containing a variety of ferns and mosses. Flowers such as yellow mountain saxifrage, globe flower and grass of Parnassus, together with several species of orchid, are common in calcareous flushes on the hill.

Timing

The reserve is mainly of interest during the nesting season, May–July.

Access

Directions to the reserve are slightly complicated. From the south, visitors should exit the A9 immediately north of Pitlochry, on the B8079. Follow this for 3 miles (4.8 km) through the wooded Pass of Killiecrankie. Turn left in Killiecrankie onto an unclassified road that crosses the railway and the river. Fork left up the hill and branch right after 200 m to the car park at Balrobbie Farm. From the north, leave the A9 1.5 miles (2.4 km) beyond Blair Atholl, and take the B8079 south to Killiecrankie (1.5 miles or 2.4 km). Turn right onto an unclassified road and follow the directions as above. The nearest railway station is at Pitlochry, 4 miles (6.4 km) away, on the Edinburgh–Inverness line. Buses run infrequently from Pitlochry to Killiecrankie. Access to the marked trails is possible at all times.

Calendar

Resident: Sparrowhawk, Buzzard, possible Long-eared Owl, Green and Great Spotted Woodpeckers in the oak woodland; Siskin and Redpoll frequent birch areas, while Black Grouse occur on the moorland fringe.

At least one pair of Kestrel occupies the crags each year, but Raven is becoming less frequent. Golden Eagle and Peregrine are seen occasionally over high ground.

May–July: Curlew, Tree Pipit, Redstart, Whinchat, Garden Warbler and Wood Warbler. Small numbers of Pied Flycatcher breed and have been further encouraged by the provision of nest boxes. Crossbill is occasionally seen.

C24 LINN OF TUMMEL

OS ref: NN 91/60
OS Landranger 43

This area, owned by the NTS, lies downstream of the Pass of Killiecrankie, at the confluence of the Rivers Garry and Tummel (see map of Loch Faskally, site T16). Access is free at all times. The mainly deciduous woodland has a good variety of breeding birds, including those to be found at the RSPB's Killiecrankie reserve. Along the rivers, Red-breasted Merganser, Goosander, Common Sandpiper, Grey Wagtail and Dipper can be seen. There is a visitor centre, open April–October, at the Pass of Killiecrankie, signposted off the B8019 some 4 miles (6.4 km) north of Pitlochry.

Dipper

ADDITIONAL SITES

Site & Grid Reference	Habitat	Main Bird Interest	Peak Season
a Carron Valley Reservoir NS 69/83 OS 64	Reservoir surrounded by coniferous woodland.	Winter wildfowl including small visiting flock of Bean Geese in October; Crossbill and Siskin breed.	Oct–Apr
b Dollar Glen NTS NS 962989 OS 58	Oak woodland in steep gorge.	Wood Warbler, Redstart, Spotted and Pied Flycatchers, Dipper.	May–Jun
c Endrick Mouth NS 42/87 OS 56	Swamp, lagoons, fen and willow carr at southeast corner of Loch Lomond.	Wintering wildfowl including up to 100 White-fronted Geese.	Oct–Mar
		Small numbers of passage waders.	Spring, autumn
d Queen Elizabeth Forest Park FC OS 56 & 57	Vast and diverse area of conifers, oakwoods, heather and bracken moorland, mountain summits.	Woodland and moorland species. Ptarmigan on some summits.	Apr–Oct
	Information about the forest park is available at the David Marshall Lodge Forest Park Visitor Centre near Aberfoyle, open 11.00 am to 7.00 pm daily, mid-March to mid-October. See also QE Forest Park Guide, available from FC.		
e Tillicoultry Glen NS 914975 OS 58	Open valley/fast-flowing stream.	Grey wagtail, Dipper, Whitethroat.	May–Jun
f Blackness Castle NT 056803 OS 65	Estuarine foreshore on either side of Blackness Castle (park in Blackness village).	Wildfowl and waders.	Oct–Mar
g Morton Lochs NO 46/26 OS 54 or 59	Artificial lochs with surrounding marsh and woodland.	Migrant wildfowl and waders.	Aug–Nov
h Newburgh NO 22/18 OS 58	Offshore island and intertidal habitats.	Roosting geese.	Oct–Apr
i Pettycur Bay NT 27/86 OS 66	Sandy, tidal bay.	Waders, terns and gulls.	Aug–Oct

C Additional sites

Site & Grid Reference	Habitat	Main Bird Interest	Peak Season
j Moonzie NO 34/17 OS 59	Open water fringed by reedbed.	Waders, gulls and geese.	Aug–Mar
k Rossie Bog NO 27/10 OS 59	Reed-fringed bog with drainage of streams.	Grasshopper Warbler. Hen Harrier, Short-eared Owl, finches.	May–Jun Sep–Dec
l Lindores Loch NO 26/16 OS 59	Open water fringed by farmland and reedbed.	Geese, ducks, Water Rail.	Oct–Mar
m Tentsmuir Pt. NO 500242 OS 59	Sandy shore.	Terns (including Little Tern), gulls, waders, ducks. Snow Bunting.	Aug–Nov Oct–Nov
n The Hermitage NTS NO 01/42 OS 53	Mixed conifer and deciduous woodland, steep gorge of River Braan.	Common woodland species; Dipper and Grey Wagtail.	Apr–Oct
o Rannoch Forest FC NN 58/55 OS 51	Birch and Caledonian pine woods on south shore of Loch Rannoch. A series of walks of 1–5.5 miles (1.6–8 km) lead through the woods and along the burns.	Black Grouse, Siskin and Scottish Crossbill Breeding visitors including Tree Pipit, Redstart, Spotted Flycatcher.	All year May–Jul
p Rannoch Moor OS 41–42, 50–51	Vast area of bogs, lochans and wet moorland.	Divers, Merlin, Peregrine, Greenshank and other moorland birds.	May–Aug
q Stormont Loch SWT Reserve NO 193422 OS 53	Inland loch with fringing fen, willow scrub and woodland.	Wintering wildfowl, especially Wigeon, Teal and Goldeneye; smaller numbers of Shoveler and Tufted Duck. Breeding duck including Pochard and Ruddy Duck; small number of resident Canada Geese.	Oct–Mar

DUMFRIES & GALLOWAY

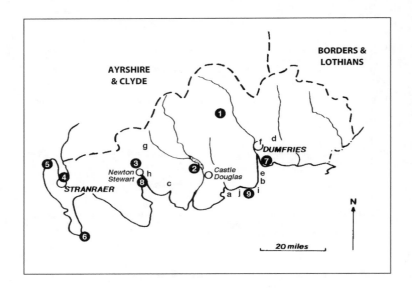

Main sites

DG1 Stenhouse Wood
DG2 Loch Ken/River Dee
DG3 Wood of Cree
DG4 Loch Ryan
DG5 Corsewall Point
DG6 Mull of Galloway
DG7 Caerlaverock
DG8 Wigtown Bay
DG9 Mersehead

Additional sites

a Auchencairn Bay
b Carsethorn
c Carstramon
d Castle Loch, Lochmaben
e Drummains Reedbed
f Fountainbleau and Ladypark
g Glen Trool
h Kirroughtree
i Southerness Point
j Southwick Coast

Habitat

This lowland woodland is situated on a northeast-facing hillside and contains deciduous trees of many types, including oak, ash, hazel, beech and willow. Stenhouse Wood covers 18 ha and is owned by the SWT. It is a designated SSSI. The wood has two main components: the lower part consists of mature broadleaf and is the best area for birds, while the upper section has recently been replanted with deciduous species following clearance of a coniferous plantation. Open scrubland with emergent trees therefore characterises the upper slopes, leading onto open hillside. The entire site is botanically very rich and trampling easily damages its rare ground flora.

Species

Sparrowhawk, Buzzard, Great Spotted and Green Woodpecker, Willow Tit and Siskin are amongst the resident birds likely to be seen. Breeding visitors include Redstart, Chiffchaff and Wood, Garden and Willow Warblers. In winter, Woodcock, Redwing and Fieldfare may be found.

Access

The reserve is approached from the village of Tynron, which lies about 1.5 miles (2.4 km) north of the A702 Penpont–Moniaive road. Once in Tynron, cross the river and turn right at the war memorial. After 0.3 mile (0.5 km) turn right into a no-through road. The reserve is on the left after about 0.5 mile (0.8 km). There are no signs to identify the reserve and parking requires care on the narrow road. The reserve is open to members and non-members of the SWT alike.

Timing

The reserve is always open, but please take care to avoid disturbance to nesting birds. Most migrants arrive late April/early May; May and June are the best months to visit.

DG2   LOCH KEN/
RIVER DEE

OS ref: NX 63/76 to 73/60
OS Landranger 84 & 77

Habitat

The construction of a hydroelectric dam across the River Dee at Glenlochar, north of Castle Douglas, in 1935 has resulted in the formation of a shallow-sided loch system just over 9 miles (14.5 km) long, flanked by marshland and meadows. Technically speaking, the southern part of the loch is still the River Dee and it is only that part north of the confluence of the Black Water of Dee, just below the old railway viaduct, that is referred to as Loch Ken. Extensive mudflats are revealed when the water level falls, especially on the southwestern shore. The loch is bordered by hillside farmland and deciduous woods, adding to the area's diversity.

The RSPB manages a total of over 162 ha of marsh, meadow and broadleaf woodland in five separate areas, although the most important holdings are at Kenmure Holms near New Galloway and also that between Mains of Duchrae and Black Water of Dee. In addition, at Threave, immediately west of Castle Douglas, the NTS has a 348-ha estate of considerable ornithological interest. Three SSSI have been designated on the Ken–Dee system between New Galloway and Glenlochar, with others at Threave and Carlingwark Loch.

Access

Good views over the area can be obtained from the roads around the loch: the A762 Laurieston–New Galloway road on the west bank, the A713 New Galloway–Castle Douglas road on the east, and the road connecting these in the south, the B795 from Townhead of Greenlaw to Laurieston. The best road for viewing the River Dee marshes is the C50 from

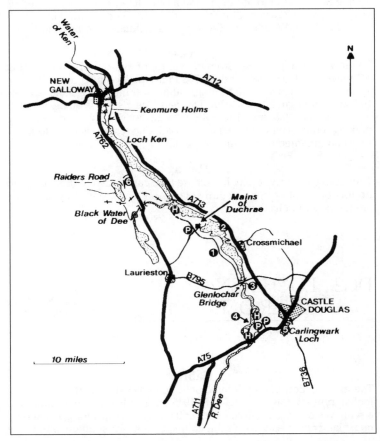

Glenlochar Bridge (see point 1, below). The RSPB have built a car park at the entrance to the Mains of Duchrae Farm (NX 699684) and from here visitors may walk to a hide on the loch shore. The round walk is 3 miles (5 km) and affords good opportunities to see the birds in this most varied part of the reserve. Fields, hedgerows, deciduous scrub and woodland and finally marshland are encountered en route. The area is good throughout the year for Willow Tit and in the breeding season for Pied Flycatcher, various warblers, field-nesting waders and breeding duck. In autumn/winter, ducks, hunting Hen Harrier and Barn Owl (always present) provide the main interest. Large groups should liaise with the RSPB warden in advance to arrange an escorted visit. Contact Paul Collin, Gairland, Old Edinburgh Road, Minnigaff, Newton Stewart DG8 6PL. Outside the RSPB reserve, the following areas are recommended.

(1) A minor road (C50) leaves the B795 north, immediately west of Glenlochar Bridge, 1 mile (1.6 km) from Townhead of Greenlaw; this affords views of the southwest part of the loch, before rejoining the A762, 0.5 mile (0.8 km) north of Laurieston. Please park considerately and do not obstruct other traffic. The area is a good one for wintering geese, especially at Mains of Duchrae, which is much favoured by Greenland Whitefronts and Greylag.

(2) The east shore between Crossmichael and Parton, especially the pasture around Cogarth, is another regular White-front haunt.

(3) Culvennan/Mains of Greenlaw area, south of the B795 between Glenlochar and the A713, is sometimes frequented by a large herd of Whooper Swan in winter, although these birds are more often seen at Threave.

(4) Threave Estate (OS ref: NX 74/62) is an area of farmland and marshes beside the River Dee, providing good feeding grounds for wildfowl in autumn and winter. The estate is entered from the A75 Castle Douglas–Bridge of Dee road at Kelton Mains Farm, 1 mile (1.6 km) west of Castle Douglas. Maps showing the location of paths and hides are displayed at the car park. There are five hides: two on the disused railway line give good views across the fields where the geese feed, one on an island overlooks fields and the river, while another two on the riverbank afford views of the river and marshes. Goosander is fairly common on the river. Kingfisher is present all year. The estate is open all year: there is no charge. A leaflet and further information are available from the visitor centre at Threave Gardens, although this is closed in winter. Ranger: Threave Gardens, Castle Douglas, Dumfries and Galloway DG7 1RX (tel: 01556 502575).

(5) Carlingwark Loch, on the southwest outskirts of Castle Douglas, can be comprehensively viewed from the A75, 0.5 mile (0.8 km) from the town centre. The loch is particularly good for diving duck in winter, including Goldeneye and Goosander.

(6) Bennan Forest (FC). The conifers west of Loch Ken and north of Mossdale, are productive for Siskin, Redpoll and Crossbill. The area also has a scattered population of Black Grouse, although these are now very scarce. Access can be gained via the Raiders Road, a 10-mile (16 km) drive through the forest which starts at the A762, about 1 mile (1.6 km)

White-fronted Geese, November

north of Mossdale and emerges onto the A712 Newton Stewart–New Galloway road at Clatteringshaws Loch. It is open from late May to October.

Timing
There is bird activity throughout the year in this area, although midsummer is probably the slackest time to visit. A winter visit is strongly recommended.

Calendar
Resident: Great Crested Grebe, Goosander and dabbling ducks. Peregrine, Buzzard and Barn Owl regularly hunt over the area. Willow Tit can be found in areas of scrubby birch, hazel and willow; Great Spotted and a few Green Woodpeckers frequent the more mature deciduous woodland, although the latter species is very localised.

March–May: Swans and geese usually depart mid-April, although the occasional Whooper remains into early May. Marshland breeders include Great Crested Grebe, Teal, Shoveler, Snipe and Redshank. Sedge and Grasshopper Warblers establish territories in emergent vegetation around the loch shore. In the scattered deciduous woods Tree Pipit, Redstart, Wood Warbler and Pied Flycatcher breed. About three pairs of Common Tern usually breed. A few waders may stopover en route north; a passage Osprey is an outside possibility.

June–July: Return migration commences in late July and generally brings a few waders to the exposed mud at the southwestern fringes of the loch. Breeding duck assume their nondescript eclipse plumage.

August–November: Wader passage continues and terns are occasionally present. Pintail is usually visible among dabbling duck in the River Dee marshes around the Mains of Duchrae; most Shoveler depart as winter approaches. A few dabbling duck occur at Kenmure Holms, north of Loch Ken. Whooper Swan may appear at any time from late September; Greenland White-fronted Geese start to arrive in early October.

December–February: Up to 300 Greenland White-fronted Geese visit the valley, together with Greylag Goose, Wigeon, Pintail, Teal, Mallard, Goosander and Goldeneye. Whooper Swan and Greylag Goose winter in the vicinity of Threave and are joined by Pink-footed Geese from Christmas. The formerly common Bean Geese is now a very rare visitor to the Threave area, usually during severe weather in January–February. There is some fall-off in swan numbers by midwinter as birds disperse, possibly to Ireland. Hen Harrier hunts over the marshes and farmland; Great Grey Shrike is occasionally seen in midwinter.

DG3   WOOD OF CREE

OS ref: NX 382708
OS Landranger 77

Habitat

An extensive area of deciduous woodland, situated on the eastern slopes above the River Cree and consisting mainly of sessile oak, birch and hazel. The RSPB owns 266 ha of woodland and some of the riverside meadows and floodplain on the opposite side of the river. Much of the area is a designated SSSI.

Species

Sparrowhawk, Buzzard, Woodcock, Great Spotted Woodpecker and Willow Tit are resident breeders in the woods. Characteristic summer visitors to the oakwoods include Wood Warbler, Pied Flycatcher and Redstart; Tree Pipit is common in areas of scattered trees and at the upper woodland fringe. Along streams and riversides Grey Wagtail and Dipper nest, joined in spring by Common Sandpiper. The wet meadows adjacent to the River Cree are good for Teal, Mallard, Oystercatcher and Snipe; Water Rail breeds. The surrounding countryside is a particularly good area in which to see Barn Owl.

Barn Owl

Access

Wood of Cree is approached from Newton Stewart via the adjacent village of Minnigaff. From here follow the unclassified road on the east side of the River Cree, running parallel with the A714 Newton Stewart–Girvan road on the opposite bank. The reserve is reached after 4 miles (6.4 km)—a parking area is marked by RSPB signs and from here a woodland track leads into the reserve. Access is possible at all times, but visitors are requested to keep to marked trails. There are regular buses to Newton Stewart, just over 4 miles (6.4 km) away.

Timing

The reserve can be of interest at any time, but a May/June visit will be most productive.

Galloway RSPB Warden

Paul Collin, Gairland, Old Edinburgh Road, Minnigaff, Newton Stewart DG8 6PL.

DG4   LOCH RYAN

OS ref: NX 05/65
OS Landranger 82

Habitat

Loch Ryan is a very large and mostly enclosed sea loch in southwest Galloway. The dimensions of the loch are approximately 8 miles (13 km) from the head of the loch to the open sea and 1.5–2.5 miles (2.44 km) in width. The loch is deep and the shore shelves steeply with only limited intertidal areas, principally at the south end and at The Wig, a small bay to the west.

Species

Wintering waterfowl provide the main interest; Red-throated and occasional Black-throated and Great Northern Divers occur; small numbers of Slavonian and Black-necked Grebes are also generally present, with the occasional Red-necked too. Eider is numerous, with over 300 often present; other sea duck include large flocks of Scaup, Red-breasted Merganser and smaller groups of Common Scoter and Goldeneye. Long-tailed Duck is sometimes present and King Eider has been recorded on occasion. Wigeon and Mallard are the most numerous dabbling duck. Moderate numbers of Oystercatcher and Lapwing overwinter and the area can be good for passage waders, including Golden Plover and Knot. Both Iceland and Glaucous Gulls are likely in winter when small numbers of Black Guillemot can be seen.

Access

Loch Ryan is easily worked from the surrounding roads: the A77 on the east and south shores, and the A718 along the west shore. There are many suitable stopping places/vantage points. Recommended areas to scan are the Cairnryan area to the east (NX 06/68), the entire south shore and The Wig (NX 03/67).

Timing

A visit between October and March is recommended. Strong afternoon sunlight can restrict viewing from the east shore of the loch.

DG5   CORSEWALL POINT

OS ref: NW 98/72
OS Landranger 76

Manx Shearwaters

This excellent seawatching point is about 3 miles (5 km) west of the entrance to Loch Ryan. It can be reached from Stranraer by taking the A718 north for 8 miles (13 km), turning right onto an unclassified road to Corsewall lighthouse, 3 miles (4.8 km) away. The optimum time to visit is autumn, from mid-August to late October, when passage of large numbers of Manx Shearwater, Gannet, Shag, Kittiwake and auks can occur. Smaller numbers of Storm and occasional Leach's Petrels and Arctic and Great Skuas are likely, especially in westerly winds. There have been several sightings of Sabine's Gull.

DG6   MULL OF GALLOWAY

OS ref: NX 157304
OS Landranger 82

Habitat

A rocky headland 22 miles (35 km) south of Stranraer, at the tip of the Rhinns peninsula. This RSPB reserve consists of 0.75 mile (1.2 km) of rugged granite cliff, rising to a maximum height of just over 80 m. The site is a designated SSSI.

Species

Nesting seabirds include Fulmar, Cormorant, Shag, Kittiwake, Guillemot, Razorbill and Black Guillemot. A few Puffin are seen most years, but no longer nest here. An offshore Gannet colony, currently numbering over 800 nests, is located on Scare Rocks, also an RSPB reserve, 7 miles (11.3 km) east of the Mull. Large numbers of Manx Shearwater regularly pass the headland in September. Passerine migrants also occur, including various warblers and occasional Black Redstart. Stonechat and Twite are resident. The Mull of Galloway is one of the few places in Dumfries and Galloway where Corn Bunting can be seen.

Access

The reserve is reached from the Stranraer–Newton Stewart road by taking the A715 or A716 south to Drummore, then the B7041 toward the Mull lighthouse. Access is possible at all times, but there is no warden (except sometimes in summer; May–July). Good views can be obtained from near the lighthouse; visitors are warned that the cliff edge is dangerous. Contact Paul Collin, Gairland, Old Edinburgh Road, Minnigaff, Newton Stewart DG8 6PL.

Timing

Breeding seabirds provide the principal interest, so the best time to visit is between May and mid-July.

DG7   CAERLAVEROCK

OS ref: NY 03/65
OS Landranger 84 & 85

Habitat

The 5500-ha NNR at Caerlaverock stretches for 6 miles (9.7 km) along the north Solway coast between the estuary of the River Nith and that of Lochar Water to the east. The extensive foreshore, saltmarsh and mudflats are internationally important for wintering wildfowl, particularly Barnacle Goose. The WWT Refuge at Eastpark (NY 05/65) covers 524 ha of saltmarsh and farmland, with excellent viewing facilities. These include 20 hides, an observatory and two observation towers. The pond immediately in front of the observatory enables up to 17 species of wildfowl to be watched at very close range. Controlled shooting is permitted over parts of the NNR.

Species

The principal attraction is the very large numbers of wintering Pink-footed and Barnacle Geese. The inner Solway holds the entire Svalbard breeding population of Barnacle Geese—these start to arrive at Caerlaverock in late September/early October and reach a peak of around 12,500 by mid-November. Pink-footed Geese are most numerous in late winter, usually in January–March, when up to 5000 roost on the merse. Both these and the smaller flocks of Greylag Geese feed on farmland managed deliberately for geese by the WWT. As well as the geese, up to 350 Whooper Swan overwinter with smaller numbers of Bewick's Swan (usually in late October) and up to 70 Mute Swan. Wintering dabbling duck include large numbers of Wigeon, Teal, Mallard and Pintail, with small numbers of Shoveler and Gadwall. Up to 400 Shelduck are present in late winter. Hen Harrier, Sparrowhawk, Peregrine and Merlin regularly hunt the saltmarsh for wintering duck, waders or passerines.

Very large numbers of Oystercatcher (up to 15,000), Golden Plover, Lapwing, Dunlin (over 5000) and Curlew (over 3000) roost on the saltmarsh. Smaller numbers of Grey Plover, Knot and Redshank are also recorded. Passage waders include large numbers of Sanderling in May and occasional Little Stint, Curlew Sandpiper, Black-tailed Godwit, Whimbrel, Ruff and Spotted Redshank in autumn. Recent rarities have included Little Egret and Red-breasted Goose.

Access

The B725 from Dumfries to Bankend affords good general views of the merse and the eastern side of the Nith estuary. There is a parking area at NY 018653. The WWT refuge at Eastpark is reached by taking the signed turning from the B725 1 mile (1.6 km) south of Bankend. Visitors should report to the observatory on arrival. A modest admission charge is levied.

Timing

Caerlaverock is an excellent area for birdwatching throughout the winter, October–March. The Eastpark refuge is open daily and the warden conducts escorted tours at 11.00 am and 2.00 pm daily.

SNH Warden

Caerlaverock Reserve Office, Hollands Farm Road, Caerlaverock, Dumfries DG1 4RS (tel: 01387 770275).

Wildfowl and Wetlands Trust Warden

Eastpark Farm, Caerlaverock, Dumfries DG1 4RS (tel: 01387 770200).

DG8 WIGTOWN BAY

OS ref: NX 45/56 etc.
OS Landranger 83

Habitat

Wigtown Bay is an area of merse and intertidal mud/sandflats formed by the estuaries of the Rivers Cree and Bladnoch. A 3500-ha LNR was established in 1992. In addition, the area is a SSSI and has been proposed for Ramsar and SPA designation. The area is bordered to the west by the Moss of Cree, while to the northeast lie the hills of Cairnsmore of Fleet.

Newton Stewart lies upstream on the River Cree; the smaller towns of Wigtown and Creetown lie on the west and east shores of the bay respectively.

Species

The area is important for wintering wildfowl and waders, including up to 10,000 Pink-footed Geese in January–May, and up to 1000 Greylag. Around 2500 Oystercatcher and 2000 Curlew winter, with lesser numbers of Shelduck, Pintail, Wigeon, Dunlin and Knot. Winter is also a good time to see various raptors hunting over the area, especially Hen Harrier, Merlin and Peregrine.

Access

Birding is difficult owing to limited access points, long-distance observation and disturbance problems. However, good views of the geese can often be obtained from the Moss of Cree road. Leave the A75 Newton Stewart–Creetown road 1 mile east of Newton Stewart and follow this loop road until it rejoins the A75 2 miles (3.2 km) later. The unclassified road leading east from the A714 Newton Stewart–Wigtown road, c. 2 miles (3.2 km) south of Newton Stewart, affords good general views of the west side of the estuary.

Warden

Wigtown Town Hall, Wigtown, Dumfries and Galloway.

DG9 MERSEHEAD

OS ref: NX 925560
OS Landranger 84

Habitat and Species

The reserve comprises 243 ha of ground owned by RSPB plus 500 ha of ground leased by RSPB from the Crown Estate. Mersehead is a relatively new reserve and now has visitor facilities. Marked walks provide good views of the reserve. Hides and further trails are presently being developed. The farmed part of the reserve mostly consists of grazed grassland with small areas of cereal and root crops.

The grassland is managed for breeding waders, such as Lapwing and Curlew, and wintering Barnacle (Svalbard population) and Pink-footed Geese. The crops provide food for wintering flocks of Chaffinch, Brambling and Linnet. Further habitat management should increase numbers of Skylark. Raptors hunting over the reserve include Peregrine, Merlin and Hen Harrier. Roe deer may be seen feeding in the fields. The saltmarsh is used by wintering geese. Grey Heron, Teal and Redshank feed in the channels. The shore and mudflats hold thousands of passage and wintering waders, comprising mostly Oystercatcher, Knot, Dunlin, Bartailed Godwit and Curlew. Shelduck feed out on the mud as well as on the merse and farmland.

The narrow strip of broadleaf woodland in the southeast of the reserve supports many common woodland birds. Management to increase the variety of tree species and shrub areas will greatly improve this habitat for birds.

Management plans for Mersehead have yet to be finalised, although work to create more grassland for geese and waders, and reversing the effects of previous land drainage, has been undertaken. A reedbed is planned.

Access

The reserve is reached via the A710 Dumfries–Dalbeattie road. Immediately east of Caulkerbush turn south and follow the road to Mersehead Farm. There is a car park to the right as you enter the farm buildings. Please keep to the paths: a route map is available at the reserve. There is a main walk of 3.5 miles (marked with blue arrows) or a shorter walk of about 2 miles (head down the farm track toward the broadleaf wood and either continue to the end of the track or turn right past the wood to reach the shore). Be aware that the tide covers the merse at times. Electric fences will be in operation when livestock are present. No dogs are allowed. The reserve is open at all times, admission free. RSPB Mersehead Reserve visitor centre (tel: 01387 780298)

ADDITIONAL SITES

Site & Grid Reference	Habitat	Main Bird Interest	Peak Season
a Auchencairn Bay NX 82/50 OS 84	Large and sheltered inter-tidal area.	Large numbers of wintering wildfowl and waders.	Oct–Mar
	View from unclassified road from Auchencraig to Balcary Bay. Path from road end to seabird cliffs at Balcary Heugh: nesting Fulmar, Cormorant, Shag, Kittiwake, Razorbill, Guillemot and Black Guillemot.		
b Carsethorn NX 98/60 OS 84	Rocky coastline and creek.	Migrant and wintering waders. Off-shore Scaup very common.	Aug–May
	See also Southerness Point.		
c Carstramon SWT Reserve NX 592605 OS 83	Mixed woodland.	Wood Warbler, Redstart, Pied Fly-catcher, Green and Great Spotted Woodpecker.	Apr–Jul
d Castle Loch, Lochmaben NY 08/81 OS 78	Loch, fringing reedbeds and woodland.	Roosting Greylag Geese and other wintering wildfowl.	Aug–May
e Drummains Reedbed SWT Reserve NX 986772 OS 84	Reedbed and marsh.	Breeding Common Tern, Sedge War-bler and Reed Bunting.	Apr–Jul
		Wintering wildfowl and waders.	Oct–Mar
f Foutainbleau and Ladypark SWT Reserve NX 986772 OS 84	Wet birch woods; hide overlooks a newly created pond. Small visitor centre.	Willow Tit, Sedge Warbler, Redpoll and Reed Bunting.	Apr–Jul
g Glen Trool FC NX 400790 OS 77	Part of Galloway Forest Park. Loch, coniferous and oak woodland.	Hen Harrier, Peregrine, Siskin and Crossbill.	All year
		Wood Warbler, Redstart and Pied Fly-catcher.	May–Jul
	A 4.5-mile (7.2 km) trail circuits Loch Trool. Leaflet available from FC.		

Site & Grid Reference	Habitat	Main Bird Interest	Peak Season
h Kirroughtree FC NX 451645 OS 83	Streamside meadows, scrub and broadleaf woodland, various conifer rotations.	Buzzard, Tawny Owl, Dipper, Grey Wagtail, Wood and Garden Warblers, Jay, small numbers of Willow Tit. Golden Pheasant.	May–Jul

From the Visitor Centre, the 'Papy Ha' bird trail leads through the valley of the Palnure Burn (trail length is 3.5 miles or 5 miles (5.6 or 8 km) depending on route). Leaflet available from centre.

i Southerness Point NX 97/54 OS 84	Peninsula extending into Solway Firth.	Good seawatching vantage point: offshore divers, Scaup, Common/Velvet Scoter and auks. Also roosting and feeding waders, including large numbers of Bar-tailed Godwit. Purple Sandpiper and Turnstone common on rocky shoreline.	Nov–Mar

Leave A710 1 mile (0.8 km) south of Kirkbean and park at end of minor road to Southerness. See also Carsethorn.

j Southwick Coast SWT Reserve NX 91/55	Saltmarsh, fen and ancient oakwood on inland cliff.	Very large numbers of wintering Greylag, Pink-footed and Barnacle Geese and other wildfowl and waders.	Oct–Mar

Car park off A710. Follow track to Needle's Eye.

HIGHLAND

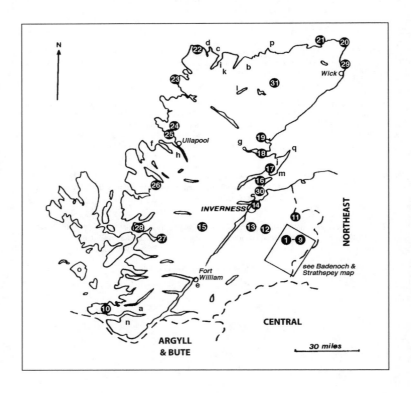

Main sites

H1	Aviemore	
H2	Abernethy Forest–Loch Garten	
H3	Rothiemurchus	
H4	Pass of Ryvoan	
H5	Cairngorm/Ben Macdui	
H6	Carn Ban Mor	
H7	Glen Feshie	
H8	Insh Marshes	
H9	Glen Tromie	
H10	Glenborrodale/	

Ardnamurchan
H11 Lochindorb
H12 Findhorn Valley
H13 Loch Ruthven
H14 Longman Point
H15 Glen Affric
H16 Udale Bay
H17 Nigg Bay
H18 Dornoch Firth
H19 Loch Fleet
H20 Duncansby Head
H21 Dunnet Head

H22 Clo Mor
H23 Handa Island
H24 Inverpolly
H25 Ben Mor Coigach
H26 Beinn Eighe
H27 Kintail and Morvich
H28 Balmacara Estate
H29 Noss Head
H30 Chanonry Point
H31 Forsinard RSPB
Reserve

Additional sites

a   Ariundle
b   Borgie Forest
c   Eilean Hoan
d   Faraid Head
e   Glen Nevis
f   Gruinard Bay

g   Kyle of Sutherland
h   Loch Broom
i   Loch Eriboll
j   Loch Eye
k   Loch Hope
l   Loch Naver

m   North Sutor
n   Rahoy Hills
o   Rum
p   Strathy Point
q   Tarbat Ness
r   Torridon

H1 AVIEMORE OS Landranger 36

Three areas are of particular interest here.

CRAIGELLACHIE (OS REF: NH 88/12)

Habitat and Access
This is a 260-ha NNR consisting mainly of birch woodland situated below sheer cliffs and open heather moorland. The crag is a well-known and freely publicised site for breeding Peregrine, which can be observed from the public footpath below. Craigellachie is on the very edge of Aviemore and can be reached from the car park next to the artificial ski-slope by walking along the path that goes under the A9 road. The Peregrine crag is now on the left. Several well-marked footpaths continue beyond this point into the woodland.

Species
The area is also notable for several woodland species: Great Spotted Woodpecker is resident, while migrant breeders include Tree Pipit, Redstart, Wood Warbler and Spotted Flycatcher. Siskin can usually be seen during autumn and winter.

Timing
Peregrine should be present in April–July, but it may be necessary to wait patiently for some time before the birds show themselves.

INVERDRUIE FISH FARM (OS REF: NH 898117)

Another site on the outskirts of Aviemore, this time famed for its Osprey which fish over the ponds on a daily basis during summer. There is a modest entrance fee.

Species
A hide overlooks the large well-stocked pool, which can attract three or four Osprey simultaneously particularly in late summer. Adults can be seen feeding young or the young themselves may come and feed. Tufted Duck and Goldeneye are often present on the pool, while Garden and Wood Warblers inhabit the surrounding scrub and trees.

Access
The entrance to the farm is reached by taking the road east from Aviemore towards Coylumbridge, then turning into the car park immediately beyond the bridge over the River Spey. It is an easy stroll from the town centre and is best reached on foot. Follow a footpath opposite the tourist information office, which leads to the fish farm via Mac's pub and a footbridge over the Spey.

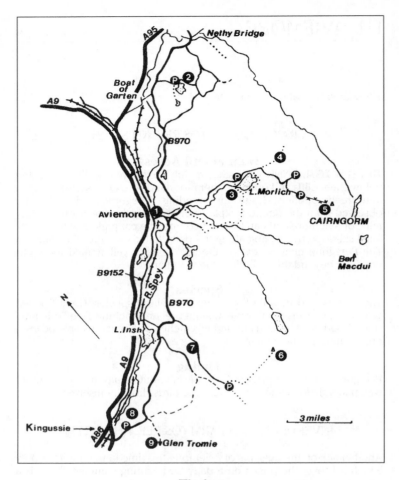

Timing

Osprey can be seen throughout the summer. The fish farm is popular with tourists and the best time for birding is therefore early in the morning (before 08.00 am) or late evening (after 6.00 pm).

LOCH AN EILEIN (OS REF: NH 895075)

This scenic loch is famous for its ruined castle, upon which Osprey once nested. It is reached by turning south onto the B970 at Inverdruie, 1 mile (1.6 km) from Aviemore. Take the unclassified road left 1 mile (1.6 km) later and follow it 0.75 mile (1.2 km) to the car park. From here a nature trail leads around the loch shore. Goldeneye is usually present and Red-throated Diver visit during summer. In the surrounding woodland, Redstart, Crested Tit, Siskin and Scottish Crossbill might be seen, and Green Woodpecker is present in some years.

H2 ABERNETHY FOREST–
LOCH GARTEN

OS ref: NH 975180
OS Landranger 36

Habitat

Loch Garten is part of the RSPB's Abernethy Forest Reserve and is world famous for its breeding Ospreys. This 12,500-ha reserve also holds several pine forest specialities. The area, a designated SSSI, is a remnant of the once more extensive Caledon Forest. The habitat includes forest bogs, lochs, heather moorland, mountain plateau and croft land.

Species

Goldeneye can be seen on Loch Garten and Loch Mallachie throughout the summer. Crested Tit is common in the woods and Scottish Crossbill usually present—the track to Loch Mallachie is probably as good a place as any to find them. Capercaillie is very scarce but can sometimes be encountered on the road early in the morning or, increasingly, in front of the Osprey hide! Woodcock is plentiful and particularly conspicuous in early April–early June, when they can be seen and heard roding in the evenings. Other interesting breeders include Sparrowhawk, Great Spotted Woodpecker, Tree Pipit, Redstart, Whinchat and Siskin.

If travelling through Boat of Garten, it is worthwhile briefly checking the River Spey as you cross the bridge—Goldeneye, Red-breasted Merganser and sometimes Dipper can be seen. Goosander is present in winter. Furthermore, the view of the Cairngorms is terrific on a clear day. In November–December up to 1500 Greylag Geese roost on Loch Garten

Osprey, spring

145

(when not frozen), along with several of the larger gulls. From October to November up to 100 Goosander have roosted, and Goldeneye is usually present. From early March a gull roost of up to 4500 Black-headed Gulls can be seen here, along with good numbers of the commoner ducks, including up to ten Red-breasted Mergansers.

Access

Loch Garten lies midway between the villages of Nethy Bridge and Boat of Garten (c. 2.5 miles or 4 km from each) and is well signed off the B970. Buses run from Aviemore and Grantown to Nethy Bridge and Boat of Garten—the best place to alight is at East Croftmore, about 1 mile (1.6 km) from the loch. The nearest mainline rail station is at Carrbridge (8 miles or 13 km distant), but the Strathspey railway, which links Aviemore to Boat of Garten, may be of use.

Contrary to most people's expectations, the Osprey eyrie is not on the loch shore, but on the opposite side of the road. Apart from obvious restrictions in the vicinity of the Osprey nest, there is open access to the reserve. From the car park a short track leads to the Osprey observation hide, which affords excellent views of the eyrie and is equipped with telescopes, binoculars and a closed-circuit television system. The hide is accessible to wheelchair users and assistance along the track is available—alternatively a post can be removed to enable cars with disabled occupants to drive to the hide. Some of the other forest tracks are also negotiable by wheelchair. In summer, an RSPB warden conducts guided walks through the reserve: make arrangements with staff at the Osprey hide. Parties are limited to 12–15 people.

Timing

Provided that the Ospreys are nesting, the observation hide is open daily from late April to August, 10.00 am to 8.00 pm. (Note: the hide is not open until some time after the birds first arrive, in order to give them a chance to re-establish themselves and settle down. Announcements in the press that 'the Ospreys are back' do not necessarily mean that they are on public view. If in doubt, contact the tourist information office in Aviemore, where up-to-date information is available. The most exciting time to visit is probably July and early August, when the birds should be feeding young.)

Warden

Abernethy Forest Lodge (tel: 01479 821409). Boat of Garten (tel: 01479 831648).

Adjacent Site

LOCH PITYOULISH (OS REF: NH 920135)

Visible from the B970 Coylumbridge–Boat of Garten road, this loch holds Goldeneye and Goosander in summer and is occasionally fished by Osprey.

H3 ROTHIEMURCHUS AND LOCH MORLICH

OS ref: NH 93/08
OS Landranger 36

Black Grouse

Habitat

A large area of the formerly extensive Caledonian pine forest, holding many of the characteristic native pinewood species. Loch Morlich is much disturbed by watersports enthusiasts, but is still a good location for waterfowl and fishing Osprey. Unfortunately, conifers have been planted right to the edge of the loch, making it unsuitable these days for nesting Greenshank. The loch is within the FC's Glenmore Forest Park, a 2,644-ha expanse of commercial woodland and heather moor. The birds of the forest park are similar to those of Rothiemurchus, but the area is not as inspiring scenically.

Species

Loch Morlich has Wigeon and small parties of Goosander throughout the year. Red-throated Diver and Goldeneye are regular in spring and summer and Osprey occasionally visit. The best time for divers is early morning and late evening, when there is no disturbance from watersports. Capercaillie is present in the woods, but is elusive and thought to be declining. Crested Tit is very common and can be found year-round, but Scottish Crossbill may need more effort to locate; it is nomadic and numbers fluctuate greatly from year to year. Other species include Sparrowhawk, Black Grouse, Woodcock and Siskin. Redstart is common in spring. A Ring-necked Duck was recorded recently.

Access

A network of footpaths lead through the area—the main access points to these are:

(1) From Coylumbridge, 1.5 miles (2.4 km) east of Aviemore on the A951. A track starts near the telephone box;
(2) From Whitewell, at the end of the minor road out of Inverdruie, 1.5 miles (2.4 km) from Aviemore;
(3) From the west end of Loch Morlich, 2.5 miles (4 km) along the Glenmore road out of Coylumbridge.

Timing
A spring visit is highly recommended, although there is bird interest all year. Late March to early May is probably the best time to locate Capercaillie, midsummer is probably the hardest. A stealthy early-morning walk in the forest is the most likely way that you will see anything more than a huge black shape explode from among the branches ahead. With a lot of luck, a dawn visit may produce a displaying male or perhaps a female taking grit or drinking from a puddle.

H4 PASS OF RYVOAN

OS ref: NH 999105
OS Landranger 36

Habitat and Access
A small (121 ha) reserve managed by the SWT. The steep-sided valley has an attractive mix of open pinewoods, juniper scrub, willow, birch and rowan, with heather and bilberry slopes above. From Aviemore, take the road to the ski-slopes as far as Glenmore. Park in the FC car park and walk up the road past Glenmore Lodge. It is a 40-minute walk to the reserve and the track then carries on through Abernethy Forest and eventually to Nethybridge, a distance of 11 miles (17.6 km).

Species
The species of greatest interest are Woodcock, Crested Tit, Siskin and Scottish Crossbill. Whinchat and Redstart can be seen in spring and summer.

Timing
The reserve makes a good excursion at any time of year, but April–July is the most rewarding time for birds.

H5 CAIRNGORM/BEN MACDUI PLATEAU

OS ref: NJ 005041
OS Landranger 36

Habitat

This is the highest mountain plateau in Britain and includes the summits of Cairngorm (1245 m) and Ben Macdui (1309 m). Not only is the area scenically impressive but also the barren-looking boulder fields are the haunt of three specialist mountain birds: Ptarmigan, Dotterel and Snow Bunting. Much of the area is a NNR and also an RSPB reserve.

Access

Because of the Cairngorm chairlift the area is very easy to visit, though it must be stressed that the weather conditions can be arctic and the trip should not be taken lightly, even in summer. Extra clothing, food, a map and compass are all important if you intend to walk any distance from the chairlift. It would be safer and a better use of time to explore around Loch Morlich and in Rothiemurchus if the cloud base is low in the morning—often it will clear by afternoon.

Take the Coylumbridge road from Aviemore and continue along the ski-road, which leads past Loch Morlich and on to the Cairngorm chairlift car park, 8 miles (13 km) beyond. There is a regular bus service from Aviemore throughout the year. The chairlift operates in all but the worst conditions. Several paths also lead onto the plateau (see OS map). (Note: Jean's Mountain Refuge Hut, marked on all but the most recent OS maps as being in Coire an Lochain, no longer exists.)

Ptarmigan, winter

From the chairlift station, head south towards Ben Macdui—in general the chances of finding birds increase with distance from the chairlift station, although it should not be necessary to walk too far. A good technique is to scan the ground with binoculars every 30–40 mm. Also check out any bird calls, as at this altitude they are all likely to be interesting! It is unfortunate that some groups of birdwatchers form a line and virtually beat across the plateau in order to locate birds—they are doing neither the birds nor birdwatching a service.

Timing
May to early July is probably the ideal time to visit, though Ptarmigan and Snow Bunting can be found year-round.

Species
Ptarmigan is resident on the plateau nearly all year, but during winter when there is a lot of snow cover it is probably easier to locate them at lower altitude, e.g. at Coire an t-Sneachda and Coire an Lochain. Dotterel is present from early May–late August; the adults' plumages start to look rather dowdy from late July, although gatherings of adults and young during August can be quite impressive. Snow Bunting is perhaps the least predictable of the Cairngorm specialities, as its population tends to fluctuate annually. During winter they are often numerous, however, and can be found feeding around the chairlift stations and car parks. Other species include Golden Eagle and Peregrine, although the plateau is not an easy area in which to locate them. Although not seen annually, Snowy Owl has been seen during late summer in several years.

H6 CARN BAN MOR

OS ref: NN 89/97
OS Landranger 35/36

Golden Plover, spring

Species

This is another good area for high-mountain species; Ptarmigan and Dotterel are very likely to be seen here, but Snow Bunting is more elusive than on Cairngorm plateau. Golden Eagle also frequents the area. A Gyrfalcon was recorded recently.

Access

Take the B970 from Inverdruie, near Aviemore, or from Kingussie. At Feshiebridge, c. 7 miles (11 km) from Kingussie, turn south on the Lagganlia road and follow it to the end, 5 miles (8 km) later, at Achlean. There is space to park a car here and the start of the well-worn track to the summit of Carn Ban Mor is obvious. This involves a long ascent of over 700 m and, once again, changeable weather conditions should not be underestimated. In addition to the birdlife is the dramatic scenery, particularly the view over Loch Einich.

H7 GLEN FESHIE

OS ref: NN 850960
OS Landranger 35/36/43

Habitat and Access

A long glen comprising open hill ground, patches of native pinewood and some birch woodland. There has been much forestation of the lower glen. Two roads lead into Glen Feshie from the B970, one each side of the river. The best approach to the upper glen is from the road end at Achlean, the starting point for the ascent of Carn Ban Mor (H6). From here a path more or less follows the river. Alternatively, turn off the B970 at Insh House, 7 miles (11.3 km) from Kingussie, and follow the minor road for 2.5 miles (4 km) until its end. Again, a track along the river leads into the upper valley.

Species

The glen is a good area for raptors: Hen Harrier, Golden Eagle, Merlin and Peregrine are all possible. Dipper and Grey Wagtail frequent the river and Ring Ouzel call from the valley sides. The pinewoods hold Crested Tit and Scottish Crossbill.

Timing

The period April to mid-July is recommended, but the area would make an interesting autumn or winter excursion as well.

Adjacent Site

VATH LOCHAN (OS REF: NH 946192)

This FC picnic area between Glen Feshie and Insh Marshes is a good site for Goldeneye, Great Spotted Woodpecker, Redstart, Crested Tit and Scottish Crossbill.

H8 INSH MARSHES

Habitat

Insh Marshes occupy the floodplain of the River Spey between Kingussie and Loch Insh, 5 miles (8 km) downriver. The reserve covers 850 ha of wetland, farmland, moorland, scrub and woodland, much of it designated a SSSI and RSPB reserve. The marshes include several pools, areas of rough pasture and scattered willow carr. They are regularly flooded in winter, sometimes to a depth of a metre or so. In summer, some of the shallower pools may dry out.

Species

The marshes and fens provide nesting habitat for a wide variety of wildfowl and waders, including Greylag Goose, Wigeon, Teal, Shoveler, Tufted Duck, Goldeneye, Snipe, Curlew and Redshank. Wood Sandpiper usually breeds and Spotted Crake call in most years. Water Rail also breed and the emergent vegetation and scrub hold Sedge and Grasshopper Warblers and Reed Bunting. In the drier birch woods, Great Spotted Woodpecker, Tree Pipit, Redstart, Pied Flycatcher and Wood Warbler occasionally nest. Up to ten species of raptor have been recorded in July and August. The principal attraction in winter is the large numbers of Whooper Swan that are usually present.

Access

The reserve reception centre and car park is entered off the B970 road from Kingussie to Insh village, 1.5 miles (2.4 km) from Kingussie. The nearest railway station is at Kingussie, on the Edinburgh–Inverness line. From the car park, access can be gained to two hides that overlook the west end of the marshes. Two nature trails, the Lynachlaggan and Invertromie, offer superb views over the reserve and are particularly recommended in late summer, when birds are often difficult to see from the hides. Good views of both the marshes and Loch Insh can be obtained from the B970 and B9152.

Timing

The reserve is open daily from 09.00 am to 9.00 pm (or sunset, if earlier). The reception centre, however, is open less frequently. There is sustained bird interest throughout the year, with the peak activity in April–May and November–March.

Calendar

April–August: Breeding wildfowl and waders, large Black-headed Gull colony. Marsh Harrier is recorded almost annually. Osprey, Hen Harrier and Short-eared Owl regularly hunt over the marsh in late summer. Summer passerines include Tree Pipit, Redstart, Spotted and sometimes Pied Flycatchers and Wood Warbler.

September–March: Migratory Greylag and Pink-footed Geese pass through during late September and throughout October. Up to 200 Whooper Swan, 500 Greylag Geese plus a variety of duck overwinter.

Hen Harrier is commonly seen, particularly in late afternoon. Great Grey Shrike occurs in some winters. Redwing and Fieldfare arrive in hundreds during early October.

RSPB Warden
Ivy Cottage, Insh, Kingussie PH21 1NT (tel: 01540 661518).

H9 GLEN TROMIE

OS ref: NN 782972
OS Landranger 35

Female Grey Wagtail

Habitat and Access
An attractive valley with a mix of birch woodland, plantations and heather moorland. Park on the track near Tromie Bridge on the B970, 3 miles (4.8 km) from Kingussie. Please take care not to block access for other vehicles. The track can be taken along the valley. Ideally, the area should be visited in spring, perhaps in conjunction with a visit to the RSPB reserve at the nearby Insh Marshes.

Species
Dipper and Grey Wagtail frequent the river. Redstart, Siskin and Redpoll should be seen among the riverside trees. Merlin and Peregrine are occasional. Hen Harrier attempt to breed each year, but usually have little success.

H10 ARDNAMURCHAN

Habitat

The Ardnamurchan Peninsula forms the most westerly land in mainland Scotland. It stretches north of Mull, Morvern and Loch Sunart and south of the Small Isles (Rum, Eigg, Canna and Muck). The fantastic views from the Ardnamurchan Point lighthouse have made this a famous place to visit. Along its rocky shores are scattered oak woodlands—remnants of those that once dominated western Britain, from Devon to Sutherland. Rough heather moorland and hill lochans characterise inland areas, with several coniferous forest plantations punctuating the landscape. Many sandy beaches and bays are dotted around the coastline. The peninsula is 17 miles (28 km) east to west and approximately 7 miles (12 km) at its widest point. Ben Hiant (528 m) and Ben Laga (512 m) are the highest points. Slightly to the east is Beinn Resipol, an 845-m mountain in the Sunart district.

Access

The peninsula has a single track road (B8007) along its southern shore, with minor roads branching off north and west. To reach the area, take the short (15 minutes) Corran Ferry crossing operated by Highland Regional Council (which runs frequently and is non-bookable) across Loch Linnhe, off the A82 from Glen Coe to Fort William. The ferry slipway is about 4 miles (6 km) north of the Ballachulish Bridge and 8 miles (13 km) south of Fort William. Once across, head south on the A861 through Strontian to Salen (23 miles or 37 km). Salachan Point, just over a mile south of Corran, is worth checking at any time of year for roosting waders, gulls and offshore divers and sea duck. The B8007 is the left branch of the road at Salen. The road beyond here is single track and can be quite busy in summer. An alternative route to Ardnamurchan is by way of the Caledonian MacBrayne ferry from Tobermory on the

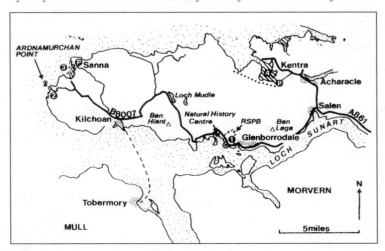

island of Mull. There is a regular (non-bookable) service to Kilchoan, on the southwest of Ardnamurchan, during the summer; this service now carries cars (but not caravans). The crossing takes 35 minutes and provides good seawatching opportunities.

Species

A wide range of species is present, including wintering and passage wildfowl and waders, oak and coniferous woodland birds, and upland heath and moorland birds. Breeders of particular importance include Red-throated Diver, Grey Heron, Teal, Hen Harrier, Golden Eagle, Buzzard, Merlin, Peregrine, Red Grouse, Golden Plover, Greenshank, Common Sandpiper, Short-eared Owl, Great Spotted Woodpecker, Tree Pipit, Dipper, Redstart, Whinchat, Stonechat, Wheatear, Ring Ouzel, Wood Warbler, Raven, Siskin and Redpoll.

In winter, the area is notable for modest numbers of Great Northern Diver offshore and a flock of wintering Greenland White-fronted Geese south of Loch Sheil. Numbers of Wigeon and Teal can be present in Kintra Bay, along with a variety of wintering waders, including small numbers of Greenshank. Goldeneye is common on sea and freshwater lochs. Passage seabirds such as divers, shearwaters, petrels, Gannet, skuas, gulls and terns are easily watched from the western end of the peninsula, or from the Tobermory–Kilchoan ferry. Passage wildfowl include Whooper Swan, White-fronted, Greylag and Barnacle Geese. Migrant waders are probably best looked for at Kintra, where Golden Plover, Dunlin, Snipe, Bar-tailed Godwit, Curlew, Redshank and Greenshank are likely. Less frequent are Grey Plover, Knot, Sanderling, Whimbrel and Green Sandpiper.

In addition to birds, the peninsula is an excellent place to see pine marten, red squirrel, fox, wildcat, otter, grey and common seals.

1 GLENBORRODALE RSPB RESERVE (OS REF: 60/61)

This 100 ha reserve comprises an interesting mosaic of habitats. About one-quarter of the reserve is coastal oak woodland, with scrub areas leading onto more open heather moorland. Two streams run through the reserve, the one to west tumbling through a steep and inaccessible gorge. To the northeast is an over-mature conifer plantation, with extensive felled areas. Below the road, the reserve encompasses a short section of the rocky shoreline. Much of the oak woodland is being cleared of invading rhododendron.

The reserve is immediately west of Glenborrodale village, with its eastern boundary adjoining that of Glenborrodale Castle. Driving west through the village, look for the black railings of the castle grounds on the right. The reserve starts where these end. A short distance beyond this the road crosses a stream running into a small bay. On the right is a path which leads through the reserve, rejoining the road at its northwestern boundary. As yet there are no parking facilities for visitors so it is best to drive further on, find a suitable parking spot (please do not park in the passing places), and walk back to the path. Regular reserve walks are organised: contact the Glenmore Natural History Centre or RSPB North Scotland Office for details.

Breeding woodland birds include Tree Pipit, Redstart, Wood Warbler and Willow Warbler. Great, Blue and Long-tailed Tits, Wren, Treecreeper, Robin and Buzzard are resident. On the hill ground, Wheatear, Stonechat, Whinchat and Meadow Pipit are common in spring/summer. There is a traditional Raven territory on the crag overlooking the wood. Others occasionally seen include Golden Eagle, Kestrel, Merlin, Skylark and Twite. Eider, Common Sandpiper and Grey Heron frequent the main bay and this is also a good place to see otter and both grey and common seal. Common and Arctic Terns can be seen fishing further out in the loch.

The Ardnamurchan Natural History Centre at Glenmore, just west of Glenborrodale, is not to be missed. Mounted displays and marine tanks, illustrating the species and habitats to be found in the area, complement an audio-visual presentation on 'The Natural History of Ardnamurchan', produced by Michael MacGregor. General information on things to do and see and details of local events are available, and the RSPB reserve walks leave from here. The centre also sells books, gifts, coffee, etc. and excellent home baking! This is an ideal information point from which to explore Ardnamurchan.

2 POINT OF ARDNAMURCHAN (OS REF: NM 67/41)

This is the most westerly point of mainland Scotland and a fantastic place to seawatch, and to view the Small Isles to the north and Coll to the southwest. A walk along the cliff south of the lighthouse may give views of Raven and possibly Peregrine. To reach the point, continue beyond Glenmore Natural History Centre along the B8007 towards Kilchoan. A car park on the left after c. 2 miles (3 km) affords fine views of Ben Hiant and an opportunity to scan the skyline for Golden Eagle, Buzzard and Raven. Continue on the B8007, stopping to check Loch Mudle after 4 miles (6 km), which often holds Red-throated Diver, with Hen Harrier and Short-eared Owl hunting over the surrounding young conifer plantations. From Loch Mudle the road carries on for 14 miles (9 km) until Achosnich, where a left fork covers the 3 miles (5 km) to Ardnamurchan Point. Park in the space available at the end and walk to the lighthouse. As well as seabirds, watch for dolphins, porpoises, whales and basking sharks.

3 SANNA BAY (OS REF: NM 69/44)

North of the Point of Ardnamurchan is the tiny village of Sanna and an extensive sand dune system. In summer, the bay can be a good place to watch diving Gannets and other seabirds. From the B8007 take the minor road to Achnaha and Sanna about 0.5 mile (1 km) out of Kilchoan. There is a large parking area at Sanna. As with the point, this is a good place to see marine mammals and basking sharks.

4 KENTRA BAY (OS REF: NM 69/64)

This is a large muddy/sandy bay in the northeast corner of the peninsula. To reach it, return to Salen and take the A861 north to Acharacle. Immediately after the church at the end of the village turn left onto the B8044 to Kentra. About half a mile (1 km) along this road there is a minor crossroads—take the left turn and drive to the end of the road, where you can go through a gate to a small parking area. From here, walk along the track for good views of the south side of the bay. Continue for just over 1 mile (2 km) through the conifer plantation to reach Camas an Lighe, a beautiful beach. The north side of the bay can be viewed from the road, by continuing along the B8044 beyond Kentra. The bay is particularly good for passage and wintering waders and wildfowl (see Species).

Also see additional sites: Ariundle National Nature Reserve (Ha) and Rahoy Hills SWT Reserve (Hn).

H11 LOCHINDORB

OS ref: NH 970360
OS Landranger 27

Habitat

A large freshwater loch, approximately 2 miles (3.2 km) long, which is surrounded by open moorland managed for Red Grouse. The northern end of the loch has recently been cordoned off for windsurfing, while fishermen use the rest of the loch; neither activity appears to have any detrimental effect on the birdlife, however, probably due to the size of the loch.

Species

Lochindorb is a very reliable place for Red-throated Diver, with up to four generally present. Small numbers of Wigeon and Red-breasted Merganser are usually found in summer, while Goldeneye is regular in April and May. Careful scanning of the surrounding moorland and skylines should reveal some of the area's raptors, which include Golden Eagle, Peregrine and Merlin. Hen Harrier is frequently seen in spring, but does not breed as successfully as might be expected. Osprey is occasionally present. One or two pairs of Short-eared Owl usually breed here. Red Grouse is plentiful and in April the territorial males give excellent opportunities for roadside viewing. Both Golden Plover and Dunlin breed on the moors and can be watched from the road; Dunlin is often seen feeding along the loch shore. Other waders include Lapwing, Curlew, Common Sandpiper and Redshank. Small numbers of Twite breed here and are often located as they fly overhead calling.

In winter, the area is generally unrewarding, although Goldeneye may be present on the loch, while groups of Raven and the occasional Golden Eagle (usually immatures) may also be seen.

Access

Lochindorb is approached either:

(1) Along the A938 road east from Carrbridge, turning north after 2 miles (3.2 km) onto the B9007. A single-track road off to the right, 6 miles (9.7 km) later, heads the final mile (1.6 km) to the loch.

(2) Along the A939 road north from Grantown-on-Spey, turning left after 6 miles (9.7 km) onto the minor road signed for Lochindorb.

Both routes lead along the minor road that closely follows the southeast shore of the loch. There are several pull-offs that enable the area to be scanned without obstructing other traffic: the area immediately north of Lochindorb Lodge is probably the best general viewpoint.

Timing
This area is mainly of interest during the period April to August.

H12 FINDHORN VALLEY
OS ref: NH 710180
OS Landranger 35

Habitat and Access
A very large area of open country given over to sheep and deer grazing, with some managed grouse moor and a scattering of plantations and birch woodland. The valley is reached from Tomatin (next to the A9, 15 miles or 24 km south of Inverness); a single-track road follows the River Findhorn upstream for c. 9 miles (14.5 km), providing good views of the surrounding terrain. The ridges above the final 3 miles (4.8 km) of this road are particularly good for soaring Golden Eagle. It is possible to walk along the track from the road end at Coignafearn, but please do not take a vehicle—there is room to park here without obstructing access to the track. Various paths lead from the track, all of which are worth exploring for birds of prey, but do not venture into the hills during the stalking or grouse-shooting seasons (i.e. early August to February). The Farr road, 5 miles (8 km) after leaving Tomatin, crosses some excellent moorland areas and can be equally good for most species.

Species
The principal attractions are the birds of prey. Sparrowhawk, Buzzard, Kestrel, Merlin and Peregrine all occur; Golden Eagle can usually be spotted with some perseverance—frequent scanning of the skyline is the tactic most likely to yield results. The eagles can be seen throughout the year and up to five individuals in a day have been known. Hen Harrier is scarce, and the Farr road is probably the best area for them. The moors hold Red Grouse and Golden Plover, while Ring Ouzel is not uncommon on the hillsides in spring. Raven is decidedly scarce, though small flocks are sometimes present in winter. The river is the haunt of small numbers of Goosander, Dipper and Grey Wagtail, joined in summer by Common Sandpiper. Osprey and Common Tern often fish here. White-tailed Eagle is an increasingly common sight during winter.

Timing
The area has a good range of residents and is worth visiting year-round.

Habitat

This 85-ha RSPB reserve is situated east of Loch Ness and 14 miles (22.5 km) south of Inverness. The relatively rich waters of the loch are backed by craggy moorland, with a narrow strip of birch wood. To the north, much of the land has been recently forested, although there is extensive farmland at Tullich to the northeast.

Slavonian Grebes, summer

Species

Slavonian Grebe is the speciality of this reserve; they breed in the emergent vegetation around the loch edge and it is therefore essential not to stray closer to the shore than the path. Red-throated Diver uses the loch for feeding, Tufted Duck and Coot are present all year, while small numbers of Common and Black-headed Gulls breed. The birch woods hold small but interesting bird communities, including Siskin and Redpoll; Sedge Warbler and Reed Bunting nest in the fringing scrub. Hen Harrier and Peregrine are regularly seen and Raven is present year-round. The area is a good one for Black Grouse.

In winter, Loch Ruthven attracts Pochard and Goldeneye, as well as occasional Smew.

Access

Loch Ruthven can be reached from the A9 by turning west on the B851, nearly 6 miles (9.7 km) from Inverness. Fork right 8 miles (13 km) later, on a minor road that leads to a parking area at the east end of the loch. Alternatively, approach directly from Inverness on the B862, turning left after c. 12 miles (19 km) at the end of Loch Duntelchaig, on the minor road to Loch Ruthven. Access is restricted to the southeast shore only— a 1.5-mile-long (0.8 km) footpath leads to the hide, which overlooks the loch.

Timing

The optimum time to visit is in spring or early summer.

H14 LONGMAN POINT, INVERNESS

OS ref: NH 66/47
OS Landranger 26

Habitat
Longman Point is on the south side of the Beauly Firth, immediately east of the mouth of the River Ness. It is overshadowed by the Kessock Bridge, which carries the A9 northbound out of Inverness and onto the Black Isle. Because of this proximity to the main road, it is a convenient place to stop when heading further north. The mud and shingle shoreline here and the waters of the firth opposite provide excellent habitat for a representative selection of the birds that occur in Beauly Firth. A sewage outfall discharges into the firth, attracting gulls and wildfowl. The shoreline is backed by a light industrial estate; to the west lies Inverness harbour and to the east a rubbish tip and reclamation area (NH 678464).

Species
Mute Swan, Mallard, Oystercatcher and the commoner gulls can be seen year-round. Breeding visitors are few, although 1–2 Shelduck and Ringed Plover nest. In winter the area is visited by a wide range of species, including up to 850 Tufted Duck, 400+ Goldeneye and large numbers of Teal. A few Scaup can usually be found among the Tufted Duck, which sometimes feed on the opposite side of the firth near Charlestown. Goosander frequents the mouth of the River Ness (mostly in autumn) and small numbers of Little Grebe and Long-tailed Duck are usually present in the harbour. Other wintering regularly recorded waterfowl include Cormorant, Wigeon, Pochard, Smew, Coot and Guillemot.

Passage waders include Knot, Dunlin, Bar-tailed and Black-tailed Godwits, Redshank and Turnstone. Up to 300 Redshank and a small number of Black-tailed Godwit overwinter. Glaucous and Iceland Gulls occur every winter and commute between the outflow and the rubbish tip to the east.

Access
From the A9/A96 Milburn Interchange head north towards Kessock Bridge, turn left at the next roundabout along Longman Road, then right at another roundabout onto Harbour Road. A right turn onto Cromwell Road leads to Longman Drive, which affords good views of the foreshore.

Timing
Access is possible at all times. August–March is the most interesting period. Visit 1–2 hours before high tide for shorebirds, although high water in midwinter is best for ducks.

Habitat

A picturesque combination of woodlands, hillsides, rivers and lochs make this a classic highland glen and one that is deservedly popular with visitors. The FC have established a 1265-ha Native Woodland reserve here, which includes an important remnant of old Caledonian pine forest. The area is a designated SSSI.

Male Capercaillie

Species

Small numbers of Capercaillie* and Black Grouse* breed in the pine-woods; Crested Tit and Scottish Crossbill are numerous all year, while Siskin and Redpoll are easier to find during winter. Migrant breeders include Tree Pipit and Redstart. On the lochs, Red-throated and (occasionally) Black-throated Divers may be seen in spring/summer, while Red-breasted Merganser and Goosander occur regularly. Dipper and Grey Wagtail frequent the burnsides. Various raptors hunt over the area, including Sparrowhawk, Buzzard, Golden Eagle and Kestrel; visiting Osprey and Merlin are seen occasionally.

Access

Approach via the A831 from Beauly or Drumnadrochit (see OS Landranger 26), turning at Cannich onto an unclassified road leading west past Fasnakyle Power Station. There are several car parks along this road (see map), including one at its end, after about 11 miles (18 km). Paths and trails, varying in length from 0.5 mile (0.8 km) upwards, lead from the parking areas: the routes to Dog Falls and Coire Loch are particularly recommended. A longer excursion (c. 11 miles or 18 km around Loch

*Please do not attempt to seek out leks of these two species as this will inevitably lead to disturbance. Leks are best watched from a good distance, and generally a car is the best hide.

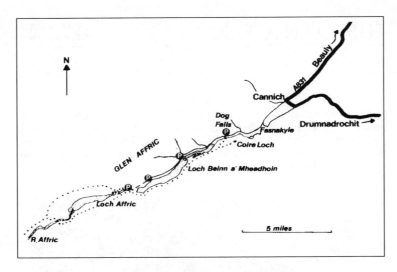

Affric or along the south shore of Loch Beinn a' Mheadhoin (7 miles or 11.3 km one way) can be very rewarding.

Timing
Access is possible at all times, although both the road and the paths can be treacherous in winter. Please take note of any specific restrictions that may apply during the stalking season. The speciality species found in the pinewoods are present all year, but many of the other interesting woodland species are only summer visitors.

References
The FC publishes a detailed booklet on the area, available from the FC or Inverness Tourist Office.

H16 UDALE BAY

OS ref: NH 71/65
OS Landranger 21/27

Habitat and Species
An open estuarine bay on the south shore of the Cromarty Firth. Like Nigg Bay on the north shore, Udale has extensive sheltered intertidal mudflats that hold a large and diverse group of passage/wintering wild-fowl and waders.

Udale Bay is best visited in September–March, during which period Wigeon is numerous and smaller numbers of Teal and Mallard can be seen. Shelduck overwinter. Large numbers of Greylag Geese sometimes visit the bay from their feeding fields at high water. Waders include Oys-tercatcher, Knot, Dunlin, Curlew, Redshank and Bar-tailed Godwit.

Small numbers of Grey Plover are often present. Sparrowhawk, Peregrine and occasional Merlin hunt overhead.

In the main channel of the Cromarty Firth, to the north of Udale Bay and visible from the unclassified road to Balblair, a flock of Scaup sometimes feed very close inshore and small numbers of Red-throated Diver, Slavonian Grebe and Long-tailed Duck can be seen.

Access

Udale Bay is situated between the small villages of Balblair and Jemimaville and can be approached from the A9 via the B9163, or from Fortrose on the A832 then the B9160. Excellent views of the bay are possible from the lay-by just west of Jemimaville, from the parking area between the road and the shore approximately 1 mile (1.6 km) east of Jemimaville or from the unclassified road to Balblair just beyond the ruined church.

H17 NIGG BAY

OS ref: NH 970730
OS Landranger 21

Habitat

An open bay on the north side of the Cromarty Firth with extensive intertidal mud and areas of poor-quality saltmarsh, much reclaimed during the last century. Over a mile (1.6 km) of the eastern shore is occupied by oil-storage and rig-fabrication sites. Nigg Bay measures around 3 miles by 4 miles (4.8 km by 6.4 km) and has been designated a SSSI.

Species

The bay holds a significant selection of the internationally important populations of wintering/passage wildfowl and waders that occur on the Cromarty Firth. Nigg Bay holds a similar suite of species to that found on the Dornoch Firth (H18), but with larger numbers of most of the commoner birds. A growth of eelgrass here attracts very large numbers of Wigeon, as well as Mute and Whooper Swans. In addition, up to 2000 Greylag and 1000 Pink-footed Geese frequent the inner bay and 200–400 Pintail can be found near the Meddat shore. The more typical waders using the bay include Oystercatcher, Knot, Dunlin, Curlew and Redshank. Moderate numbers of Scaup and Goldeneye winter on the firth.

Access

The best areas for birds are at the inner end of the bay between Pitcalnie and Meddat. From Tain, take the A9 south for 4 miles (6.4 km), turning onto the B9175 towards Nigg. After a further 4 miles an old coastguard station is reached and this and the adjacent banks make good observation points. Parking is possible on the roadside, but care must be taken—the road can be extremely busy with traffic to the nearby fabrication yard. All of the surrounding farmland is privately owned. The paths to the two old coastguard huts (NH 795739 and 803724) are rights of way to an old fording point.

Timing
Nigg Bay is a good birding location throughout the winter, from late September to late March. The best time to visit is 1–3 hours before high tide, although large wader roosts can be seen at high water. A southeast wind is best if watching from the old coastguard station.

H18 DORNOCH FIRTH
OS ref: NH 609915–900900
OS Landranger 21

Habitat
The Dornoch is the only east coast firth that has no industrial development. The combined flow of the rivers Shin, Oykel and Carron, plus their many tributaries, enter the firth via glaciated valleys. A series of points and promontories naturally divide the firth into several distinct areas and a complex of sand bars—Gizzen Briggs—guards the mouth of the estuary from the Moray Firth and almost connects Dornoch Point on the north shore with Morrich More on the south. This narrow mouth feeds into a wide bay separated from the rest of the Moray Firth by the Tarbat Ness peninsula.

The Dornoch Firth is about 16 miles (26 km) long and varies in width from around 0.5 mile (0.8 km) at Bonar Bridge to almost 4 miles (6.4 km) across Tain Bay/Dornoch Sands. The outer bay from Embo to Tarbat Ness is approximately 10 miles (16 km) wide.

The extensive estuarine mudflats are the principal habitat of interest, there being few saltmarshes. East of Tain lie the sand dune and sandflats areas of Morrich More, which are important for breeding waders but form a part of RAF Tain's bombing range. The Tarbat Ness coast of the outer firth is rocky, whereas that on the north side at Dornoch is sandy. There is a brackish-water lagoon cut off from the estuary by the railway midway along the south shore (Mid-Fearn Mere). Both Morrich More and the Outer Dornoch Firth are designated SSSI. The only noteworthy surrounding bird habitats are at Spinningdale where there is a small and rather over-grazed oakwood and at Easter Fearn, opposite the base of the Struie Hill road, where there is a locally important area of juniper scrub.

Species and Calendar
Dornoch Firth is of great importance for passage and wintering wildfowl and waders. Outstanding among the visiting duck populations are a flock of 150–300 Shelduck in Tain Bay, up to 7000 Wigeon and 1000 Teal at Ardjackie/Tain Bays (peak numbers occur in October), up to 150 Pintail and up to 400 Scaup in Edderton Bay. Up to 1000 Common and 400 Velvet Scoters winter off the Dornoch/Embo coastline; 2–3 Surf Scoters and (in recent years) Black Scoter have also been present. The period late March–early May is probably the best time for these birds.

Oystercatcher numbers peak at around 2000 in November, with a similar number of Redshank present in October. Approximately 3000 Dunlin can be found in September. Other passage waders include up to 50 Grey and 100 Golden Plovers, 400 Curlew, 200 Bar-tailed Godwit and around 70 Knot. Small numbers of Greenshank and occasional Black-tailed Godwit, Ruff and Spotted Redshank also occur. Modest numbers of Sanderling and Turnstone overwinter at Portmahomack and Dornoch.

The firth is very quiet from March until July, although small numbers of non-breeding ducks and waders are present and there is often a significant spring passage of geese and Whooper Swan. Osprey is regularly seen fishing over the estuary in late spring/summer.

Return wader passage commences in July, with the main movement occurring between late August and early November.

Access
The A9 provides access to both the north and south shores and there are many good vantage points from roadside lay-bys. The bridge across the Dornoch Firth west of Tain affords good views of the outer estuary.

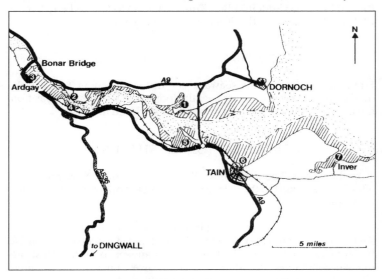

1 SKIBO ESTUARY (OS REF: NH 73/88)

Turn off the A9 at Clashmore, then turn right at the junction 1 mile (1.6 km) later to Ferrytown. Park in the gorse area and walk to the pier, which is a good general vantage point. Large numbers of Teal can be present on the estuary in late autumn. Tufted Duck occurs on Lochs Evelix and Ospisdale all year.

2 NEWTON'S POINT (OS REF: NH 711877)

Further along the A9 towards Bonar Bridge turn off to Newton's Point, a good viewpoint over the estuary. There is space to park at the point and also by the inner bay west of the point.

3 ARDGAY STATION (OS REF: NH 601904)

The station platform is a useful vantage point. The railway line between Ardgay and Tain follows the south shore closely and gives good views of the firth; there are four trains per day during summer, but fewer in winter. Tain Station is also a good vantage point, being conveniently situated on the edge of Tain Bay.

4 MID-FEARN MERE (OS REF: NH 638873)

A lagoon visible from a lay-by on the A9 Bonar Bridge–Tain road immediately after the Dingwall turn.

5 CAMBUSCURRIE BAY (OS REF: NH 725852)

Known locally as Edderton Bay. Turn off the A9 to Meikle Ferry 2 miles (3.2 km) west of Tain. This is an excellent viewpoint.

6 TAIN BAY (OS REF: NH 785840)

From the car park on the seaward side of the railway in Tain (on the road to the golf course), cross over the footbridge and view the bay from the opposite bank of the inlet. Morrich More lies to the east.

7 INVER BAY (OS REF: NH 864832)

Take the unclassified road out of Tain towards Tarbat Ness, turning off after 5 miles (8 km) to the village of Inver. A car park overlooks the sheltered inlet.

Timing
August–March is the best time to visit. Waders are most easily seen 1–3 hours before high water. Southerly winds appear to be the most productive conditions. Disturbance is at its lowest on Sunday mornings, although afternoon light is preferable on sunny days.

References
Nature Conservation within the Moray Firth Area. NCC (1978).
Birdwatching in Sutherland. T Mainwood (1992). Scottish Bird News 27.

Habitat

The large tidal basin of Loch Fleet is the most northerly inlet on the east coast of Scotland. Only a narrow channel between the shingle and dune bars of Ferry and Coul Links connects the loch with the open sea. At low tide, an extensive area of intertidal mud is exposed; dunes and coastal heath bound the estuarine habitat to the east and pinewoods to the north. To the west, beyond the Mound, lies an area of alder carr which formed as a result of an abortive attempt to drain the loch.

The SWT manages the loch and some of the surrounding habitats as a reserve, totalling 1163 ha. A summer warden is employed from April until August and organises guided walks to explore the woodland, estuary and sand dunes. Much of the site is a designated a SSSI.

Species

Large numbers of dabbling duck overwinter in the loch, including over 2000 Wigeon with smaller numbers of Teal and Mallard. The coastline between Embo and Golspie holds important concentrations of waterfowl, including three species of diver, Slavonian and occasional Red-necked Grebes, up to 2000 Eider and several hundred Long-tailed Duck, Common Scoter and Red-breasted Merganser. Smaller numbers of Goldeneye and Velvet Scoter can also be seen. Drake King Eiders were annual between 1973 and the late 1990s. Up to three have been seen at once, although they have been more elusive in recent years. If not present in the entrance to the loch, try the coast off Embo or Brora, although they can be some distance offshore. Surf Scoter can also be seen year-round, although their movements are less predictable. Green-winged Teal and American Wigeon have both been recorded in recent years.

P.Snow ©

Eiders and King Eider

A moderate flock of Greylag Geese uses the area and a flock of more than 50 Whooper Swan feeds in the surrounding fields in winter. Sparrowhawk and Buzzard are resident and seen often. Osprey may occur in summer, while Hen Harrier and Peregrine visit occasionally. Short-eared Owl regularly hunts over the dunes and heathland.

Waders roost at three main places: Skelbo Point, the beach at the mouth of the Fleet and Balblair saltmarsh. Up to 1800 Oystercatcher, c. 250 Curlew, 400 Redshank and 150 Ringed Plover can be present at Loch Fleet, with Dunlin numbers sometimes exceeding 1000, and Knot and Bar-tailed Godwit numbers occasionally reaching 1000. The loch is not generally considered to be an especially good place for passage waders, but many species do pass through, including large numbers of Curlew, Golden Plover and Knot. Greenshank is regular in spring and autumn at the Mound Pool.

Redstart, Goldcrest, Coal Tit, Siskin and Scottish Crossbill breed in the pinewoods at Balblair, but Capercaillie has probably now disappeared.

Access

Loch Fleet is 5 miles (8 km) north of Dornoch and is accessible from the A9 and unclassified roads along the south shore and to Littleferry from Golspie. There are several good vantage points

1 SKELBO (OS REF: NH 790950)

Take the minor road east off the A9 along the south shore of the loch. There is a car park and information board at Skelbo, 1.5 miles (2.4 km) later.

2 COUL LINKS (OS REF: NH 803952)

Half a mile (0.8 km) east of Skelbo, take a track north onto the links and park overlooking the estuary. It is possible to explore the links on foot from here.

3 THE MOUND (OS REF: NH 770979)

There are two parking bays on the A9 at the head of the loch which overlook both the upper estuary and the freshwater pools and alder carr to the west.

4 BALBLAIR AND FERRY LINKS (OS REF: NH 80/96)

Take the minor road south from Golspie past the golf course towards Littleferry. There are car parks at Balblair Wood where the road first comes alongside the estuary, and at Littleferry itself. Eider and Long-tailed Duck can sometimes be watched at very close quarters here; most sea duck tend to congregate north of the loch mouth and can be viewed by taking the paths east from Littleferry. A permit is required from the SWT in order to wander off the paths in Balblair pinewoods and at Ferry Links. Please note that there is a very high fire risk on this reserve.

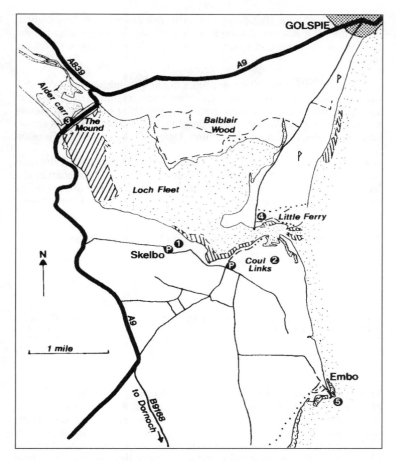

5 EMBO PIER (OS REF: NH 820922)

This is reached via the caravan site at Embo. It is probably the best place for close views of Velvet/Common Scoters and is a favourite area for King Eider in some years. White-winged gulls are occasionally present in winter and Purple Sandpiper frequents the rocky shore adjacent to the pier. Other good vantage points include the pier at Golspie, Brora and at Dornoch caravan park.

There are bus and train services to Golspie from Inverness.

Timing
The reserve is of most interest to birders in October–April, when large numbers of waterfowl and waders are present, although a summer visit is pleasant and can also be productive for birds.

Calendar
March–May: Up to 2000 Long-tailed Duck can be present by late May, prior to their departure to breeding grounds.

June–July: Shelduck, Redshank and Oystercatcher feed on the intertidal mud; Eider is numerous throughout the summer, feeding on the mussel beds in the river channel. Common and Arctic Terns can be seen fishing for sand eels.

August–November: Sea duck numbers decline to midwinter levels, following peak counts in October. Shelduck numbers start to increase from late November as they return from their moulting grounds. Moderate numbers of passage waders occur. Passage shearwaters and skuas are occasionally present offshore in autumn, especially when visibility is poor.

December–February: Red-throated and smaller numbers of Black-throated and Great Northern Divers occur offshore. Glaucous and the scarcer Iceland Gull, and small numbers of Snow Bunting and Twite are occasionally present. Purple Sandpiper and Turnstone frequent rocky shorelines.

Reference
Birdwatching in Sutherland. T Mainwood (1992). *Scottish Bird News* 27.

H20 DUNCANSBY HEAD
OS ref: ND 406733
OS Landranger 12

This headland forms the extreme northeast corner of Caithness. Coastal cliffs are backed by maritime heath; the area is a designated SSSI. An unclassified road off the A9 at John O'Groats covers the 2.5 miles (4 km) to the head. There is a car park near the lighthouse—a rough path leads to the cliff-top. The best vantage point for nesting seabirds is at the Geo of Sclaites. Late April to mid-July is the optimum time to visit. Sea mist is not infrequent. The cliffs hold breeding Fulmar, Shag, Kittiwake, Guillemot, Razorbill and Puffin.

H21 DUNNET HEAD
OS ref: ND 20/76
OS Landranger 7 & 12

Habitat and Access
The cliff-girt moors of Dunnet Head lie on the northernmost headland in Britain, some 13 miles (21 km) to the west of Duncansby Head. The area can be reached by taking the B855 turning off the main A836 Thurso–John O'Groats road in the village of Dunnet and following this north to the lighthouse, almost 5 miles (8 km) away.

Species

Fulmar, Kittiwake, Guillemot, Razorbill, Black Guillemot and Puffin all breed on the sea cliffs on the north and east sides of the headland. A few Great Skua usually attempt to breed on the moors. Other miscellaneous breeding birds include Rock Dove, Raven and Twite.

Dunnet Bay to the southwest is an important winter resort for waterfowl, including Red-throated Diver, a few Black-throated and Great Northern Divers, Common Scoter, Goldeneye, Eider, Long-tailed Duck and Red-breasted Merganser. Glaucous and Iceland Gulls can often be found here too. Around 100 Greenland White-fronted Geese overwinter in the Loch of Mey area east of Dunnet.

Timing

There is year-round bird interest, with the seabird colonies of Dunnet Head being the main attraction from mid-May to mid-July and divers, sea duck and gulls providing the interest during autumn, winter and early spring.

H22 CLO MOR

OS ref: NC 32/72
OS Landranger 9

Habitat

Clo Mor is situated about 4 miles (6.4 km) east of Cape Wrath, in extreme northwest Sutherland. The Torridonian sandstone cliffs here are the highest on mainland Britain, rising to nearly 300 m; inland are extensive tracts of open moorland and hills. The MOD uses the Cape Wrath area as a bombing range and access restrictions are sometimes in force.

Ravens at play

Species

The cliffs hold considerable numbers of Fulmar (an estimated 5000 occupied sites), Kittiwake, Guillemot, Razorbill, Black Guillemot and one of the largest Puffin colonies in Britain. Other cliff-nesting species include Peregrine and Rock Dove. Inland, Red Grouse and even Ptarmigan occur; Greenshank can also be seen, but Golden Plover is scarce.

Access

Clo Mor is reached by taking the ferry across the Kyle of Durness (pedestrians and bicycles only) at Keoldale, 1 mile (1.6 km) southwest of Durness and just off the A838. A connecting minibus service on the far side operates to Cape Wrath, 11 miles (16 km) away (tel: 01971 81287)—arrange to be dropped off at the Kearvaig track and picked up later at Inshore. Walk to the coast at Kearvaig, and then around the cliffs eastward for about 3 miles (5 km), cutting inland along the eastern flanks of Sgribhis-bheinn to the road at Inshore. This is a tough walk and should not be underestimated! The ferry across the Kyle of Durness operates several times daily during summer, except in bad weather (tel: 01971 511376 for details).

H23 HANDA ISLAND

OS ref: NC 13/48
OS Landranger 9

Habitat

Handa lies off the northwest coast of Scotland, 18 miles (29 km) south of Cape Wrath. Near-vertical cliffs of Torridonian sandstone over 120 m high in places bound the island on three sides; only in the south do these diminish and give way to lower cliffs and sandy bays. The interior comprises 363 ha of rough pasture, moorland and a few lochans, although there is a small plantation of Lodgepole pine and alder near the warden's bothy. Handa is a SSSI and has long been a bird reserve, previously under the management of the RSPB but now managed by SWT.

Species

Over 170 species have been recorded on/from the reserve; 30 are regular breeders and another 20 nest occasionally. An estimated total of 98,000 pairs of Guillemot and 9000 pairs of Razorbill breed on the ledges and crevices of the cliffs, best seen on the Great Stack in the northwest of the island. Large populations of Fulmar (c. 3000 pairs) and Kittiwake (c. 10,000 pairs) also occur, with about 200 pairs of Shag and 700–800 pairs of Puffin. Black Guillemot is often seen on the crossing to Handa, but do not regularly breed. Skuas have recently colonised Handa: currently about 30 pairs of Arctic Skua and 100 pairs of Great Skua breed on the moorland, although many non-breeders are also present. No raptors at present breed on Handa, but visiting Buzzard and Peregrine are regular and passage Sparrowhawk and Merlin may be seen in spring and autumn.

Puffins—breeding cliffs

Access

Boats for Handa leave from Tarbet, which is reached via an unclassified road off the A894 Laxford Bridge–Scourie road, 3 miles (4.8 km) north of Scourie. Boats operate daily (except Sunday) between 1 April and 10 September (contact Charles Thompson: 01971 502077 or Stephen Mac-Leod: 01971 502340). The first boat usually departs at around 10.00 am. Please note the crossing should be undertaken only in calm weather. The boat service is not connected with the SWT and the Trust accepts no liability for the safety of visitors on the crossing. Once ashore on Handa, visitors are asked to keep to the marked paths and take care near the cliff edge. Very close views of nesting skuas are possible from the marked path which passes through what has now become a breeding area, the birds seemingly very tolerant of human visitors. There are many good vantage points from which to overlook cliff-nesting seabirds. A warden is present from April to August.

Timing

The best time to visit is between early May and mid-July.

Calendar

The auks start to come ashore in large numbers during April and lay their eggs in early May. Most of the young Guillemot and Razorbill will have left their nest ledges by late July, but Puffin will be present until early August. Kittiwake lay in the third week of May and the first young start to leave their nests in mid-July. Apart from the breeding seabirds, many other interesting species frequent Handa.

Overwintering Great Northern Diver is often still present in early May and a few Black-throated Diver occur in the sound throughout summer. Small numbers of Red-throated Diver, Eider and Shelduck breed in the area and can be seen off Handa's southeast coast. The bays here hold small numbers of nesting Oystercatcher and Ringed Plover. A small colony of Common and Arctic Terns is located on the skerries in Port an Eilein, near the boat landing point. In addition to Kittiwake, four other species of gull breed on the cliffs, as does Rock Dove. Inland, breeding birds include Snipe, Wheatear, Stonechat and occasionally Red Grouse, Golden Plover and Reed Bunting.

Regular passage migrants include parties of Pink-footed and Greylag Geese flying north in April and early May, small numbers of waders such as Dunlin, Greenshank, Turnstone, Sanderling and Whimbrel which feed along the tideline during spring and autumn; Pomarine Skua offshore in early May and movements of Manx and a few Sooty Shearwaters in autumn. The plantation in the east of the island provides welcome cover for passerine migrants.

In winter a small flock of Barnacle Geese visits the island.

SWT Warden (summer only)
Contacted through the Inverness office of SWT (tel: 01463 714746).

H24 INVERPOLLY

OS ref: NC 13/12
OS Landranger 15

Habitat
The 10,856-ha Inverpolly NNR is a vast wilderness area bordered to the east by the A835 Drumrunie–Elphin road and extending northwest to Enard Bay. The undulating moorland plateau is interspersed by a mosaic of freshwater lochs, lochans and boggy hollows, punctuated by the sharply defined sandstone peaks of Stac Pollaidh (613 m), Cul Mor (849 m) and Cul Beag (769 m). Small remnants of the formerly extensive birch/hazel woodlands cling to the valley sides in a landscape otherwise dominated by heather and grass moorland, excepting the relatively barren mountain summits.

Species
Black-throated and Red-throated Divers, Red-breasted Merganser, Goosander, Wigeon and small numbers of Greylag Geese can be seen on the freshwater lochs in spring and summer. These are best worked

Skylark, spring

from the roadside so as to minimise disturbance to breeding species. Repeated scanning of the skyline should eventually produce views of Golden Eagle, and Buzzard, Merlin, Peregrine and Raven can also be seen. Ptarmigan is present in small numbers on the high tops, with the more numerous Red Grouse occurring on the lower moors, Snow Bunting sometimes frequents the roadsides in winter and many linger on the summits until well into spring. Moorland breeders include Golden Plover, Greenshank, Ring Ouzel, Wheatear and Stonechat. A few Twite are often seen around crofts. In the birch woods, look for Woodcock, Wood Warbler, Treecreeper, Long-tailed Tit and Spotted Flycatcher. Fulmar, Shag, Eider and Black Guillemot breed on the coast and small numbers of Barnacle Geese use the offshore island in winter.

Access

The challenging nature of the environment requires that any exploration away from the roadside is taken very seriously—adequate clothing/footwear are necessary and experience in hill walking and navigation essential. Fortunately, many interesting birds can be seen either from the roadside (the A835, plus the unclassified road alongside Loch Lurgainn and the connecting road north to Lochinver) or from one of the few short tracks that lead into the area. One of the best of these is alongside the River Kirkaig in the west of the reserve. Please note that dogs are not allowed on the reserve.

There is an information centre at Knockan (NC 187904), 2.5 miles (4 km) southwest of Elphin on the A835. Open Monday–Friday 10.00 am–6.00 pm, between May and mid-September. The Knockan Cliff Nature Trail, adjacent to the centre, gives fine views over the area.

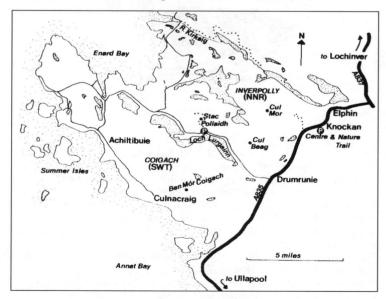

Timing

April–June is the best time for birds, although scenically the area is absolutely superb in autumn and winter. There is unrestricted access to the hill ground for most of the year, except from 15 July to 21 October when permission should be sought from the Assynt Estate Office (tel: 01571 844203) to visit the Drumrunie area. Between 1 September and 21 October it is advisable to contact the SNH warden (see below) for advice on the access situation.

SNH Warden
Knockan Cottage, Elphin, Lairg, Sutherland IV27 4H (tel: 01854 666234).

H25 BEN MOR COIGACH

OS ref: NC 10/04
OS Landranger 15

(See map of Inverpolly, H24)

Great Northern Divers

Habitat and Access
This is the largest of SWT reserves, covering more than 6000 ha of mountain, moorland, coastline and islets on the north shore of Annat Bay. To the north, a chain of large freshwater lochs separates this area from the adjacent Inverpolly NNR. The SWT reserve takes its name from, and is dominated by, the 743 m-high summit of Ben Mor Coigach, which rises steeply above the moorlands and peat bog inland from the croft township of Achiltibuie.

In common with Inverpolly, this area has few tracks and expeditions into the more remote parts of the reserve should not be taken lightly. Many of the birds characteristic of the area can be seen from the road to Achiltibuie and by continuing to the road end at Culnacraig.

Species
Breeding birds include Red Grouse, Ptarmigan, Golden Plover, Greenshank, Whinchat, Stonechat, Wheatear, Ring Ouzel, Raven and Twite.

Look for Golden Eagle over the skylines and check the roadside lochs for divers. The fields and offshore islands at Achiltibuie are used by Barnacle Geese in winter, while Great Northern Diver is generally present in the bay from October to May.

H26 BEINN EIGHE

OS ref: NG 001650
OS Landranger 19 & 25

Habitat

The Beinn Eighe NNR covers 4800 ha of remote and rugged terrain south of Loch Maree. The area comprises a rich mixture of upland habitats, including about 182 ha of natural pinewoods which extend from the shores of Loch Maree up to c. 300 m. Birch, rowan and holly trees grow among the relic Scots pines and the area has an understorey of heather and bilberry. In addition to this woodland, a further 486 ha has been planted with native tree species. The hills south of Loch Maree rise to around 1000 m. Heather, grass moorland and bog dominate the landscape, with dwarf shrubs on the high ground giving way to arctic–alpine heath on the summits.

Species

The woodlands hold limited but interesting bird communities including resident Buzzard, Sparrowhawk, Great Spotted Woodpecker, Coat Tit,

Golden Eagles—immature and adult

177

Goldcrest, Long-tailed Tit, Siskin, Redpoll and Crossbill, which are joined by Tree Pipit, Redstart, Wood Warbler and Willow Warbler in summer. Above the treeline, Golden Eagle, occasional Merlin, Peregrine and Raven occur; small numbers of Golden Plover, Ring Ouzel, Wheatear and Whinchat are present during the breeding season. Red Grouse may be seen on the lower moorlands, while the summits have small populations of Ptarmigan. Loch Maree is the haunt of Red-throated and Black-throated Divers, Red-breasted Merganser, Goosander and Greylag Geese. Common Sandpiper breeds around the loch shore, Greenshank is occasionally seen, while Dipper and Grey Wagtail frequent the burns.

Timing

The optimum time to visit is between May and July. From mid-August to 21 October red deer stalking is in progress and access to the hill ground is therefore restricted to the main footpaths and nature trails. For details contact SNH, Dingwall Business Park, Strathpeffer Road, Dingwall, Ross-shire IV15 9QF (tel: 01349 865333).

Access

The A832 runs along the south shore of Loch Maree and there are several car parks that afford good views across the loch. There are two nature trails—one is a short (c. 1 mile/1.6 km) mainly woodland route, the other a long (c. 4 mile/6.4 km) path that climbs above the treeline through a variety of upland habitats. Both commence from a car park at Glas Leitire (NH 000650), c. 3 miles (5 km) northwest of Kinlochewe. If venturing further afield, please note that the terrain demands a high level of competence in hill walking and that adequate weatherproof clothing and footwear are essential. Please also note that dogs are not allowed on the reserve. The Aultroy Visitor Centre near Kinlochewe (tel: 01445 760258) can supply trail leaflets, further information and advice. It is open daily between May and September.

SNH Reserve Manager

Anancaun Field Station, Kinlochewe, Ross-shire IV22 2PA (tel: 01445 760244).

Buzzard and Hooded Crow

H27 KINTAIL AND MORVICH

OS ref: NH 00/19
OS Landranger 33

Habitat and Access

The magnificent highland scenery of this 18,000-ha NTS property includes the peaks of the Five Sisters of Kintail, rising from sea level at the head of Loch Duich to over 1000 m. There is a Countryside Centre at Morvich Farm, just off the A87 north of Shiel Bridge; this is also the best access point into the hills. The centre is open June–September and a ranger/naturalist leads guided walks in the area and can give advice on the best routes to take in the hills.

Species

Kintail is a particularly good place in which to see Golden Eagle and the mountain skyline should be scanned frequently. Peregrine is present year-round and again, regular vigilance should be rewarded. Ptarmigan breeds on many of the summits, however, only experienced and adequately equipped groups should contemplate the ascent of any of the Kintail peaks. Three or four pairs each of Red-breasted Merganser and Goosander breed and can be seen between March and July in Glen Lichd and Glen Shiel. The mergansers also frequent Loch Duich. Scarcer breeding visitors include Black-throated Diver and Greenshank.

The area is poor for passage birds, but the sea and freshwater lochs support modest numbers of wintering wildfowl, including occasional Whooper Swan. A few Crossbill are usually present in the Glenshiel forestry between December and March.

Ranger/Naturalist

William Fraser, Morvich Farm, Inverinate, Kyle, Ross-shire IV40 8HQ (tel: 01599 511219).

H28 BALMACARA ESTATE

OS ref: NC 79/29
OS Landranger 33

This is another NTS property, covering some 2274 ha of the Kyle/Plockton Peninsula north of Loch Alsh. The habitat comprises seacoast, rugged moorland with scattered hill lochs and both deciduous and coniferous woodland. The woodland at Coille Mhor is a SSSI. There is a visitor centre at Lochalsh, open April–October. Although not an outstanding area for birds, there is good selection of woodland and moorland species that typify west coast birdlife. Hen Harrier has bred in recent years and Grasshopper Warbler can be heard in Coille Mhor, but the area is poor for passage and wintering species.

Ranger/Naturalist
Morvich Farm, Inverinate, Kyle, Ross-shire IV40 8HQ (tel: 01599 511219).

Grey Heron

H29 NOSS HEAD

OS ref: ND 388550

Habitat and Access
This important seawatching and migrant bird headland is situated 3 miles (5 km) north of Wick, at the southern end of Sinclair's Bay. It can be reached by taking the unclassified road from Wick to Stoxigoe and then following the signs for Noss Head (note: the alternative route across Wick Airport is now closed to vehicles). Park at the car park approximately 400 m from the lighthouse.

Species
The bird interest at the headland is divided between the migrant passerines that can sometimes be found in the numerous gorse-overgrown ditches and the old lighthouse garden, and passage seabirds that can be watched from the lighthouse. Spring migrants have included Bluethroat, Red-backed Shrike, Great Reed Warbler and Thrush Nightingale. In autumn the area is good for passage thrushes, chats and warblers (especially *Sylvia* warblers); Bluethroat, Wryneck, Red-breasted Flycatcher, Yellow-browed Warbler and Little Bunting have been recorded in recent years. Seawatching can be very good for shearwaters, petrels and skuas. Possible species include Sooty, Great and Cory's Shearwaters, plus Pomarine and Long-tailed Skuas.

H30 CHANONRY POINT OS ref: NH 75/56

Habitat and Access
This point provides a good viewpoint over the narrowest part of the Moray Firth. Turn south off the A832 just east of Fortrose and continue past the golf course to a car park at the point.

Species
Northeast winds in late summer and autumn can prompt excellent seabird passage, including Great, Arctic, Pomarine and Long-tailed Skuas, Razorbill, Guillemot, Black Guillemot, Puffin and Little Auk, divers, waders, Leach's and Storm Petrels, Fulmar and Kittiwake. In winter, Rock Pipit and Turnstone can be seen on the shore, while divers, Long-tailed Duck and Common Scoter occur at sea.

H31 FORSINARD RSPB RESERVE

Habitat and Species
This 7000-ha reserve is located in the Flow Country of northern Scotland. The landscape is one of rolling peat bog, interspersed with numerous bog pools. The peatlands hold breeding Red-throated and Black-throated Divers, Hen Harrier, Merlin, Greenshank, Dunlin and Golden Plover. These species are sensitive to disturbance and walking across the open bogs should therefore be avoided between April and July.

Access
By car the reserve is reached via the A897, Helmsdale–Melvich road. Turn inland at Helmsdale and follow the road for 26 miles. From Melvich, turn inland 2 miles east of the Melvich Hotel and follow the A897 for 14 miles. Forsinard can also be reached by train from Inverness (tel: 01463 238 9241 for details). The reserve is open at all times. There is a visitor centre at Forsinard station, open daily April–October, which has facilities for the disabled. A 1-mile trail takes visitors past a cluster of bog pools. Regular guided walks are arranged.

RSPB Warden
Forsinard Station, Forsinard, Sutherland KW13 6YT (tel: 01641 571225).

ADDITIONAL SITES

Site & Grid Reference	Habitat	Main Bird Interest	Peak Season
a Ariundle SNH/FC NM 830635 OS 40	Oakwood and pines, streamside.	Woodland species including Redstart and Wood Warbler. Dipper and Grey Wagtail.	May–Jul
b Borgie Forest FC NC 66/58 OS 10	Only large area of mature woodland on the north Sutherland coast.	Common woodland birds.	All year
c Eilean Hoan RSPB Reserve NC 44/67 OS 9	Low-lying offshore island.	Great Northern Diver gathers late in winter. Barnacle Goose.	Oct–Apr
	Access to this island is very difficult—the divers and geese can be 'scoped from the A838 Durness–Tongue road.		
d Faraid Head NC 38/71 OS 9	Headland/sea cliffs.	Breeding Fulmar, Kittiwake, Black Guillemot, Guillemot.	May–Jul
		Razorbill and Puffin; passage seabirds including Sooty Shearwater.	Aug–Oct
e Glen Nevis NN 16/69 OS 41	Mountain and steep valley.	Golden Eagle.	All year
f Gruinard Bay NG 95/93 OS 19	Open sea loch.	Great Northern Diver.	Oct–May
g Kyle of Sutherland NH 59/93 OS 21	Enclosed tidal basin with surrounding conifer woodland.	Wintering wildfowl.	Oct–Mar
		Common woodland species including Scottish Crossbill.	All year
	There are a number of FC trails in this area—booklet available from the Tourist Office in Dornoch.		
h Loch Broom NH 12/93 OS 19	Long, deep sea loch, used by trawlers landing fish at Ullapool and visiting fish-factory ships.	Wintering divers and gulls, especially Glaucous and Iceland.	Nov–May

H Additional sites

Site & Grid Reference	Habitat	Main Bird Interest	Peak Season
i Loch Eriboll NC 43/59 OS 9	Long, deep sea loch; A838 follows shore.	Divers and sea duck.	Oct–May
j Loch Eye NH 830795 OS 21	Only large (c.165 ha) eutrophic loch in East Ross.	Passage and wintering geese roost including up to 20,000 Greylag and 2,000 Pink-footed; also up to 700 Whooper Swan.	End Oct

Note: all the land surrounding Loch Eye is privately owned. Reasonable views can be obtained from the road north and west of the loch. Visit in the last 2 hours of daylight (3.30 pm–5.30 pm in October). During the day many feeding geese and swans can be found in the area between Arabella and Balmuchy (on stubble in autumn, winter wheat/barley in spring).

k Loch Hope NC 46/54 OS 16	Long freshwater loch surrounded by open moor and birch scrub; vegetated crags of Ben Hope (927 m) to southeast.	Divers, Golden Eagle, Merlin, Peregrine, Whinchat, Stonechat, Wheatear, Ring Ouzel, Raven.	May–Aug

Good views of surrounding terrain and across loch from unclassified road along east shore.

l Loch Naver NC 61/36 OS 16	Long freshwater loch with birch scrub on west shore; heather, bracken and some conifers to east.	Divers, raptors and moorland birds.	May–Aug
m North Sutor NH 822688 OS 21 or 27	Steep 100 m cliffs on the seaward side of the entrance to the Cromarty Firth.	Nesting Guillemot, Razorbill, Black Guillemot and over 400 pairs of Cormorant.	Jun–Jul
n Rahoy Hills SWT Reserve NM 690530 OS 49	Mountain, oak woods, hill lochans.	Red-throated Diver, Golden Eagle, Snipe, Common Sandpiper, Pied Flycatcher; also pine marten and wildcat.	May–Jul

Permit required—contact Donald Kennedy (tel: 01967 421327).

o Rum SNH Reserve OS 39	Mountain and coastal habitats, some woodland around Kinloch.	Variety of upland species including Golden and White-tailed Eagles; seabird colonies on south and northeast coasts.	Apr–Oct

Permits are required to visit all areas away from the Loch Scresort area—contact SNH Inverness Office.

p Strathy Point NC 82/69 OS 10	Exposed northerly peninsula.	Seawatching vantage point, Sooty Shearwater regularly recorded.	Aug–Sep

Site & Grid Reference	Habitat	Main Bird Interest	Peak Season
q Tarbat Ness NH 949877 OS 21	Rocky promontory extending into Moray Firth.	Excellent seawatching point especially in southeast gales: Fulmar, Sooty and Manx Shearwaters, geese, waders, Pomarine, Arctic and Great Skuas, gulls, terns and auks.	Aug–Sep
r Torridon NTS NG 90/59 OS 24 & 25	Vast mountainous areas adjacent to Beinn Eighe NNR.	Breeding divers, birds of prey, Ptarmigan and moorland species.	May–Aug

NORTH EAST SCOTLAND

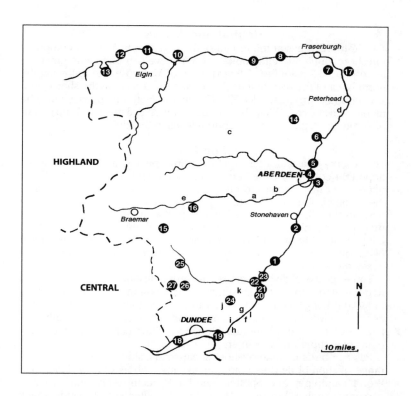

Main sites

NE1 St Cyrus
NE2 Fowlsheugh
NE3 Girdle Ness
NE4 Mouth of Don
NE5 Black Dog
NE6 Ythan Estuary and Sands of Forvie
NE7 Loch of Strathbeg
NE8 Troup Head
NE9 Banff/Macduff Harbour
NE10 Spey Bay
NE11 Lossiemouth
NE12 Burghead
NE13 Findhorn Bay
NE14 Haddo Country Park
NE15 Glen Muick and Lochnagar
NE16 Glen Tanar
NE17 Rattray Head
NE18 Tay Estuary
NE19 Outer Tay
NE20 Lunan Bay

NE21 Fishtown of Usan
NE22 Montrose Basin
NE23 Kinnaber Links
NE24 Balgavies Loch
NE25 Angus Glens
NE26 Loch of Kinnordy
NE27 Loch of Lintrathen

Additional sites

a Crathes Castle
b Drum
c Leith Hall
d Longhaven Cliffs
e Muir of Dinnet
f Arbroath
g Auchmithie
h Carnoustie
i East Haven
j Forfar Loch
k Montreathmont Forest
l Seaton Cliffs

NE1 ST CYRUS

Habitat and Access

This 92-ha NNR lies at the mouth of the River North Esk and comprises foreshore, dune and cliff habitats. The reserve can be reached by turning off the A92 3.5 miles (5.6 km) north of Montrose and following the north bank of the river to a track entering the reserve at the sharp bend 1.5 miles (2.4 km) later (NO 743635). Alternatively, an approach may be made from St Cyrus village by turning off the A92, 6 miles (9.7 km) north of Montrose. A path from the church leads to the cliff-top.

Species

The reserve boasts a total of 47 breeding species, including a locally important colony of Little Terns at the south end of the reserve. These often suffer heavy losses to predators. In order to reduce disturbance, the colony is fenced off from May to August. Fulmar and Herring Gull nest on the cliffs, while Eider breeds in the dunes. Other noteworthy breeders include Stonechat, Grasshopper Warbler and Whitethroat. Large concentrations of Eider, Goosander and Red-breasted Merganser occur offshore in spring and autumn—the river mouth is the best place to see these.

Three species of diver have been recorded offshore in winter, although Red-throated is by far the most numerous. Common and Velvet Scoters, Eider and Long-tailed Duck winter in the bay, there being much interchange between the sea duck here and at Lunan Bay further south. Dipper and Grey Wagtail frequent the river; Short-eared Owl frequently hunts over the dunes in winter.

Passage birds include offshore shearwaters, skuas and terns, a good range of shorebirds (less common species such as Curlew Sandpiper, Wood Sandpiper and Spotted Redshank occur every autumn) and passerines such as Wheatear, Whinchat and (after easterly winds) Black Redstart.

Timing

Breeding birds provide the interest in April–July; migrants are best sought September–November. Further information is obtainable from SNH Area Officer, The Old Lifeboat Station, Nether Warburton, St Cyrus, by Montrose, DD10 OAD (tel: 01674 830736).

NE2 FOWLSHEUGH

OS ref: NO 880798
OS Landranger 45

Habitat

The RSPB reserve at Fowlsheugh is home to one of the largest and most accessible seabird colonies in Britain: approximately 80,000 pairs of six species breed on the 1.5 miles (2.4 km) of old red sandstone cliffs. These cliffs, up to 65 m high in places, are deeply indented, making it possible to closely observe nesting birds without causing disturbance. The reserve is a SSSI of international importance.

Access

The reserve is reached via a minor road leading east off the A92, 3 miles (4.8 km) south of Stonehaven, signed for Crawton. There is a bus service along the A92, between Montrose and Stonehaven. The nearest railway station is at Stonehaven, on the Perth–Aberdeen line. From the car park at Crawton, walk north along the cliff-top footpath for 0.5 mile (0.8 km). Visitors are requested to take care at the cliff edge. Superb views of the nesting seabirds can be obtained at several vantage points. The reserve is open at all times.

Timing

The seabirds are ashore April to mid-July; there is little of interest during the rest of the year.

Calendar

May–July: Fulmar, Herring Gull and small numbers of Puffin occupy the upper cliff, while the niches and lower ledges are crammed with about 30,000 pairs each of Kittiwake and Guillemot, and c. 5000 pairs of Razorbill. Recent studies indicate that just over 2 per cent of the Guillemot are the bridled form. Many Shag nest in the caves at the foot of the cliffs and small numbers of Eider can be seen close inshore.

Fowlsheugh is not noted for seawatching, but passage shearwaters and skuas can be seen offshore, especially during onshore winds in late summer/autumn.

NE3 GIRDLE NESS

OS ref: NJ 973054
OS Landranger 38

Habitat and Access

This promontory lies on the south side of the mouth of the River Dee in Aberdeen. A lighthouse is situated at its end, about 1.5 miles (2.4 km) from the city centre. This is backed by a golf course, with short grass, some rough areas and gorse bushes. Travelling south through Aberdeen, cross the River Dee on the A956 to Torry then take the second road on the left, which leads past the docks and golf course to the lighthouse. There are two car-parking areas—that by the foghorn offers the best sea-watching opportunities.

Species

Passage seabirds are the main attraction. Arctic and Great Skuas are numerous, while Pomarine is annual and Long-tailed almost annual. Shearwaters are common in the autumn; sea duck (especially Eider), white-winged gulls and waders provide interest in the winter. King Eider is occasionally recorded. Large numbers of passage Wheatear some-times occur on the short grass of the golf course. The limited amount of cover provides temporary shelter for migrant passerines such as Whin-chat and Redstart and occasionally scarcer ones too, for instance: Bluethroat (recorded annually, mainly in spring), Lesser Whitethroat, Yellow-browed Warbler (six records in 1988), Greenish Warbler, Wood-chat Shrike, Nightingale, Melodious Warbler and Arctic Redpoll. On the rocky foreshore, Purple Sandpiper is present well into spring, while Turnstone can be seen year-round.

Timing

Easterly winds following a strong northwesterly blow are best for seabird passage. Direct sunlight can cause visibility problems in the morning. In both spring and autumn, a southeasterly might produce passerine migrants, especially Bluethroat.

Calendar

March–May: Passage skuas, Iceland Gull, one or two Little Gull, possible Bluethroat, Wheatear, Whinchat and Redstart.

Purple Sandpipers and Oystercatchers, winter

May–July: Black Tern.

August–November: During late August–September passage Manx and some Sooty Shearwaters can be seen, together with up to four species of skua and occasional Little Gull. Mediterranean Shearwater is almost annual and a few Great and Cory's Shearwaters have occurred in recent years. Wader passage includes Ruff (up to 80), Black-tailed Godwit and Curlew Sandpiper. In August–September the site is increasingly used by c. 200 Eider coming out of eclipse plumage. Miscellaneous species also be seen at this time include infrequent Blue Fulmar, Velvet Scoter, Ring Ouzel and Snow Bunting. A Woodchat Shrike was recorded in 1996.

December–February: Up to 300 Goldeneye formerly overwintered in Greyhope Bay but due to a change in the sewage outflow into the bay perhaps only 40 birds currently use the area. Iceland and Glaucous Gulls can be seen in the river mouth. On the rocky foreshore excellent views of Purple Sandpiper and Turnstone can be obtained. Very high counts of Little Auk (e.g. over 2000 in a day) may occur in easterly winds. Slavonian and Red-necked Grebes are possible.

NE4 MOUTH OF DON

OS ref: NJ 951095
OS Landranger 38

Habitat and Access

A greenbelt on the northern outskirts of Aberdeen, which has become a LNR. The river mouth is 3 miles (4.8 km) north of the city centre, on the A92. On reaching the Bridge of Don turn right onto Beach Boulevard, where there are plenty of parking places. About 200 m along the Boulevard is a hide, open in daylight hours in summer and by arrangement with the district council in winter. It is possible to walk from here along the estuary foreshore to Aberdeen beach. On the opposite side of the Bridge of Don lies Seaton Park; this continues along an embankment high above the river as far as Brig o'Balgownie, affording excellent views of ducks (especially Goosander) and waders. A lower track on the opposite bank returns to Bridge of Don.

Timing

There is year-round interest owing to the attraction of the area for terns in summer, migrants during spring and autumn, and duck in winter.

Calendar

Resident: Sparrowhawk, Kestrel and Grey Wagtail can usually be found in the area.

May–July: Feeding Sandwich, Common and Arctic Terns can be seen. Little Tern is regular offshore and occasionally seen on the beach. Black Tern has been recorded but is better seen at Girdle Ness, where it is almost annual. In late summer, Arctic and Great Skuas sometimes harass the terns in the estuary mouth. Riverside bushes provide cover for passerine migrants and Redstart, Goldcrest, Chiffchaff, Willow Warbler and Blackcap are annual. During May, Spotted and even Pied Flycatchers are possible, while Yellow Wagtail should be sought on the short grasslands.

August–October: Passage Manx Shearwater, Gannet and skuas can be seen offshore. Wader passage can be good (especially for an urban site!) and includes large numbers of Ringed Plover, plus occasional rarities: Pectoral Sandpiper and Greater Sand Plover have been recorded. The golf course opposite the hide regularly floods in autumn and can hold good numbers of passage waders, including Ruff and Little Stint. Curlew Sandpiper may occur on the mud. A Pied Wheatear was recorded recently.

November–April: Large numbers of diving duck are present, including Goldeneye, Tufted Duck and Goosander. Scaup (up to 15) and Long-tailed Duck are possible in midwinter and Smew is an occasional visitor. Watch for Slavonian and Red-necked Grebes in the bay and at sea. Pink-footed Geese can be seen flying over in the evenings.

Between September and March there is a large gull roost at the mouth of the river. This regularly includes Glaucous and Iceland Gulls. Up to four Mediterranean Gull have been present, including an adult which has returned each year since 1991. A Ring-billed Gull was seen in 1995.

NE5 BLACK DOG

OS ref: NJ 965137
OS Landranger 38

Habitat
A sandy shore backed by a marram-dominated dune system with a few boggy dune slacks; these have been largely 'improved' for a golf course. To the south, the beach stretches for 3 miles (4.8 km) to the Don estuary, while the Ythan estuary lies 7 miles (11 km) to the north.

Access
The beach at Black Dog is reached by way of the A92, turning off east onto a driveable track c. 5 miles (8 km) north of Aberdeen at NJ 955143. There is room for a few vehicles to park near the cottages after 1 mile (1.6 km). From here, walk 100 m to the beach. Offshore duck can be viewed from anywhere along the beach. There is a bus route from Aberdeen to Ellon/Peterhead, along the A92.

Species
The principal attraction here is a large flock of moulting sea duck, present in summer and early autumn.

Timing
Calm sea conditions are needed for viewing sea duck. The afternoon is the best time to visit on a bright day, so that the light is behind you.

Calendar
June–September: From late June to early September up to 10,000 Eider, 2000 Common Scoter and perhaps 250 Velvet Scoter may be seen. King Eider and Surf Scoter are present most summers. In autumn, Scaup may also appear, while Sandwich, Common and Arctic Terns from nearby colonies feed at sea and rest on the beach, attracting marauding Arctic and Great Skuas.

November–March: Sea duck numbers are much reduced, but many Red-throated Diver occur and Long-tailed Duck is present. Sanderling may be found on the shoreline, while Short-eared Owl and Snow Buntings frequent the dunes.

NE6 YTHAN ESTUARY AND SANDS OF FORVIE

OS ref: NK 00/24
OS Landranger 38

Habitat
The Ythan estuary is around 5 miles (8 km) long by 300–400 m wide and is situated 12 miles (19 km) north of Aberdeen. It is bordered by agri-cultural land to the west and by the dunes and moorland of the Sands of Forvie to the east. The estuary is composed of intertidal mud- and sandflats, with pebbles, shingle and mussel beds largely confined to the areas of faster-moving water, especially below Waterside Bridge. Areas of saltmarsh occur mainly at the mouth of the Tarty Burn and near Waterside Bridge. The area is a NNR totalling 1018 ha and includes the best example of coastal moorland in northern Britain. Although gener-ally undisturbed, the outer estuary in particular is becoming increasing-ly popular as a windsurfing location.

Access
The estuary can be reached by taking the A92 north from Aberdeen, then turning east onto the A975 Newburgh road after c. 10 miles (16 km). This road crosses the estuary 3 miles (4.8 km) later. Access to the foreshore and along footpaths is allowed at all times. Visitors are not per-mitted in the ternery or to enter the moorland during April to August. There are a number of good vantage points.

1 NEWBURGH (OS REF: NJ 997252)

Heading north along the A975, turn right immediately after the Ythan Hotel at the southern end of Newburgh (signposted to the beach) and

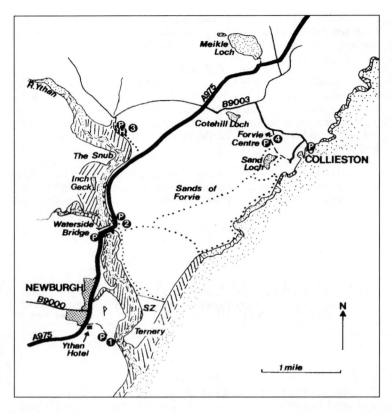

follow this track to the car park near the golf course. Good views over the river mouth and the tern breeding area opposite can be obtained by walking 100 m across the dunes. Little Tern has bred on this shore recently—please obey any signs to avoid disturbance. A right turn after the Udny Arms leads to Inches Point, another good viewpoint.

2 WATERSIDE BRIDGE (OS REF: NK 002268)

There are several lay-bys on the A975 north of Newburgh, both near the bridge and beyond, where the road follows the river for a mile or so. These are good viewpoints for feeding and roosting waders. From a parking area near the east end of the bridge, two tracks lead into the Forvie NNR. Tawny and Long-eared and Short-eared Owls can be seen here, often during the day. SNH wardens are on hand during the breeding season.

3 WAULKMILL HIDE (OS REF: NK 003290)

Follow the A975 north from Newburgh for 3 miles (4.8 km); turn left along an unclassified road (opposite the B9003 turn for Collieston) and after 1.5 miles (2.4 km) take another left onto a track on the east side of a stream leading into the Ythan. A car-parking area and large comfort-able hide with wheelchair access is reached within 200 m. This hide, built by Gordon District Council, affords excellent views of the inner estuary. Little Egret and Grasshopper Warbler have occurred recently.

4 FORVIE CENTRE (OS REF: NK 034289)

Take the B9003 turn, 3 miles (4.8 km) north of Newburgh, towards Col-lieston. After 1.5 miles (2.4 km) a track on the right leads to a car park and the Forvie Centre, where information about the reserve is displayed. Tracks lead from here into the moorland areas and Sands of Forvie NNR. Nearby Sand Loch sometimes has Shoveler, Gadwall and (very rarely) in spring Garganey and perhaps Ruddy Duck. There is a regular bus ser-vice to Newburgh from Aberdeen.

Timing

Apart from the restrictions mentioned above, the area is accessible at all times. Bird interest is sustained throughout the year (see Calendar). A rising or falling tide, two hours either side of high water, is best for observing the waders at close quarters. High tide should be avoided, as waders will probably either be feeding in the surrounding fields or roost-ing on the inaccessible Inch Geck Island. Note that high water above Waterside Bridge occurs approximately one hour later than at the estu-ary mouth. The Eiders at Newburgh are most easily watched at low tide however, while they feed on the submerged mussel beds.

Species

Numbers and diversity of birds are outstanding at all times of year. Approximately 2000 pairs of Eider have bred on the moor, making this the largest breeding concentration in Britain. However, predation by foxes, crows and gulls has led to an alarming decline in productivity. Around 50 pairs of Shelduck also breed, using abandoned rabbit bur-rows. At the southern end of the Sands of Forvie there is a large mixed tern colony, including Sandwich, Common, Arctic and Little Terns. Like the Eider, these are all faring badly and the colonies are much reduced. Curlew, Skylark and Meadow Pipit also breed on the moorland, while Oystercatcher and Ringed Plover prefer shoreline sites. Cliffs in the north-ern part of the reserve are used by Fulmar, Herring Gull, Kittiwake and (in recent years) Razorbill.

The Ythan is a major staging post for migrating geese. Up to 10,000 Pink-footed, 3000 Greylag and smaller parties of Brent, Barnacle and White-fronted Geese occur during late autumn and early spring. Smaller numbers overwinter. In addition, moderate numbers of Whooper Swan may also be present. Large numbers of duck also pass through, includ-ing Teal, Wigeon and Mallard, with smaller numbers of Goldeneye and Long-tailed Duck. Drake King Eider has been recorded in both summer and winter in recent years.

The estuarine part of the reserve is an excellent feeding and roosting site for a variety of waders and during spring and autumn passage counts of up to 1500 each of Golden Plover and Lapwing have been recorded, as well as 1000 each of Curlew and Redshank, while smaller but significant numbers of Ringed Plover, Knot, Dunlin, Bar-tailed God-wit and Whimbrel occur. Scarcer, but still regular, passage waders in-

Snow Buntings and immature male Merlin, winter

clude Little Stint, Curlew Sandpiper, Ruff, Black-tailed Godwit, Spotted Redshank, Greenshank and Green Sandpiper. Wildfowl are generally most numerous around the Snub and Inches Point, while large high-tide roosts of waders occur at Inch Geck, a favoured roosting site for Cormorant.

Calendar

Resident: Eider, Shelduck and Red Grouse.

March–May: Courting Eiders are prominent on the river and by early May most of the ducks will have laid. Goosander moves into the river during late spring. Passage waders may stopover on the river. Skeins of northbound geese arrive and depart throughout April and into early May. Sandwich Tern arrives in late March and from April the area at the south end of the Sands of Forvie is fenced off to permit Sandwich, Common, Arctic and Little Terns to breed undisturbed.

June–July: The four species of breeding tern can be viewed from the golf course vantage point near Newburgh. A rising tide brings shoals of herring fry and sand eels into the estuary, resulting in frenzied tern activity. In July, skuas (mainly Arctic) enter the estuary mouth to harry the terns.

August–November: Eider numbers decline as many depart for their moulting grounds. About 1000 remain and overwinter. The return passage of waders means that there is usually much activity on the river. Migrant geese start to appear from mid-September and numbers peak during late autumn.

December–February: Overwintering geese use the fields and estuary, and large herds of Whooper Swan are sometimes present. Wigeon, Teal, Goldeneye and Red-breasted Merganser are present on the river, while Long-tailed Duck may be seen in the estuary mouth, especially in rough sea conditions. Offshore, Red-throated Diver, and Common and Velvet Scoters can usually be found in small numbers. Short-eared Owl is a common sight over the moor whereas Hen Harrier is rare. Rough-legged Buzzard is an occasional winter visitor. Peregrine and Merlin can regularly be seen hunting over the river. Snow Bunting is a common winter visitor to the coast and Twite is regular in varying numbers. Look for Sanderling on the beaches.

Rarities seen in recent years include Hudsonian Godwit (in an area known as Slains Pools, just northeast of Meikle Loch and north of the Ythan estuary mouth, in September 1988), American Golden Plover, Great White and Little Egrets, Pectoral Sandpiper, Bee-eater and Booted Warbler.

SNH Reserves Manager
Forvie Centre, Collieston, Ellon, Aberdeenshire (tel: 01358 751330).

Adjacent Sites

COTEHILL LOCH (OS REF: NK 027293)

Visible from the B9003 road to Collieston, mentioned above, c. 0.25 mile (0.4 km) after the turn-off from the A975, the loch is worth checking quickly for passage waders during spring and autumn and it can hold wildfowl (sometimes including Garganey) in spring. Ruddy Duck is frequently present. It is also a good Gadwall and Shoveler site. Rarities seen in recent years include Marsh Sandpiper and Ring-necked Duck.

COLLIESTON (OS REF: NK 043287)

At the end of the B9003, the car park here can be a good seawatching vantage point. This site is good for passerines in autumn, e.g. Wryneck, Red-backed Shrike, Yellow-browed and Icterine Warblers. Rarities have included Booted Warbler.

MEIKLE LOCH (OS REF: NK 028309, OS LANDRANGER 30)

Reached by continuing north on the A975 for 1 mile (1.6 km) past the Collieston turn-off, a rough track on the left leads to a viewpoint over the loch, immediately before the next crossroads. The loch is the main roost for wintering Pink-footed Geese, but also holds Whooper Swan, Tufted Duck and Goldeneye. Canada Goose and Ruddy Duck are present all year. In May/June and from late July into autumn it is sometimes visited by Black Tern; Little Gull is also possible in autumn. Passage waders occur, but can be hard to find around the vegetated edges. Pink-footed numbers can reach tens of thousands in early autumn, while several thousand Greylag Geese are present in spring. A visit just before sunset for the roost flight can be spectacular. In good light occasional Snow, White-fronted or Brent Geese may be discernible.

References
Birdwatching around the Ythan Estuary, Newburgh, Aberdeenshire. S Anderson (1991). *Scottish Bird News* 24.

Habitat

On the northeast coast approximately midway between Peterhead and Fraserburgh, this shallow 222-ha loch is separated from the North Sea by an area of sand dunes only a few hundred metres wide. The RSPB manage the loch and much of the surrounding marsh, dune, farmland and wooded habitats, totalling 1012 ha. Extensive areas of reed-grass and other emergent vegetation fringe much of the loch; there are also scattered areas of willow scrub. Widely fluctuating water levels mean that much of the surrounding land is frequently flooded. Loch of Strathbeg is listed as a SSSI by SNH. The reserve has a visitor centre, several hides and a loch-side boardwalk. Some of the hides overlook the loch, while others provide views of wader scrapes.

Species

The size and location of Loch of Strathbeg combine to make it of great importance for staging and wintering wildfowl; at times more than 35,000 swans, geese and duck can be present, using the area for both feeding and roosting. Greylag and Pink-footed Geese are predominant, but smaller numbers of Barnacle Geese also visit and now winter, while Brent and White-fronted Goose are seen annually in early and late winter. Snow Geese are regular visitors.

Whooper Swans

Breeding duck include Shelduck, Shoveler, Teal, Tufted Duck and Eider, and Garganey has attempted to breed, while 2–3 pairs of Great Crested Grebe nest. Water Rail breeds in the marshland, while Sedge Warbler and Reed Bunting nest in the reedbeds at the northwest end of the loch. An island supports an expanding colony of Sandwich Tern, while Common Tern also breeds. A newly acquired part of the reserve has a rookery containing over 150 nests. Marsh Harrier and Black-tailed Godwit are present in summer.

Loch of Strathbeg is an outstanding site for wader passage, especially in August when large numbers of Ruff and Black-tailed Godwit pass through, plus several species of rarer wader. It is the best site in northeast Scotland for Pectoral Sandpiper. Both the marshes and scrub attract migrant passerines, and Sparrowhawk, Merlin and Short-eared Owl often hunt over the reserve. Rarities are regular and in recent years have included Bittern, Purple Heron, Glossy Ibis, Spoonbill, American Wigeon, Ring-necked Duck, Honey Buzzard, White-rumped and Buff-breasted Sandpipers, Lesser Yellowlegs and White-winged Black Tern.

Access

The reserve is entered from the A952 Peterhead–Fraserburgh road, some 7 miles (11.3 km) northwest of Peterhead, at the village of Crimond. The nature reserve is Thistle signposted from here. Buses from Peterhead to Fraserburgh pass the turn to the reserve near Crimond.

Timing

The prime period to visit for wildfowl is October–April, but May and June are of interest for breeding species. The nature centre and hides are open daily throughout the year. Please note that dogs are not welcome.

Calendar

March–June: Pink-footed and Greylag Geese begin to move north in late March–April, with all but a very few gone by early May. Other wildfowl also disperse, leaving only breeders by mid-May. Terns and warblers arrive. Spring wader passage occurs in May and continues until early June. Up to six Wood Sandpipers have been recorded in some years, while Temminck's Stint is almost annual. An increasing population of terns breed on the islands at the east side of the loch.

July–August: Breeding species present and ducks enter eclipse plumage. Wader passage can be very good, especially in August; large numbers of Ruff (up to 140), Black-tailed Godwit (up to 60) and Greenshank (up to 12) can occur, while small numbers of Spotted Redshank, Green, Wood and Curlew Sandpipers and Little Stint are regular. Pectoral Sandpiper is an annual visitor.

September–November: The first Pink-footed Geese generally arrive during early September and numbers increase steadily towards the end of the month. From September diving duck numbers start to build up, followed by an increase in the dabbling duck in October. Barnacle Geese often stage at Strathbeg during early October, on their way from Spitsbergen to wintering grounds on the Solway. Flocks of several hundred Whooper Swan are present in early November. More unusual wildfowl species, including Snow Goose, White-fronted Goose and Gadwall, are seen annually in small numbers.

December–February: All wintering wildfowl present, including Whooper Swan, Pink-footed and Greylag Geese, Wigeon, Teal, Mallard, Pochard, Tufted Duck, Goldeneye, Red-breasted Merganser and Goosander. Smew has been regular in recent years. Great Crested, Slavonian, Black-necked and Red-necked Grebes may be present.

RSPB Warden
Starnafin Farmhouse, Crimond, Fraserburgh AB4 4YN (tel: 01346 532017).

References
Strathbeg Reserve. RSPB leaflet.

NE8 TROUP HEAD
OS ref: NJ 825673
OS Landranger 29 or 30

Habitat
The rocky north-facing sea cliffs of Troup Head extend for 5 miles (8 km) between Aberdour Bay and Crovie, 10 miles (16 km) east of Banff. Large numbers of seabirds are present during the breeding season and the bays hold wintering divers and sea duck. The area includes Troup and Lion's Head to the west of Pennan village and Pennan Head to the east. Rising to around 100 m in height, the cliffs and steep, vegetated slopes consist mainly of sheer gritstone in the west and spectacularly eroded sandstone/conglomerate to the east. Agricultural land extends to the cliff edge along virtually the whole length, although there are some interesting areas of maritime heath and grassland vegetation. The coast is designated a SSSI.

Species
About 1500 pairs of Fulmar breed, scattered throughout both the eastern and western cliffs. West of Pennan, approximately 125 pairs of Shag, over 16,000 pairs of Kittiwake, 16,000 Guillemot and 1200 Razorbill have been counted. In excess of 60 Puffin and 1–2 pairs of Black Guillemot also occur, mainly east of Pennan village. Eider is visible year-round.

Access
All of the cliff-top is privately owned and the only public access points are at Lion's Head and Aberdour Bay. These are approached from either New Aberdour or Macduff along the B9031. If visiting Lion's Head, there is a car park at Cullykhan, between the Gardenstown and Pennan turn-offs, or alternatively, car parking is possible at Northfield Farm, 1.5 miles (2.4 km) east of the Gardenstown signpost (please ask at the farm for permission). From here the coast can be reached by walking north to the head of a large gully, then by following its left bank to the headland. The car park at Aberdour Bay lies immediately north of New Aberdour on the B9031. There is a vague path along the cliff-top. Several promontories between Lion's Head and Troup Head provide good views of nesting seabirds. There are fewer good vantage points on the eastern cliffs.

Timing
The optimum time to visit is between May and mid-July, when seabird activity is at its peak. Relatively calm conditions are essential for viewing seabirds here, owing to the exposed situation of the vantage points.

Calendar
April–June: Breeding seabirds dominate the interest (see above).

July–August: Breeding birds start to disperse; Great and Arctic Skuas visible offshore.

November–March: Offshore divers and sea duck join the Eider in the sheltered bays.

References
Seabirds of Troup and Pennan Heads 1979–86. CS Lloyd & SG North (1987). *Scottish Birds*, vol. 14, no. 4.

NE9 BANFF/MACDUFF HARBOUR

OS ref: NJ 69/64
OS Landranger 29

Habitat and Access
This is a renowned location for winter sea duck and gulls. Banff is situated on Grampian's north-facing coastline, some 25 miles (40 km) west of Fraserburgh. The harbour and rocky coastline around Banff can be viewed from any number of vantage points along the coast.

Great Black-backed Gulls and Glaucous Gull

Species

Winter sees Red-throated Diver, Velvet Scoter, Eider, Iceland and Glaucous Gulls, with Purple Sandpiper and Turnstone on the rocky foreshore. Great Northern and Black-throated Divers are sometimes present. Passage birds include divers, Common and Velvet Scoters, Eider and skuas. Little Auk is numerous during late autumn in some years.

NE10 SPEY BAY

OS ref: NJ 335658
OS Landranger 28

Habitat

This very wide, shallow bay is situated east of Lossiemouth. There are about 6 miles (9.7 km) of shoreline on both sides of the mouth of the River Spey at Kingston. The inter-tidal area is predominantly sand and shingle in the western half of the bay, while rocky substrates characterise the eastern part. Lossie Forest, to the east of Lossiemouth, is a mixed plantation of Scots and Corsican pines.

Species

Numbers of wintering sea duck in Spey Bay are substantially lower than formerly. Currently up to 1000 Common Scoter and Long-tailed Duck overwinter, with around 500 Velvet Scoter. A few hundred Eider and small numbers of Scaup, Red-breasted Merganser and an occasional Surf Scoter are recorded most years. Up to 700 Red-throated Diver have been counted in late autumn/early winter, while very small numbers of Great Northern and Black-throated Divers are sometimes present.

The tidal area at the mouth of the Spey can be good for passage waders in autumn, including Whimbrel and Greenshank. To the east, the rocky shoreline around Portessie can hold up to 300 Purple Sandpiper and large numbers of Turnstone.

Long-tailed Duck, winter

Large flocks of Snow Bunting may be found along the shoreline in winter, particularly nearer Lossiemouth. Goosander can be seen off-shore during summer and large numbers of Sandwich Tern may be present in late summer/early autumn. Osprey is a regular feature of summer. Spey Bay is also a good place to watch bottlenose dolphin, which gather at the mouth of the river to catch salmon. Crested Tit and Scottish Crossbill are present throughout the year at Lossie Forest.

Access

The following access points are recommended.

1 FROM LOSSIEMOUTH (OS REF: NJ 238705)

(See G11.) Cross the wooden footbridge over the River Lossie and walk east along the shore. The Lossie estuary is best worked for waders at low tide.

2 BOAR'S HEAD ROCK (OS REF: NJ 285678)

Take the B9013 from Lossiemouth for 2 miles (3.2 km) to NJ 255670 (just over the River Lossie at Arthur's Bridge). From here a forestry track leads through Lossie Forest to Boar's Head Rock, a favourite feeding area for wintering sea duck. This is a 2-mile (3.2 km) walk and there are a number of potentially confusing tracks—an OS map is therefore essential.

3 KINGSTON (OS REF: NJ 340657)

One mile (1.6 km) west of Fochabers take the B9015 turning off the main A96 at Mosstodloch. Kingston is reached after 3.5 miles (5.6 km). The tidal area at the mouth of the river is good for migrant waders. Access is

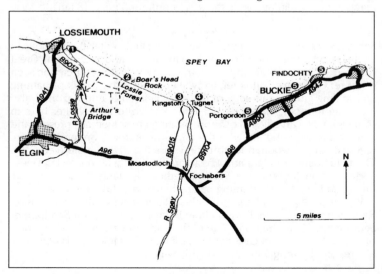

easily obtained from the picnic site overlooking the estuary. A low tide is essential for watching birds in the estuary. Calm conditions are preferable for the sea duck, which may be rather distant.

4 TUGNET (OS REF: NJ 348656)

This is on the opposite side of the river to Kingston and is reached via the B9104 from Fochabers. Again, the river mouth should be checked for waders, then walk east along the shore.

5 PORTGORDON, BUCKIE AND FINDOCHTY

The harbours along the A990/A942 are worth checking in winter for white-winged gulls and sheltering waterfowl.

Timing

Spey Bay is mainly of interest between autumn and spring, although many sea duck are present throughout the year.

NE11 LOSSIEMOUTH

OS ref: NJ 239712
OS Landranger 28

Branderburgh pier and harbour at Lossiemouth are excellent sites for observing wintering waterfowl and passage seabirds. The area is reached from Elgin by taking the A941 north for 5 miles (8 km).

Species

Sea duck, especially Eider and Long-tailed Duck, enter the harbour in winter, while small numbers of Red-throated (and occasional Great Northern) Divers, Common Scoter and a few Velvet Scoter can be seen offshore. Glaucous Gull is regularly seen among the flocks of bathing and loafing gulls at the edge of the river. Guillemot and Razorbill also enter the harbour; Little Auk has been known to take shelter here in some winters. Large flocks of Snow Bunting are sometimes present and can usually be found either in the dunes or on the shore east of town, reached via the wooden footbridge across the River Lossie (see G10). The fields between Elgin and Lossiemouth usually hold Greylag Geese and occasionally Whooper Swan, together with large flocks of Greenfinch and Linnet. Corn Bunting occurs here throughout the year.

Wader passage can be good in the tidal reaches of the River Lossie. Rarities in recent years have included Marsh and Pectoral Sandpipers. Seawatching from the north side of the harbour can produce numbers of Great, Arctic and occasional Pomarine Skuas. Little Auk is occasionally reported during autumn and early winter.

NE12 BURGHEAD

OS ref: NJ 110690
OS Landranger 28

Burghead lies west of Lossiemouth and has a similar range of species. It can be reached by taking the A96 west from Elgin, turning north after 3 miles (4.8 km) on the B9013. Burghead is reached 4.5 miles (7.2 km) further on.

Species

Eider and Long-tailed Duck regularly enter the harbour and in late winter the latter can be watched displaying at very close range. Glaucous and Iceland Gulls can occur among the commoner gulls that frequent the harbour. A few Black Guillemots are generally present and in some winters Little Auk use the harbour for shelter. Both Common and Velvet Scoters occur offshore and Surf Scoter is seen in most winters. Small numbers of Red-throated (and occasionally Great Northern) Divers are usually present. The harbour and headland make good viewpoints. The headland itself is an excellent place for watching waders, including Dunlin, Turnstone, Oystercatcher, Redshank and, in winter, Purple Sandpiper (at high water these roost on the harbour wall).

NE13 FINDHORN BAY

OS ref: NJ 045625
OS Landranger 27

Habitat and Access

This large tidal basin is almost completely land-locked, there being only a narrow northern outlet into the Moray Firth. The most straightforward approach to the bay is along the B9011 from Forres, via Kinloss. After 2 miles (3.2 km) this road more or less follows the east side of the bay and good views can be obtained from the roadside. Continue to Findhorn village, where it is possible to walk to the mouth of the bay—offshore is the best area for wintering sea duck and terns in summer. Access to the west side of the bay is more complicated: 1 mile (1.6 km) west of Forres an unclassified road turns north off the A96, immediately after the bridge over the River Findhorn. Follow this, without turning off, for 2.5 miles (4 km) until just past Wellside Farm. Park here, taking care not to obstruct access, and walk c. 0.75 mile (1.2 km) along the track to the bay.

Species

Small numbers of Eider, Oystercatcher and Ringed Plover breed nearby, and Sandwich, Common and Arctic Terns can be watched feeding in the entrance to the bay in summer. The bay is also a favourite fishing haunt of Osprey. Crested Tit breeds in the forest to the west.

Migrant waders include large numbers of Oystercatcher, Redshank, Knot, Ringed Plover and Dunlin, with smaller numbers of Greenshank, Whimbrel, Curlew Sandpiper and Black-tailed Godwit. Spotted Redshank and Little Stint are occasional. Sandwich Tern can be seen in the bay during late summer/early autumn, while offshore, Gannet and skuas occur.

Wintering waterfowl are represented by large numbers of Long-tailed Duck, Common and Velvet Scoters, Red-breasted Merganser and Eider. Red-throated, Great Northern and Black-throated Divers are regular offshore, particularly in late autumn.

Timing

Findhorn Bay has year-round attractions. The large numbers of waterfowl that gather at sea between autumn and early spring, or the passage waders that move through in spring and autumn, tend to be the prime attractions for birders.

NE14 HADDO COUNTRY PARK

OS ref: NJ 875345
OS Landranger 30

Habitat

Formerly part of the policies of Haddo House, this 73-ha country park contains parkland, woodland and wetland, including a loch and several ponds. Both broadleaf and coniferous trees are present. In recent years over 2000 mainly broadleaved trees have been planted, greatly enhancing the wildlife potential of the area.

Species

A few pairs each of Grey Heron, feral Greylag Goose, Mallard, Tufted Duck and Stock Dove breed at Haddo. One pair of Mute Swan occupies Middle Lake throughout the year. Other residents include Buzzard, Sparrowhawk, Kestrel, Grey Partridge, Pheasant, Moorhen, Great Spotted Woodpecker, Grey Wagtail and Goldcrest. In spring and summer these are joined by around 7–8 pairs of Sedge Warbler and 1–2 pairs of Blackcap and Chiffchaff. Small numbers of Oystercatcher and Lapwing breed. Osprey is a regular visitor to the loch.

The area is not particularly noted for migrants, although significant records in recent years have included Wood Sandpiper in spring and small flocks of Crossbill in the pines during July and August. In late summer, Sand and House Martins gather in large numbers over Middle Lake.

Wintering wildfowl are dominated by large numbers of roosting Greylag Geese, especially in November/December when staging birds are present. Depending on the weather conditions, up to 5000 Greylag can be present throughout much of the winter. In addition, over 100 Teal are usually present, mostly frequenting the reedbeds. Fifty or so Wigeon and up to ten Pochard and a similar number of Goldeneye can be seen among the Tufted Duck, which number about 40 during winter. Middle Lake can host as many as 60 Goosander in late winter. Water Rail has been seen in the reedbeds at this season, and small numbers of Brambling and Siskin have been recorded.

Access

Take the A92 from Aberdeen to Peterhead, turning onto the B999 after Bridge of Don, 3 miles (4.8 km) later. Follow this road to Tarves (c. 13 miles/20 km) and then follow signs for Haddo House. There is ample parking space. Two bird hides overlook the loch and wetland areas and there are several paths through the woodlands. A leaflet describing the park is available from the Ranger's Office and country park display at the Stables Block adjacent to Haddo House itself. Special facilities are available for handicapped visitors—contact the Ranger Service in advance (see below). Please note that dogs must be kept on a lead at all times. There is a bus service from Aberdeen to Tarves, about 2 miles (3.2 km) from the park entrance.

Timing

The country park is best visited October–April, when a range of wintering wildfowl can be seen. Weekends, especially Sunday afternoons, can be very busy and are best avoided. The park is open daily dawn to dusk. For further information, contact Aberdeenshire Ranger Service (tel: 01651 851489).

NE15 GLEN MUICK
AND LOCHNAGAR

OS ref: NO 300850
OS Landranger 44

Habitat

This is one of the grandest parts of the eastern Grampians. Under an agreement with the Balmoral Estate, the SWT manages a total of 2570 ha, including Loch Muick, the plateau summit of Lochnagar and its spectacular northern corries, acres of open moorland and the craggy valley sides above Dubh Loch. The area has been designated a SSSI. Further information is available from the visitor centre at Spittal of Glenmuick. The estate operates a ranger service and a reserve information booklet is on sale at the centre.

Species

Ptarmigan, Red and Black Grouse breed in the area. Breeding waders include Dotterel, Golden Plover and Dunlin, while Common Sandpiper frequents the shoreline of Loch Muick. Lochnagar is an excellent area for raptors and a regular watch should be kept for Golden Eagle and Peregrine; Hen Harrier, and Merlin too, can be seen. Short-eared Owl frequents the glen. White-tailed Eagles have been seen in recent years.

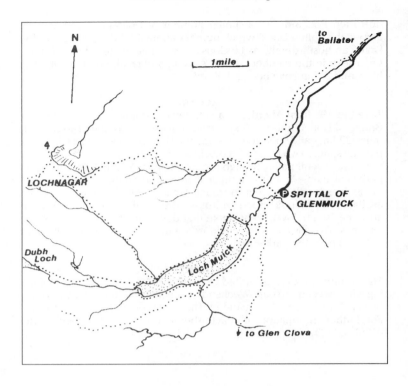

Meadow Pipit and Cuckoo, spring

Access

Lochnagar is reached by taking the B976 west from Ballater, then turning left on an unclassified road at Bridge of Glen Muick, just over 0.5
mile (0.8 km) further. From here it is 8 miles (13 km) to a car park at the
road end at Spittal of Glenmuick. There are several paths leading from
the visitor centre, varying from the straightforward route along the
shores of Loch Muick to the more arduous climb to the summit of
Lochnagar. A useful compromise is to tackle the moderate gradients of
the track that leads south towards Glen Clova. Alternatively, cross the
River Muick and take the track north from Allt-na-guibhsaich through
the woods. Please note that all visitors must keep to the paths, especially during the stalking season. Weatherproof footwear and clothing, and
a map and compass are essential if venturing onto high ground.

Timing

The optimum time to visit Lochnagar is May–September. A winter visit is
recommended to see large numbers of red deer and Ptarmigan, especially on the scree slope left of the track before Dubh Loch Corrie.

NE16 GLEN TANAR
OS ref: 47/96
OS Landranger 44

Habitat

The Glen Tanar NNR covers 4185 ha of pine forest and moorland habitats, managed jointly by the Glen Tanar estate and EN. It is an important
remnant of the old Caledonian forest and contains many fine mature
trees with an understorey of heather, bilberry and cowberry. Juniper,
some rowan, aspen and birch also occur. Extensive, high-quality
heather moorland blankets the lower mountains, although there is
much natural regeneration of Scots pine in places. To the south, the
ground rises gradually to the Grampian/Angus watershed, whose summits include Mount Keen (939 m), Hill of Gaimey (756 m) and Hill of Cat
(742 m). This ancient massif is bisected by the Waters of Tanar, Gaimey
and Allachy, which combine to flow north into the Dee.

Species

Capercaillie and Scottish and Common Crossbills are reasonably common in the old pinewoods. Crested Tit, however, is noticeable for its
absence—there were records from Deeside in 1973–75 and 1977, but
none since. Other breeding species of interest include Sparrowhawk,
Black Grouse, Woodcock and Siskin in the pines, Dipper and Grey Wagtail on rivers and Ptarmigan on the summits. Regular scanning of the
open ground and ridges should produce raptors, especially Hen Harrier, Golden Eagle and Merlin.

Access

From Aboyne, on the main A93 Banchory–Braemar road, turn south
across the River Dee, then west on the B976, following the south bank of

Red Grouse

the river. At Bridge o'Ess, 1.5 miles (2.4 km) later, take the minor road left to Braeloine (1.5 miles/2.4 km), where there is a car park. A visitor centre, open April–September on the opposite bank of the Tanar, gives information about the reserve. A little further upstream there are a number of trails leading from Glen Tanar House into the surrounding woods, any of which can be good for birds. Two old high-level drove roads—Mounth Road and Firmounth Road—lead south along Glen Tanar and Water of Allachy respectively and eventually climb to the Grampian/Angus watershed. These are the best routes for seeing open-country species such as raptors and grouse. However, the full expedition onto the watershed or to the summits of Mount Keen, Cock Caim or Hill of Cat is a considerable undertaking, and should only be planned by fit, experienced and equipped hill walkers. Please note that access is permitted only along marked trails and the drove roads. Other restrictions may be enforced during the grouse shooting/stalking seasons—details are posted at the visitor centre. A ranger is present all year, tel: 01339 886072

Timing
The best time to visit is between May and September.

NE17 RATTRAY HEAD

OS ref: NK 010570
OS Landranger 30

Habitat
A coastal site halfway between Peterhead and Fraserburgh, off the A952. It is primarily notable for migrants and has a good record for rarities. Among the more common east coast birds are Spotted and Pied Flycatchers, Redstart, Willow Warbler, Chiffchaff and Goldcrest.

Species and Timing

Corn Bunting is a common sight in spring and summer, perching on telephone wires at regular intervals on the way to Rattray, after Greenmyre
Cottage. Marsh Harrier usually occurs around this time. Other than the
dunes there is very little cover for migrants, which can make them very
easy to see but means they tend not to stay long. Best views are around
the houses. If there is a fall you literally have to be careful where you
step because the ground can be covered with birds—this can happen in
both spring and autumn.

The flash pools are usually in good condition in spring and Little
Ringed Plover and Garganey can both occur. Coastal species include
divers, Eider, Long-tailed Duck and many waders. Kentish Plover and
White-rumped Sandpiper have been seen.

In spring, Bluethroat, Red-backed Shrike and Black Redstart are annual visitors while Dotterel, Short-toed and Shore Larks, Yellow and Blue-
headed Wagtails, Subalpine and Greenish Warblers, Rustic and Little
Buntings, and Woodchat Shrike have all occurred.

Summer is fairly quiet although offshore there are plenty of Eider,
Sandwich, Common and Arctic Terns, some divers and Manx Shearwater on passage. Late summer sees skuas and various waders, notably
Sanderling. Late August can bring migrants, including Greenish Warbler.
Merlin and Peregrine are present. The flashes are dry in summer and are
usually still empty in autumn. Cover is plentiful, in the form of nettles,
dock and burdock in the field behind the houses. Red-breasted Flycatcher and Yellow-browed Warbler are almost annual. Jack Snipe, Wryneck, Richard's Pipit, Grey-headed Wagtail, Siberian Stonechat, Barred,
Dusky and Pallas's Warblers, Red-breasted Flycatcher, Arctic Redpoll,
Snow Bunting and Common Rosefinch have all occurred. Seawatching
from the dunes can be productive for skuas, waders, divers, ducks, geese
and occasional grebes.

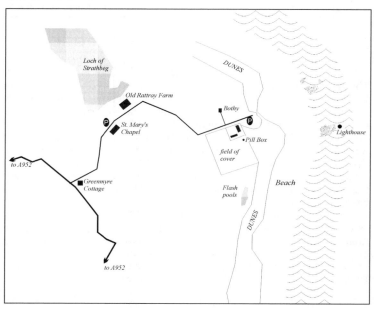

The main interest in winter is geese and seabirds. In the fields around Rattray there are large gatherings of Pink-footed Geese but also good numbers of Greylag and Barnacle and regular appearances by Bean, White-fronted and Brent Geese and occasional Snow Goose. A car park at St Mary's Chapel affords good views of the south end of the Loch of Strathbeg. Smew is annual here and in recent years Bittern has also been annual. Watch also for grebes. On the sea there are plenty of Eider, Long-tailed Duck, Red-throated and Great Northern Divers, with occasional Black-throated Diver. An adult Glaucous Gull has been resident for the past couple of winters and Iceland Gull is regularly seen. Little Auk is often seen offshore. Flocks of Snow Bunting are frequently present in the dunes. Peregrine and Merlin are regular. The flash pools host Whooper and occasional Bewick's Swans.

Access
From the A952 both north and south access roads are signposted 'Rattray 2 miles'. Follow the road to the very end (it deteriorates beyond Old Rattray Farm) and park in the area beyond the houses. The field by the track here can be very good for larks and pipits (note: it should not be entered). For the beach, walk through the gap in the dunes at the end of the car park. For migrants, walk beside the garden fence and into the field by the pillbox. For the flash pool follow the fence adjacent to the dunes and view the pools from a distance (otherwise all the birds flush). Please respect the rights of local landowners.

NE18 TAY ESTUARY

OS ref: NO 15/01
OS Landranger 58 & 59

Habitat
The inner Tay estuary is considered here to extend downstream from Perth as far as the rail bridge at Dundee, a total length of approximately 18 miles (29 km). This is one of the cleanest and least spoilt of the country's larger estuaries, having the highest volume of freshwater outflow of any in Britain. It is the extensive mudflats on the north bank that mainly interest the birder. The largest reedbed (*Phragmites australis*) in Great Britain is found along this bank, much of it commercially harvested. Inland, the heavy clay soils support an intensive agricultural regime, giving way to rich sandstone loams and some wooded hillsides on the Braes of the Carse of Gowrie.

The area is of international significance for roosting geese, as well as of national importance for its numbers of wintering Goldeneye. The tidal flats are the feeding ground for a large local breeding Shelduck population and of other migrant, wintering and breeding wildfowl and waders. Much of the shoreline is designated a SSSI and is a proposed LNR.

Species

The Tay is particularly important for passage and wintering wildfowl and waders. Around 2000 Greylag geese feed on the Carse of Gowrie and roost on the estuary; 500 or more Pink-footed Geese and small numbers of Whooper Swan are also present. Common wintering waders include Redshank, Dunlin, Bar-tailed Godwit, Curlew, Golden Plover, Lapwing, Snipe and Jack Snipe. Migrants regularly include Curlew Sandpiper, Ruff, Greenshank and Little Stint. Small numbers of Whimbrel and Green Sandpiper occur regularly in spring. Very large mixed flocks of hirundines occur on passage, sometimes forming roosts (near Errol) in excess of 10,000 birds.

Shelduck breeds along the inner fringe of the reedbed and inland on the 'Braes'. In the reeds, Water Rail and Reed Bunting are resident breeders, joined in summer by Sedge Warbler—the populations of all three are among the largest in Scotland. The harvested areas permit Snipe, Redshank, Curlew and Lapwing to breed successfully within the reedbeds.

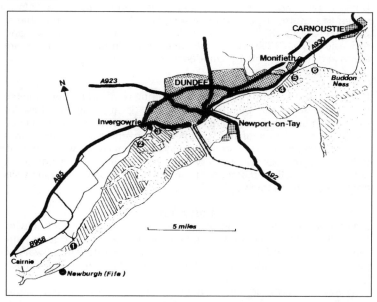

Access

Access to this coast is difficult, there being few roads down to the shore and the generally narrow but dense reedbeds effectively block visibility of much of the estuary. Parking, too, is problematical and care must be taken not to prevent access to gateways, impede traffic on roads and tracks, etc. if stopping on road verges. Please note that there is no access to Dundee Airport. The following vantage points can be recommended.

1 PORT ALLEN (OS REF: NO 252212)

Continue along the B958, past the Cairnie turn-off and take the minor road to the shore just beyond Mains of Errol, 3 miles (4.8 km) later.

Please park considerately at the farm near the end of this road—do not block the track leading to the shore. A series of mudbanks, used by a variety of passage waders, can be viewed from the embankment on the west side of Port Allen. Late summer/early autumn is the best time of year.

2 KINGOODIE (OS REF: NO 33/29)

This is by far the best general viewpoint over the estuary. An unclassified road, leading south from Invergowrie, runs along the foreshore immediately west of Kingoodie and there is a lay-by for parking. This area is best worked at high tide.

3 INVERGOWRIE BAY (OS REF: NO 35/29)

Both the pier and Invergowrie Station make good vantage points from which to scan this busy and interesting bay. Access is also possible at Cairnie Pier (NO 197192) via an unclassified road from St Madoes, and at Seaside (NO 283243) via a public right of way from Grange. There are buses and trains from Perth/Dundee to Invergowrie.

Timing
It is spring and autumn passage and wintering wildfowl that provide the main interest on this picturesque estuary. 'Spring' tides are best for bringing waders close to vantage points, but with the exception of overcast days, early morning and late afternoon/evening are the best times to visit. Otherwise direct strong sunlight may make viewing difficult. Between September and January there is a great deal of wildfowling activity both on the embankments and in the reedbeds—Sunday visits are therefore recommended.

Calendar
March–May: This is the time of greatest species diversity and activity, with both winter visitors and summer migrants present. Grey geese, wintering wildfowl and waders are joined by migrant thrushes, Swallow, Sand Martin, Sedge and Willow Warblers and other summer migrants.

July–September: Hirundines and migrant warblers move through. During the latter part of this period, Ruff, Greenshank, Spotted Redshank, Arctic Skua, Sandwich, Common and Arctic Terns occur regularly. Curlew Sandpiper and Little Stint also occur, but numbers are more variable.

October–February: Greylag and Pink-footed Geese, Whooper Swan, Mallard, Teal, Pochard, Tufted Duck and Goldeneye are present, as are small numbers of Great Crested Grebe and a few Pintail. Overwintering waders are abundant and sometimes include a few Black-tailed Godwit. Redwing and Fieldfare frequent the disused orchards and hawthorn hedges/scrub along the length of the estuary. Kingoodie and Invergowrie usually attract Waxwing in irruption years.

Habitat
This area comprises the 5 miles (8 km) of urbanised north shore of the Firth of Tay, from Stannergate in the west to Buddon Burn. The deep-water channel offshore contains large mussel beds, which are especially attractive to Eider. The intertidal zone of the north shore is characterised by a mixture of substrates, with areas of mussel beds and eelgrass. Freshwater and sewage outflows discharge onto the sand- and mudflats. A dune system extending into the mouth of the firth to the east is a rare example of a lowland heath bounded by dunes involving mobile sands. Monifieth Bay and Barry Buddon Ranges are both SSSI.

Species
Up to 300 Little Gull can be seen in Monifieth Bay and at Carnoustie, to the east. These birds can be seen year-round; the flock mostly comprises juveniles, but adults are generally also present. In winter, over 20,000 Eider can sometimes be seen in the mouth of the firth. In addition, small numbers of Red-throated and occasional Black-throated and Great Northern Divers occur, with up to 250 Red-breasted Merganser; some Great Crested Grebe, Goldeneye and a few Long-tailed Duck. Common and Velvet Scoters are also seen occasionally. Wader numbers are equally impressive, with around 1000 Oystercatcher, 50–200 Ringed Plover, 300–400 Sanderling and 500–2000 Bar-tailed Godwit. A few Black-tailed Godwit may also be present. Small numbers of Turnstone, Redshank and Dunlin also occur. Knot numbers vary considerably, but the species regularly overwinters. Passerines include Tree Sparrow, Linnet, Goldfinch, Redpoll and Yellowhammer. A few Snow Buntings can usually be found in the Carnoustie/Buddon area each winter.

The area is not especially noted for its passage birds, but Green Sandpiper are regular migrants in spring and autumn, while offshore, Great and Arctic skuas often enter the firth in late summer and autumn, pursuing the fishing terns, which at this season include Sandwich Tern.

Little Gulls—immature and adult, late summer

Access

The area can be worked from the A930 Dundee–Carnoustie road; the foreshore is easily accessible at many points, using public roads and pavements. There are very good bus and train services between Dundee, Broughty Ferry, Balmossie, Monifieth and Barry Links. Note that access to the Barry/Buddon MOD area is not permissible when the red flags are flying but is otherwise unrestricted to pedestrians. Park at Riverview football pitches and walk. The following vantage points, numbered on the Tay estuary map, page 211, are recommended.

4 BROUGHTY FERRY HARBOUR/ESPLANADE
(OS REF: NO 462305)

5 FORESHORE AT DIGHTY WATER OUTFLOW
(OS REF: NO 487318)

6 BUDDON BURN/MONIFIETH LINKS
(OS REF: NO 516323)

Timing

The main interest here is during winter, although Common, Arctic and Little Terns can be seen in summer. 'Spring' tides are usually best, especially when high water is around midday. Ideally, visit during slightly overcast conditions or in the morning and evening, thus avoiding having to look directly against the light.

Calendar

March–May: Displaying Eider, Goldeneye and Red-breasted Merganser are conspicuous, as too are many of the breeding-plumaged waders.

June: The quietest month of the year, although breeding Eider, terns and small numbers of Redshank, Curlew and Ringed Plover occupy territories on Barry Links.

July–September: Return passage of waders occurs, many of them (Bartailed Godwit, Sanderling and Dunlin for example) still in breeding plumage. Offshore, the terns and gulls are harassed by Great, Arctic and occasional Pomarine Skuas. Other obvious passage migrants include Swallow and Meadow Pipit.

October–February: Wintering wader populations increase; large gull roosts (comprising Black-headed, Common, Herring and Great Black-backed Gulls) form; wintering wildfowl (Goldeneye, scoters, Red-breasted Merganser, etc.) gather offshore; divers and auks move into the shelter of the outer firth. Short-eared Owl hunts over Barry Links.

NE20 LUNAN BAY

OS ref: NO 69/51
OS Landranger 54

Habitat and Access

This broad, sandy bay is located between Montrose and Arbroath on the Angus coast. It is backed by dunes and divided by Lunan Water, which enters the bay midway along the 2.5-mile (4 km) beach—at high tide the river here cannot be forded. The Water is flanked by deciduous woodland and a small conifer plantation. The bay is accessible at three points:

(1) Car park at NO 692516, reached by a private road (with speed ramps) just north of the entrance to Lunan Bay Hotel (now a hospital for the mentally disabled).

(2) On foot via Red Castle. Parking on the roadside is awkward, but feasible, at NO 688510.

(3) Ethie Haven, at the south end of the bay, NO 699488. Again, narrow roads and limited space make parking awkward.

The southern end of the bay is probably the best area, but the easiest access is via the public car park, setting up a telescope on the dunes nearby. Early-morning visitors may have visibility problems due to viewing against the light.

Species and Calendar

There is year-round bird interest at Lunan Bay. From late July, up to 2000 scoters (mostly Velvet) gather in the bay. One or two Surf Scoter are usually present in this flock. In late summer and early autumn large numbers of Gannet, Kittiwake and terns occur offshore, with a few Arctic, Great and, occasionally, Pomarine Skuas. Little Gull also occurs. Numbers of Red-throated Diver and Great Crested Grebe increase at this time, with about 100 of each present. Other divers and grebes are occasional, especially in winter. Scoter numbers decline after October, but numbers of Long-tailed Duck increase, usually to a maximum of around 100. In spring and summer the bay is busy with fishing Gannet and terns; a few Red-throated Diver, Great Crested Grebe, Common and Velvet Scoters may still be found.

The woodland around Lunan Water is good for passerine migrants in spring and autumn. Kingfisher occurs on the river in autumn. Short-eared Owl often hunts over the dunes in winter and Snow Bunting may be present.

Habitat and Access

This is the best seawatching site in Angus and is a relatively easy area to work. Follow unclassified roads through the farm of Seaton of Usan and park by the road (dead end) overlooking the bay. The promontory south of the small bay is a good vantage point. From May to October there is plenty to see—northerly winds are best for seabird passage, while in spring, a southeasterly is best for passerine migrants.

Bluethroat

Species

Passage seabirds are the main attraction. Arctic and Great Skuas are numerous, while Pomarine is annual. Manx Shearwater is common in autumn and a few Sooty are annual; sea duck (especially Eider) and waders provide interest in the winter. Willows on the sloping ground and cliffs surrounding the bay provide cover for passerine migrants. The small boats, piles of creels and drying nets on the slopes are also used. The limited cover provides only temporary shelter for migrant passerines and these tend to move inland to the woods surrounding Usan House (NO 723553) following landfall. Many birds have been seen adjacent to the unclassified road through this area. In addition to the more expected species, several scarce birds have occurred, such as Yellow-browed Warbler and Red-breasted Flycatcher, while rarities like Thrush Nightingale, Radde's, Aquatic and Arctic Warblers have been recorded.

Habitat

A large enclosed estuary immediately inland from Montrose and fed by the River South Esk. The basin comprises extensive tidal mud/sandflats, with a fringe of reedbeds, wet pasture and riverine habitats to the west. Montrose Basin is a LNR and SSSI covering 1012 ha, administered by Angus District Council and managed by the SWT, the major landowner within the reserve. Unlike many of the productive and sheltered inlets on the Scottish east coast, which have suffered from pollution and industrial development, Montrose Basin is a relatively clean and unspoilt estuarine area. The intertidal mud is exceptionally rich in invertebrates, particularly the *Hydrobia* snail, and this attracts very large numbers of waders. Glasswort and eelgrass attract important populations of wintering dabbling duck, while mussel beds in the river channel support Eider throughout the year. Controlled wildfowling is allowed under a permit system. Shooting takes place between one hour before and two hours after sunrise and sunset, 1 September–20 February. There is a fantastic wildlife centre 1 mile (1.6 km) south of Montrose, off the A92, on the south shore.

Species and Calendar

In winter, Montrose Basin holds a major roost of Pink-footed Geese. The main roost occurs in the east–central part of the basin and can be seen from the railway station and Rossie Island. Numbers peak in October–November, when 20,000–30,000 birds may be present. In very cold conditions, up to 3000 Greylag Geese roost in the main channel at the west end of the basin. Around 5000 Wigeon occupy the area in early winter, with approximately 1000 Mallard and 2000 Eider. Other wintering wildfowl include 300–400 Shelduck, c. 120 Pintail and small numbers of Shoveler, Teal, Red-breasted Merganser and Goosander. Scaup and Tufted Duck sometimes occur in freezing conditions. Sparrowhawk, Merlin, Peregrine and Short-eared Owl regularly hunt the area in winter. Waders can include up to 4000 Oystercatcher, large numbers of Dunlin, 10,000 Knot (more usually 2000–3000), 1000 Golden Plover and 1000+ Redshank. Knot numbers generally peak in January and Dunlin in February.

There is an excellent wader passage at the basin, particularly in July–September. Regulars at this time include Green and Wood Sandpipers, Spotted Redshank, Ruff and both godwits. Spring passage peaks in May. There are strong passages of Curlew in March and August, Redshank in March and September, and Oystercatcher in October and November.

Post-breeding terns make extensive use of the basin, and numbers often reach several thousand, including Common, Arctic, Sandwich and a few Little Terns. Osprey can often been seen fishing for flounder in late summer. More than 200 pairs of Eider nest around the basin. Other breeders include Oystercatcher, Redshank and Lapwing. Sedge Warbler and Reed Bunting nest in the reedbeds. Recent rarities have included Montagu's Harrier and Long-billed Dowitcher.

Access

1 MAINS OF DUN (OS REF: NO 669592)

A car park at the old mill, just off the reserve, marks the start of a track leading to three hides overlooking the west side of the basin (see map). These hides are kept locked, and the keys must be obtained in advance from the SWT Ranger/Naturalist (address below). A deposit of £5 (for life) per key is levied. The most northerly of these hides overlooks the corner of the basin that is the last part to flood, so is best visited near high tide when large numbers of roosting waders may be seen.

2 BRIDGE OF DUN–OLD MONTROSE PIER (OS REF: NO 663585–676572)

Walk along the south side of the river to the old pier. There is limited parking space at either end. The pier is a good general viewpoint for the southeastern basin: best at low water or mid-tide.

3 ROSSIE BRAES (OS REF: NO 703565)

The A92 roadside here is a good vantage point for the south side of the basin. The new wildlife centre here is excellent. There is a high-tide wader roost at Rossie Point.

4 RAILWAY VIADUCT (OS REF: NO 707568)

The eastern basin can be viewed from the no-through road on the west side of Rossie Island, approached either on foot from the parking area immediately south of New Bridge or by driving under the south span of the viaduct to a small car park west of the railway. Visit at low water for feeding waders.

5 TAYOCK BURN (OS REF: NO 708590)

Take the A935 Brechin road west from Montrose and turn south onto the old town rubbish dump immediately after crossing the railway. This is an excellent vantage point for the northeast basin. Ideally, visit one hour either side of high tide, when close views of feeding waders should be possible. This area has the best selection of waders, as well as most of the basin's Shelduck. Roosting geese may be found here very early on winter mornings. Observation becomes difficult around midday, due to strong backlight. Montrose is connected by bus and rail services to Aberdeen and Dundee.

Timing

No season is a dull one at Montrose Basin. Wildfowl provide the main winter interest and waders in spring and autumn. In summer, breeding Eider and gatherings of post-breeding terns are of note. Wader activity is often most easily observable, especially from the south, when the river

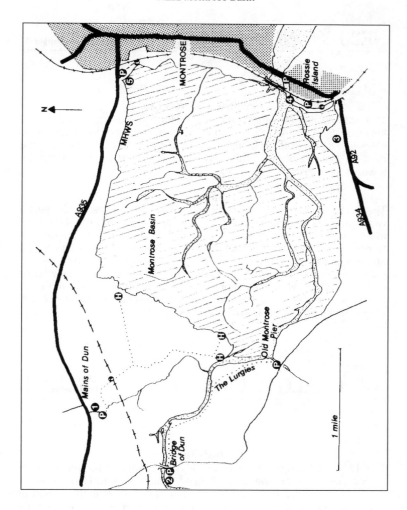

channels are full but there are still plenty of exposed mudflats. Dawn and dusk observation is inadvisable at the west end of the basin in winter, due to wildfowling activity (see above).

SWT Ranger/Naturalist

Full information on parking, access and birdlife in the basin can be obtained from Rick Goater, The Wildlife Centre, Montrose, Angus DD10 9LE (tel: 01674 676336/676555).

Habitat and Access

This area lies immediately south of the North Esk estuary, 2 miles (3.2 km) from St Cyrus. Access is via the A92, turning east onto a minor road 3 miles (4.8 km) north of Montrose (NO 724616). Park at the bend in the road at Fisherhills and walk downstream alongside the North Esk towards the coast.

Species

The river is good for Dipper, Grey Wagtail and Red-breasted Merganser (a moulting flock of around 400 birds gathers at the mouth of the river in late summer). Tidal pools at NO 736622 are very good in autumn for waders, including species such as Curlew and Wood Sandpipers and Spotted Redshank. Autumn passerines include Wheatear, Whinchat and (after easterly winds) Black Redstart. Short-eared Owl frequently hunts over the Links in winter. Offshore, a range of sea duck similar to that at Lunan Bay occurs and there may be much interchange of divers, Long-tailed Duck and scoters between the two bays.

NE24 BALGAVIES LOCH

Habitat

This 46-ha SWT reserve is one of a series of wetlands in the Upper Lunan Valley, east of Forfar. The loch is fringed by reedbeds and woodland; to the west there is an extensive area of fen. Unfortunately, the run-off of dissolved phosphates and nitrates from the surrounding agricultural land is having a detrimental effect on the aquatic life of the loch.

Access

Take the A932 from Forfar towards Arbroath/Montrose and turn into a parking lay-by that overlooks the loch 5 miles (8 km) later. This commands a good general view; there is also a hide at the southwest corner, accessible from a small car park 0.25 mile (0.4 km) to the west. This is open to the public 1.00 pm–4.00 pm on the first Sunday of each month, but is otherwise normally locked—SWT members can obtain a key ($5 deposit) from the warden or Rick Goater (tel: 01674 676555/676336). Permits to visit any other part of the reserve are issued by the warden (free of charge).

Species

Balgavies Loch is mainly of interest to birders between October and March, when moderate numbers of wintering wildfowl including Wigeon, Shoveler, Pochard, Tufted Duck, Goldeneye and Goosander, can be seen. Large numbers of Greylag and Pink-footed Geese roost on the loch; Grey Heron and Cormorant roost in trees around the shore and on a large island. Water Rail, Woodcock, Snipe and Kingfisher are sometimes seen. Little Grebe is frequent and Great Crested Grebe breeds. Long-tailed, Great, Blue and Coal Tits are usually around the hide in winter, while Bullfinch frequents the hide car park.

NE25 ANGUS GLENS OS Landranger 43 & 44

Habitat and Species

The glens of Isla, Prosen, Clova and Esk, together with their numerous minor side valleys cut deep into the Grampian plateau. The hills at the head of these glens rise steeply to well over 800 m—high enough for birds such as Ptarmigan and Dotterel. Lower moorland terrain supports large numbers of Red Grouse, breeding Hen Harrier, Merlin (both at lower densities than one might expect, given the quality of the habitat), Golden Plover, Dunlin and Short-eared Owl. The steep corries and rocky hillsides hold crag-nesting species such as Golden Eagle, Peregrine and Raven; Ring Ouzel is not uncommon among the scree slopes. Wheatear and Whinchat are reasonably numerous; Dipper and Grey Wagtail frequent the burns; and Siskin and Crossbill occur in some of the woods.

Short-eared Owl—display

The Caenlochan NNR, stretching from the Devil's Elbow to the heads of Glens Isla and Clova, covers 3,639 ha of the upland plateau and steep glens.

Access

This is an immense area and accessible only to dedicated hill walkers. There are restrictions upon access to many upland areas between 1 June and 20 October. However, one of the attractions of these glens to the birdwatcher is that a good cross-section of species typical of upland eastern Scotland can be seen from the roads through the valleys. Golden Eagle in particular can be seen relatively easily by regularly scanning the skylines with binoculars. Glen Isla is one of the better glens to explore in this way: it is remote and sparsely populated, with a good mix of habitats and species. Glen Esk is particularly noted for Buzzard and also as a place to see Black Grouse. Glen Clova is the only glen where Twite is regularly recorded, especially in the arable fields around Braedownie near the head of the glen. The adjacent woods hold Siskin and Crossbill. April and May are probably the best months to visit, although October is often a good month for soaring eagles. Please park considerately and do not obstruct access.

NE26 LOCH OF KINNORDY

OS ref: NO 361539
OS Landranger 54

Habitat

Loch of Kinnordy is an 81-ha RSPB reserve consisting primarily of open water and freshwater marsh. Willow and alder scrub fringe much of the loch, with some mature Scots pine on drier ground. The loch is extremely nutrient rich, due to the combination of the underlying geology, drainage from the surrounding farmland and the enrichment effects of the droppings of the large bird population. The reserve is a SSSI.

Timing

Access is restricted to 09.00 am–9.00 pm (or sunset if earlier), April–August inclusive. During September to November, the reserve is open similar hours but only on Sundays. It is closed December–March. In addition to the breeding birds found in April–July, the reserve can be good for passage waders in autumn and wintering wildfowl from October.

Access

The reserve is 1.5 miles (2.4 km) west of Kirriemuir, adjacent to the B951 to Glen Isla. There is a regular bus service from Dundee to Kirriemuir. Paths lead from the car park to the two hides, a short distance away. Please do not venture beyond these hides. There is a warden present from April to August. Contact the RSPB, 17 Regent Terrace, Edinburgh.

Black-necked Grebes—summer (left) and winter plumages

Species

Great Crested, Black-necked and Little Grebes all breed on the loch and are usually easy to see from the hide. Eight species of duck have bred, including Wigeon, Gadwall, Shoveler, Pochard and, since 1979, Scotland's first Ruddy Ducks. However, the latter appear to have had poor fledging success so far. A Black-headed Gull colony, numbering almost 7000 pairs, breeds on the islands of floating vegetation. Water Rail, Snipe, Curlew and Redshank breed in marshy areas. Sedge Warbler and Reed Bunting nest in the scrub. Sparrowhawk regularly hunts over the reserve, and Marsh Harrier summers. Osprey is often seen in late summer. Otter is frequently spotted in the loch. The woodlands hold Blue, Great, Coal and Long-tailed Tits, Treecreeper, Goldcrest, and Great Spotted and Green Woodpeckers.

Calendar

April–July: Breeding grebes and wildfowl, Water Rail, Moorhen, Coot, Snipe, Redshank and passage waders such as Ruff, Black and Bar-tailed Godwits and Greenshank. Breeding passerines include Sedge Warbler, Goldcrest, Spotted Flycatcher and Long-tailed Tit. Marsh Harrier is regular.

August–November: Several species of migrant wader may pass through during August and September, feeding on any exposed mud around the edge of the loch. Ruff, Greenshank and Spotted Redshank are all possible. Greylag Geese start to appear from October—up to 5000 use the loch as a roost in winter. An increasing number of Pink-footed Geese and occasional Barnacle Geese also occur. Short-eared Owl and Hen Harrier often hunt over the reserve in autumn and winter.

NE27 LOCH OF LINTRATHEN

Habitat
This 162-ha SWT reserve is situated in the foothills of the Braes of Angus, north of the A926 Rattray–Kirriemuir road. The loch was created in the 19th century by damming Melgam Water and is the principal water supply for Dundee and Angus. Fertile farmland surrounds the loch, which is largely fringed by coniferous woodland.

Access
Loch of Lintrathen is reached by taking either the B951 from Kirriemuir, which runs along the north shore after 7 miles (11.3 km), or via the B954 from Alyth, turning right at Bridge of Craigisla onto the minor road that circumnavigates the loch, which is best viewed from a lay-by on the southeastern shore. The SWT has a hide on the peninsula which juts into the northwestern loch, but this is kept locked. Keys are available to SWT members only—contact Rick Goater (tel: 01674 676336/676555) ($5 deposit).

Species
Of most interest are the large numbers of Greylag Geese that roost on the loch in autumn and winter—up to 5000 can be seen arriving from the adjacent farmland at dusk during late October and November. Other wintering wildfowl include large numbers of Mallard, several hundred Tufted Duck and modest numbers of Goldeneye. Whooper Swan is regularly present, often in large numbers, and Teal and Wigeon occur in small numbers.

In summer, Great Crested Grebe, Mallard and Tufted Duck can be found, Grey Heron nests nearby and Osprey occasionally fishes the loch. If the water level is low, the exposed mud can attract large numbers of Lapwing and a few passage Dunlin and Redshank.

ADDITIONAL SITES

Site & Grid Reference	Habitat	Main Bird Interest	Peak Season
a Crathes Castle NTS NO 73/96 OS 38 or 45	About 240 ha of mixed woodland, ponds and farmland.	Woodland species including Buzzard, Woodcock, Green and Great Spotted Woodpeckers, Jay.	All year
	A ranger service provides information and a guided walks programme. There are five waymarked trails including one suitable for wheelchair users.		
b Drum NTS NJ 70/00 OS 38	About 47 ha of mixed woodland including ancient oakwood.	Resident woodland birds including Green and Great Spotted Woodpeckers, Jay and *c.* 500 pairs of Rook.	All year
		Breeding visitors including Blackcap and Garden Warbler.	Apr–Jul
c Leith Hall NTS NJ 54/29 OS 37	Farm and woodland, some hill ground, two ponds.	Common woodland and open ground species; small number of waterfowl.	Apr–Aug
	There are three trails through the grounds and a bird hide.		
d Longhaven Cliffs SWT Reserve NK 117394 OS 40	Coastal granite cliffs.	Breeding seabirds—total of *c.* 23,000 pairs of nine species.	May–Jul
e Muir of Dinnet SNH Reserve NO 43/99 OS 37 or 44	Moorland, woodland, lochs and bog.	Wintering wildfowl including Whooper Swan, Greylag and Pink-footed Geese, small numbers of Pintail, Gadwall and Shoveler; Water Rail and otter. Osprey often present in summer; Hen Harrier all year.	Oct–Mar
f Arbroath NO 643405 OS 54	Fishing harbour—best on weekdays, when the boats are returning to port.	Glaucous and occasionally Iceland Gulls.	Oct–May
		Good for Purple Sandpiper and Turnstone.	Aug–Apr
g Auchmithie NO 683443 OS 54	Beach and harbour.	Kittiwake, terns and auks commuting offshore.	Apr–Aug
	Cliffs to north.	Breeding Fulmar and Puffin.	May–Aug

Site & Grid Reference	Habitat	Main Bird Interest	Peak Season
h Carnoustie NO 560340–583352 OS 54	Coast of Carnoustie, West Haven and Penbride.	Passage and wintering waders.	Aug–May
	Pitairlie Burn outflow.	Large numbers of Little Gull.	Jul
	Craigmill Den/Penbridge House grounds.	Migrant warblers such as Chiffchaff, Willow Warbler and Blackcap.	Apr–May
	Craigmill Burn (579353).	Dipper and Grey Wagtail.	All year
i East Haven NO 591362 OS 54	Beach car park on seaward side of railway line (reached via tunnel).	Offshore divers, Little gull often present.	Oct–May
	Bushes and waste ground.	Passerine migrants have included Yellow-browed and Barred Warblers.	Sep–Oct
j Forfar Loch NO 440505 OS 54	Small loch immediately west of the town of Forfar.	Wintering wildfowl, including roosting Greylag, Shoveler, Tufted Duck, Pochard.	Oct–Mar
		Build-up of Coot.	Jul–Aug
		Migrant waders.	Aug–Oct
k Montreathmont Forest FC NO 575545 OS 54	Extensive area of old conifer plantations.	Small numbers of Capercaillie (north-central sector best); Chiffchaff, Long-eared Owl, Great Spotted and Green Woodpeckers.	All year
l Seaton Cliffs SWT Reserve NO 665415 OS 54	Sandstone cliffs with many caves, arches and stacks.	Spring and autumn migrants.	Mar–May
		Cliff-nesting House Martin.	May–Aug
		Good seawatching point.	May–Sep

ORKNEY

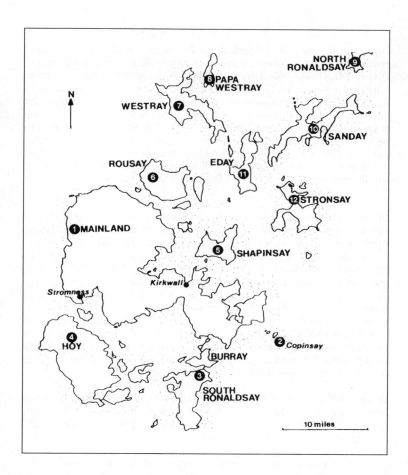

Main sites

INTRODUCTION
TO ORKNEY

Orkney comprises an archipelago of 75 islands, 20 of them inhabited, covering a total of 376 square miles (974 km^2). At their nearest point the Orkney islands are only 6 miles (9.7 km) from the mainland, yet extend northeast for 53 miles (85 km) and span 23 miles (37 km) west to east. Apart from Hoy, the islands are mostly low lying and characterised by fertile farmland and moorland. Maritime heath is found only in relatively small parts of the west of the islands. The islands can fairly claim to be an ornithological paradise; over 330 species have been recorded, many of them rare and recorded on only a handful of occasions within the British Isles. We are grateful to Eric Meek, RSPB Orkney officer, for supplying most of the details for this account.

Access

By sea: P&O ferries operate a two-hour roll-on/roll-off service from Scrabster to Stromness, on the Orkney mainland. There is a Sunday sailing April–October, but otherwise a six-day-week schedule (tel: 01856 850655 for details). P&O also operate a twice-weekly route from Aberdeen to Stromness to Shetland. This runs on Tuesdays and Saturdays May–August, and Saturdays only in September (tel: 01224 572615 for details). Orcargo Ltd operates a roll-on/roll-off service between Invergordon and Kirkwall six days a week. This is primarily a cargo service but cars/passengers are carried. Book through Orcargo Ltd, 10a Junction Road, Kirkwall, Orkney KW15 1LB (tel: 01856 873838). John O'Groats Ferries run a passenger-only ferry service from John O'Groats to Burwick at the southern tip of South Ronaldsay (a 40-minute trip), April–September. Contact John O'Groats Ferries (tel: 01955 611353).

By air: British Airways/Loganair fly daily except Sundays to Kirkwall from Glasgow, Edinburgh and Inverness, with additional flights from Aberdeen and Wick. Tel: Kirkwall Airport 01856 873457 or 01856 872233 or Ridgeway Travel on 01856 873359.

Inter-island ferries: Orkney Ferries operate a roll-on/roll-off ferry service from Tingwall to Rousay, Egilsay and Wyre. They also operate services from Kirkwall to the northern isles, on a daily or more frequent basis: Westray, Stronsay, Sanday, Papa Westray, Eday, Shapinsay and North Ronaldsay (once a week). Ferries run from Stromness to Moness on Hoy, 4–5 times a day (including Sundays in summer) and also to Flotta, Longhope (on South Walls) and Graemsay. A roll-on/roll-off service runs from Houton on Mainland to Lyness on southern Hoy and to Flotta. For details of all Orkney Ferries routes tel: 01856 872044.

Inter-island flights: These operate on a daily/twice daily basis (except Sunday) from Mainland to North Ronaldsay, Stronsay, Sanday, Westray and Papa Westray. Contact Kirkwall Airport on 01856 873457 for details.

Public transport within the islands consists of four bus companies. J & D Peace run a bus service between Kirkwall and Stromness, Houton and Dounby (tel: 01856 872866). Causeway Coaches travel from Kirkwall to St Margaret's Hope on South Ronaldsay (tel: 01856 831444). WJ Stove's bus route is between Kirkwall and Deerness (tel: 01856 741215). The Kirkwall–Tingwall route is run by Rosie Coaches (tel: 01856 751227). There are also bicycle-hire facilities and taxi services. In addition there are four tour bus operators. Sinclair Dunnet runs 'Go Orkney', a mini-bus service that specialises in ornithological, botanical and archaeological tours (tel: 01856 871871). 'Wild About' is run by Michael Hartley (tel: 01856 851011), 'Roads and Tracks' by John Philips (tel: 01856 831297) and Hazel Goar runs tours for small groups (tel: 01856 781327). The Orkney Tourist Board is very helpful and can be found at 6 Broad Street, Kirkwall, Orkney KW15 1NX (tel: 01856 872856).

Timing

No season is a dull one on Orkney. Breeding birds dominate the interest between May and early July, with the additional bonus of spring migrants during April, May and early June. Autumn passage is best from late August until mid-October; wintering species start to increase in late October and are present until March/April, with a few lingering into May.

Calendar

May–July: The moorlands, maritime heaths and sea cliffs are the most obvious centres of activity, although wetland and scrub habitat should not be neglected. Whimbrel and Greenshank pass through during May and early June, together with a few less common waders such as Black-tailed Godwit, Spotted Redshank and Green Sandpiper. A number of rare migrants have been recorded on Orkney during spring in recent years, including Black Stork, Little Bustard, Terek Sandpiper, Laughing Gull, Needle-tailed Swift, Collared Flycatcher, Trumpeter Finch and Pallas's Rosefinch (although the latter was not considered to have been wild).

August–October: This is the peak migration period, and that when some hapless vagrant or other is most likely to make landfall. The eastern islands are probably those with the highest chance of producing a rarity, particularly during a southeast wind. The passage waders mentioned for spring are also regularly seen during autumn. A wide variety of chats, warblers, flycatchers, buntings and other passerines can occur, sometimes including extreme vagrants. Some of the more regular scarce migrants are Wryneck, Bluethroat, Yellow-browed Warbler, Red-breasted Flycatcher, Red-backed Shrike, Common Rosefinch and Ortolan Bunting. Seawatching can be excellent, with a large passage of Sooty Shearwater being especially noteworthy—the rarer shearwaters and skuas are possibilities.

October–April: Winter is a generally unproductive time of year on the moors, although Red Grouse and Short-eared Owl should be visible, while a Rough-legged Buzzard may put in an appearance. Wildfowl numbers greatly increase in winter, with the arrival of northern breeding birds—Loch of Harray and Loch of Stenness on the Mainland of Orkney are particularly good areas. Skeins of Greylag and other geese can be seen flying south during October. Barnacle Geese (c. 400–600) can be found on Switha, Swona and in the South Walls area. They also occasionally visit South Ronaldsay and Flotta. There are three flocks of Greenland White-fronted Geese: c. 100 at Birsay (northwest Mainland), c. 50 on Stronsay and c. 30 on East Mainland. Offshore, major concentrations of waterfowl can be found in Scapa Flow, including large numbers of Eider and Red-breasted Merganser. Around 2500 Long-tailed Duck feed in the relatively shallow inshore waters here during the day and fly to roost communally in deeper waters at night. In addition, c. 200 Great Northern Diver and small numbers of Slavonian Grebe and Velvet Scoter are usually present. A few Little Auk winter around the islands. Waulkmill Bay, part of the Hobbister RSPB reserve, is an ideal location from which to see a selection of these offshore species. Here, as in many other situations on Orkney, a telescope can be a great advantage.

The islands are of considerable importance for winter waders; huge numbers of Curlew—nearly a quarter of the British wintering population—occupy Orkney at the time, using the fields and shoreline. Among other wintering shorebirds, Grey Plover, Knot, Sanderling, Purple Sandpiper and Turnstone are of especial interest, the last two reaching numbers that are nationally significant.

Iceland and Glaucous Gulls can often be found in the harbours at Stromness and Kirkwall. Small numbers of Long-eared Owl are sometimes present, while Snow Bunting is a regular winter visitor.

O1 MAINLAND OS Landranger 6

Mainland is by far the largest of the Orkney islands. Irregularly shaped, it measures just less than 25 miles (40 km) at its widest and a maximum of slightly over 15 miles (24 km) north to south. It is best considered in two parts, east and west, divided by a line through Kirkwall, since each are important but different bird regions.

WEST MAINLAND

Habitat

The breeding bird interest here is concentrated upon three areas of heather moorland, totalling some 39 square miles (100 km^2), which between them support one of the finest moorland bird communities in Britain. Numerous freshwater lochs adorn the West Mainland landscape. Despite much drainage, a number of important wetland areas survive providing nesting habitat for ducks and waders. Another important haunt of breeding birds are the old red sandstone cliffs of the west and north, which hold large colonies of nesting seabirds. Elsewhere, West Mainland is characterised by fertile fields of sown grass for hay or silage, grazed by cattle in summer and supporting an abundance of waders and gulls in winter.

Species

The moorland lochans support breeding Red-throated Diver, Wigeon, Teal and Red-breasted Merganser. Hen Harrier is a speciality of the moors of West Mainland—the species is generally polygamous here, with up to 100 females breeding in some years. Important populations of another vole predator, the Short-eared Owl, also occur. Small numbers of Red Grouse and several pairs of Merlin nest. Both Arctic and Great Skuas breed, as do a wide range of waders, including Golden Plover, Dunlin, Snipe and exceptionally high densities of Curlew. Breeding passerines include Reed Bunting, which is common, and smaller numbers of Wheatear, Stonechat, Sedge Warbler and Twite. In the absence of ground predators such as fox, stoat and weasel, species such as Kestrel, Woodpigeon and Hooded Crow regularly nest on the ground. On the larger lochs and in other wetlands, Mallard is the most numerous of the breeding wildfowl, but Shelduck, Wigeon, Teal, Pintail, Shoveler, Tufted Duck and Red-breasted Merganser also breed. Several species of wader nest, including Dunlin, Snipe and Redshank. Rushy areas, iris beds and more cultivated ground are favoured by the few Corncrake that occur on West Mainland, and of the more widespread Sedge Warbler and Reed Bunting.

Wildfowl numbers greatly increase in winter with the arrival of northern breeding birds, while a wide variety of waterfowl and waders occur on passage. Breeding seabird activity is concentrated on the west coast at Marwick Head, where large colonies of Kittiwake and Guillemot occur, with lesser numbers of Fulmar, Razorbill and a few Puffin. Substantial colonies also exist at Costa Head and Row Head.

In winter, the West Mainland coast is home to a variety of visiting shorebirds. Turnstone and Purple Sandpiper feed on the rocky shores, while Dunlin, Bar-tailed Godwit, Redshank and Curlew are found in estuarine areas. Inland, Curlew is undoubtedly the most conspicuous of the waders using the fields as feeding and roosting sites. Peregrine and Merlin can sometimes be seen hunting over both coastal and farm habitats.

Male and female Hen Harriers

Access

1 BIRSAY MOORS AND COTTASCARTH RSPB RESERVE (OS REF: HY 37/19)

This is a 2340-ha moorland reserve in the north of the island. It can be reached by turning left off the A966 Finstown–Evie road, just north of Norseman Garage, 3 miles (4.8 km) from Finstown. Turn right along the track signposted Cottascarth and follow this to the hide. Further north, a second hide on Burgar Hill, near the wind generators, overlooks Lowrie's Water where Red-throated Diver and other waterfowl can be observed. To reach this, turn off the A966 at Evie, 1.5 miles (0.8 km) northwest of the B9057 junction. The Birsay moors are perhaps best viewed from the B9057 Evie–Dounby road. In the west of the area, access can be gained to the Dee of Durkadale by turning right along a rough track at the south end of Loch Hundland and following this to the ruined farm of Durkadale.

Hen Harrier and Short-eared Owl both breed; there are a few pairs of Merlin and small colonies of Arctic and Great Skuas. The reserve is best visited between mid-April and mid-July.

2 LOCH OF BANKS (OS REF: HY 27/23)

This is a roosting site for Hen Harrier in October–March, and holds wild-fowl and wader interest throughout the year. It is best observed from the A967/A986 roads on either side, thus reducing disturbance. Please park considerately.

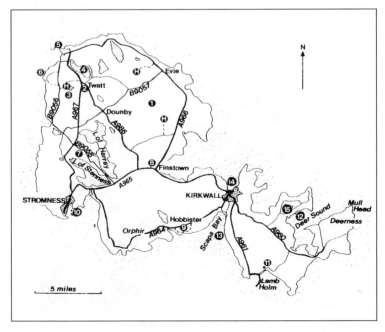

3 THE LOONS RSPB RESERVE (OS REF: HY 27/23)

Located adjacent to Loch of Ibister in northwest of Mainland this 64-ha reserve, a SSSI, is basically a waterlogged marsh within a basin of old red sandstone hills. It can be approached along the unclassified road leading west off the A986, just north of Twatt and 3 miles (4.8 km) from Dounby. There is a hide open at all times on the west side of the reserve, but access to the rest of the area is not permissible. Emergent vegetation provides nesting habitat for both wildfowl and waders, including Wigeon, Pintail, Shoveler, Snipe and Redshank. Arctic Tern and Sedge Warbler also breed. In winter, visiting wildfowl include a flock of about 100 Greenland White-fronted Geese.

4 LOCH OF BOARDHOUSE (OS REF: HY 27/25)

Located in the northwest of the island, the loch can be viewed from the A967 along the western shore and an unclassified road to the east. It is an important winter wildfowl site, especially for Pochard.

5 BROUGH OF BIRSAY (OS REF: HY 23/28)

This headland in extreme northwest Mainland can be reached via a pedestrian causeway (closed for three hours either side of high water) but many birds can be seen from the car park on Mainland. It is a good seawatching point: July–October is the best time, especially in a northwesterly wind. Species include shearwaters, petrels, skuas, gulls, terns and auks. Note: when visiting the Brough be very watchful of the tides closing the causeway (tide details are available from tourist information centres).

6 MARWICK HEAD RSPB RESERVE (OS REF: HY 22/24)

A mile-long (1.6 km) cliff reserve on the west coast, including a part of Marwick Bay. The old red sandstone cliffs rise to almost 100 m and have weathered to produce abundant flat ledges for nesting seabirds. Access is possible at all times from either the end of the minor road off the B9056 to Marwick Bay or from the car park at Cumiaquoy, also reached by a minor road off the B9056, 1 mile (1.6 km) north of the Marwick turning. There are several good viewpoints overlooking the breeding ledges, but a large part of the cliffs is not visible from land and care should be taken when near the cliff edge. Approximately 5000 pairs of Kittiwake and 32,000 Guillemot nest; other breeding species include Fulmar, Razorbill, a few Puffin, Rock Dove and Raven.

7 LOCH OF HARRAY AND LOCH OF STENNESS
(OS REF: HY 29/15 AND 28/12)

These two lochs, the largest in Orkney, are separated by a narrow peninsula which carries the B9055 road. The lochs can be viewed from surrounding roads and tracks. The car park at Ring of Brodgar is a good general observation point. Between them, the lochs hold a breeding population of around 30 pairs of Mute Swan. In winter, Greylag Geese and Whooper Swan can be seen in the fields between the lochs and those adjacent to Loch of Skaill to the northwest. Loch of Harray can hold over 10,000 wintering duck on occasion, and is one of Britain's most important sites for overwintering Pochard. By contrast, Loch of Stenness is tidal and therefore attracts birds such as Long-tailed Duck and Goldeneye.

8 BINSCARTH WOOD (OS REF: HY 348140)

Apart from areas of willow scrub and a few scattered bushes and stunted trees, the only woodland on West Mainland is at Binscarth, near Finstown. A track though the wood leaves the A965 on the western outskirts of Finstown. Essentially a mixture of sycamores and conifers, the wood can be attractive to passerine migrants. It contains a large rookery and often holds a Long-eared Owl roost in winter.

9 HOBBISTER RSPB RESERVE (OS REF: HY 38/06)

Though primarily a moorland reserve, Hobbister is more diverse than Birsay and Cottascarth moors and includes elements of cliff, sandflats and saltmarsh habitat. Access to this 759-ha reserve is possible at any time, but is restricted to the area between the A964 and the sea. It is 4 miles (6.4 km) southwest of Kirkwall, on the A964 road to Orphir and is entered either via the minor road on the east side of Waulkmill Bay, or along a rough track at HY 396070. The area is one of the best in Orkney for moorland breeders, and is also of interest in autumn and winter when passage waders and wintering waterfowl can be seen in Waulkmill Bay.

10 STROMNESS HARBOUR (OS REF: HY 25/09)

Considerable numbers of gulls feed in the harbour, often including white-winged gulls such as Glaucous and Iceland Gulls in winter, with the possibility of Ring-billed Gull also.

EAST MAINLAND

Habitat and Species

The East Mainland landscape is more cultivated than that of the West. Only a narrow band of moorland remains, plus some coastal heaths such as those at Rose Ness and at the Mull Head in Deerness. Despite this restricted habitat, small numbers of moorland breeding birds still breed, although Herring and Lesser Black-backed Gulls tend to predominate.

Virtually all of the remainder of the area is farmed, and apart from the large seabird colonies at Mull Head and the Cliffs of Noster, East Mainland has relatively limited breeding bird communities. It is, however, of great significance for migrants. Rarities are regularly recorded among the large numbers of commoner species such as thrushes and warblers, which sometimes arrive. Due to the extent of available habitat, passerine migrants tend not to be concentrated in any particular area. It is advisable to check all suitable areas of scrub, crop and other vegetation in spring and autumn.

In common with West Mainland, the coastline is an important winter habitat for visiting waders; the 1983 winter shorebird count recorded a total of 21,000 waders around the Mainland coast, dominated by huge numbers of Curlew.

Access

11 GRAEMESHALL LOCH (OS REF: HY 489020)

Located immediately northeast of Churchill No. 1 barrier, which connects East Mainland with Lamb Holm, this inland loch is easily viewed from the road. Several species of duck and wader breed, and the extensive reedbed is good for Sedge Warbler.

12 DEER SOUND (OS REF: HY 53/07)

A large inlet in the northeast, separating Deerness from the rest of East Mainland. This is an excellent area for wintering Great Northern Diver and sea duck. The following shallow bays/inlets in Deer Sound are good places for migrant waders in April and September: Mill Sands (HY 515080, view from the minor road from Tankerness to Toab), Bay of Suckquoy (HY 52/04) and St Peter's Pool (HY 54/04). The latter two can be seen from the main A960.

13 SCAPA BAY (OS REF: HY 43/07)

Inlet on the south coast dividing East from West Mainland. This area can be viewed from the B9053 Scapa road at the head of the bay, just over 1 mile (1.6 km) from Kirkwall. Similar range of species as Deer Sound, with wintering waterfowl providing the main interest.

14 KIRKWALL HARBOUR (OS REF: HY 45/11)

As with Stromness harbour, large numbers of gulls can be found, often including Glaucous and Iceland Gulls. The abattoir on the Hatston Industrial Estate to the west of the harbour is also useful in this respect. Immediately inland from the harbour lies the enclosed Peedie Sea—a good place to watch Long-tailed Duck and Goldeneye in winter.

15 LOCH OF TANKERNESS (OS REF: HY 51/09)

A large inland loch, situated on the wide peninsula which separates Inganess Bay and Deer Sound. The loch can be viewed from the road at its northeast corner. Permission from local farmers must be sought in order to cross the fields to reach the shore. The loch is good for wildfowl from August to March, and attracts migrant waders between April and September.

Timing

The bird interest of Mainland is sustained throughout the year; from May to July activity is focused upon the moorland and sea cliffs, then from August to October, wetland habitats and areas of crops or scrub become the all-important places. Coastal and offshore areas hold the main interest from late October until early May.

O2 COPINSAY

OS ref: HY 60/01
OS Landranger 6

Habitat and Species

The 152-ha island of Copinsay lies 2 miles (3.2 km) off the coast of the East Mainland. The southeast cliffs, nearly a mile (1.6 km) long and reaching about 75 m in height, hold approximately 10,000 pairs of Kittiwake, 30,000 Guillemot and 1000 Razorbill. Large numbers of Fulmar nest; Eider, Ringed Plover, Rock Dove, Raven and Twite also breed.

Three adjacent holms, accessible from Copinsay at low tide, have good numbers of Arctic Tern, Puffin and Black Guillemot, together with a few pairs of Common Tern. The Horse, 0.5 mile (0.8 km) to the northeast, holds more gulls and auks.

Access

It is possible to visit Copinsay by making arrangements with the local boatman at Skaill in Deerness, East Mainland (contact S Foubister, tel: 01856 741252). Nesting seabirds can be seen well from various cliff-top vantage points, or by getting the boatman to take you underneath the cliffs if weather conditions are suitable.

Timing

The optimum time to visit is May–July, although an autumn trip could turn up any number of migrant species.

O3 BURRAY AND SOUTH RONALDSAY

OS Landranger 7

Habitat and Species

Burray and South Ronaldsay are similar in character and birdlife to the East Mainland, to which they are linked by the Churchill Barriers. Vestiges of the former heathland support small gull and tern colonies, plus a few pairs of skuas; the remaining small lochs and wetland areas hold nesting duck and waders. On South Ronaldsay, moderately large seabird colonies exist on both the east and west coasts. For the most part, however, farming dominates the scene and the islands are of note for migrant rather than breeding birds. In common with East Mainland, a number of rarities have occurred in recent years.

Access

THE CHURCHILL BARRIERS

The A961 road over these four causeways offers unrivalled opportunities for watching offshore wintering divers, grebes and sea duck. Late April–early May is probably the best time to visit, as birds like Great Northern Diver and Slavonian Grebe should still be present and will have acquired their summer plumage. This is the most likely time of year to find Black-throated Diver too, an otherwise scarce bird on Orkney.

ECHNALOCH BAY (OS REF: ND 47/97)

An open bay on the west coast of Burray which, like the barriers, can be viewed from the A961. Again, waterfowl provide the main interest.

Timing

It is probably during autumn and winter that this area offers the best opportunities for birdwatching. A visit between late October and early May is recommended.

O4 HOY

OS Landranger 7

Habitat

Hoy is a sparsely populated island, largely dominated by heather moorland. It is the hilliest of the Orkney isles, reaching a maximum height of nearly 500 m at Ward Hill in the north. The 300-m-high sea cliffs at St John's Head in the northwest are among the highest in Britain, and the rock architecture includes the spectacular 150-m sea stack, the Old Man of Hoy. A limited amount of arable land exists in a few areas along the east coast, and on South Walls.

Species

The moorland birdlife of Hoy is characterised by Red Grouse, Golden Plover, Dunlin, Snipe and Curlew. Small numbers of Hen Harrier, Merlin and Short-eared Owl breed, while the island has some of the most important populations of skuas in Britain; 210–220 pairs of Arctic and c.

Great Skua harrying Arctic Tern

1750 pairs of Great Skua were censused in 1992. In addition, the hill lochans of Hoy account for about a half of the 110 pairs of Red-throated Diver that nest on Orkney. Stonechat, Wheatear and Twite enhance the bird interest of the island's interior.

On the cliffs, large numbers of Fulmar, Kittiwake, Guillemot, Razorbill and Puffin breed, together with many Shag, Black Guillemot and Rock Dove. Other cliff-nesting species include Buzzard, Peregrine and Raven; Golden Eagle has not bred since 1982 however, and is now very rarely recorded. A small but significant woodland bird community inhabits the patches of woodland/scrub (willows, birch, rowan and aspen) on Hoy, most notably at Berriedale, the most northerly native wood in Britain.

Connected to the south of Hoy is the more agricultural island of South Walls, notable for a visiting flock of over 1000 Barnacle Geese in late winter.

Access

NORTH HOY RSPB RESERVE (OS REF: HY 20/03)

This 3,926-ha reserve occupies the entire northwest of Hoy, and includes both the summit of Ward Hill and the immense sea cliffs of St John's Head. The moorland habitats are best explored via a footpath through the glen that leads to Rackwick. From here, a second footpath heads towards the Old May of Hoy and affords fine views from the cliff-top. There are no access restrictions, but visitors are asked to take special care near the cliff edge as it is very unstable in places. During spring and early summer, it should be possible to see most of the moorland and coastal species mentioned above. Small numbers of Manx Shearwater often gather off Rackwick Bay in late evening prior to coming ashore to their nesting burrows.

Timing

The ideal time to visit is May through to July for breeding species. Hoy also attracts many migrants in autumn, including the occasional vag-

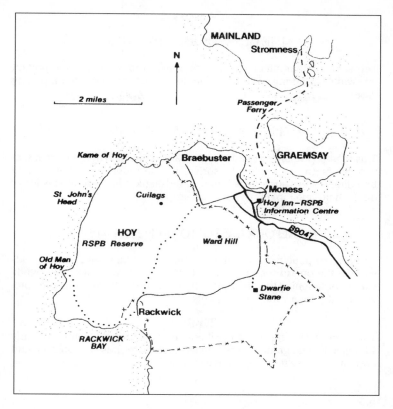

rant; offshore movements of the rarer shearwaters and skuas are possible. An out-of-season trip to Hoy can therefore be very worthwhile.

RSPB Warden

For all Orkney reserves, please telephone 01856 850176.

O5 SHAPINSAY

OS Landranger 6

Habitat and Species

Shapinsay is almost entirely given over to agriculture, with only a small remnant of moorland in the southeast. Oystercatcher, Lapwing and Curlew nest on the farmland, but apart from a few skuas, gulls and terns in the southeast the inland habitats are disappointing for breeding species.

Access

THE OUSE (OS REF: HY 505190)

This shallow tidal inlet in the centre of the north coast is an important late-winter gathering ground for Shelduck returning from their moulting grounds.

MILL LOCH (OS REF: HY 510190)

This loch is primarily notable for the large herd of Whooper Swan that visit Shapinsay in winter. In spring, the surrounding wetlands hold breeding waders such as Snipe and Redshank, plus several species of duck, including Pintail.

BALFOUR CASTLE (OS REF: HY 47/16)

The general paucity of woodland habitats in Orkney mean that woods such as the one in the grounds of Balfour Castle are extremely significant in broadening the diversity of breeding birds. In addition, they provide shelter for a variety of migrants.

Timing
The most interesting time to visit Shapinsay is probably winter or early spring, when migrant swans, ducks and shorebirds are present and breeding ducks and waders have returned.

O6 ROUSAY AND EGILSAY   OS Landranger 6

Habitat and Species
Rousay is a hilly and generally uncultivated island. The breeding bird community of the island's interior is impressive, with Red-throated Diver on the hill lochs and Hen Harrier, Merlin, Curlew, Golden Plover, five species of gull and Short-eared Owl on the heather moor. The numerous small crags have encouraged Fulmar to nest inland. A few Common Sandpiper nest—a relatively scarce breeder on Orkney. Woodland at Trumland House and Westness serves to further diversify the bird interest of the island.

Egilsay, 1 mile (1.6 km) east of Rousay, is one of the least intensively farmed islands in Orkney, and for that reason has retained significant populations of birds, especially Lapwing and Redshank. It is also notable for its important numbers of breeding Corncrake. There are many small lochs holding breeding ducks, waders and Black-headed Gull. In winter the coastline of Egilsay can support up to 1000 waders,

Fulmars

including large populations of Purple Sandpiper and Turnstone. Large numbers of divers and sea duck also winter, using the relatively sheltered sounds between Rousay, Egilsay and Wyre. This was the wintering area of a single adult White-billed Diver in recent years.

Access
A ferry service operated by Orkney Islands Shipping Company connects Tingwall (Mainland) with Rousay, Egilsay and Wyre (see Introduction).

QUANDALE AND BRINGS HEATHLANDS (OS REF: HY 38/34)

These two maritime heaths in the northwest of Rousay are the breeding haunt of up to 4000 pairs of Arctic Tern and 100 pairs of Arctic Skua. A few Great Skua also nest. The western cliffs hold large numbers of seabirds, including Fulmar, Kittiwake, Guillemot and Razorbill.

TRUMLAND RSPB RESERVE (OS REF: HY 430280)

This 433-ha moorland reserve lies in the south of the island, above Trumland House. Access is possible at all times. Red-throated Diver, Hen Harrier and Golden Plover breed, while Merlin, Arctic and Great Skuas, and Short-eared Owl may also be seen.

EYNHALLOW SOUND (OS REF: HY 38/27)

The mile-wide (1.6 km) sound between Rousay and Mainland is an important wintering area for Great Northern Diver, Eider and Long-tailed Duck; smaller numbers of Velvet Scoter and Red-breasted Merganser are also usually present. The sound can be viewed from either the Broch of Gurness (HY 382269) on Mainland or from the south Rousay coastline. The ferry also makes a good observation platform.

ONZIEBUST AND NORTH TOFTS FARM

Onziebust lies toward the south of Egilsay, the farm comprising all of the land in the southern part of the island together with a more recently acquired block in the north-central area, east of the famous Round Church. The total area of the farm is about 145 ha. The site comprises a range of habitats, primarily low-intensity pastoral farmland, coastal grasslands, naturally eutrophic lochs and surrounding wetlands. There is also a small reedbed. The abundant iris beds provide important early-season cover for Corncrake. In addition, species nesting on the farm include Curlew, Arctic Tern, Twite, Lapwing, Snipe, Redshank, Rock Dove, Wheatear, Sedge Warbler and possibly Pintail. Otter is known to occur around the lochs. The site is viewable from the public road and from along several tracks. A cenotaph to St Magnus stands at the place where he was killed, within the farmland, and there is unrestricted public access to this area.

Timing

The best time for moorland species and seabirds is mid-May until July, but the chance of a rare migrant could make a September/October visit worthwhile. Wintering waterfowl and shorebirds complete the year-round attractions of these islands. Great Northern Diver and Long-tailed Duck numbers increase considerably in late April, prior to their departure. There is a good display of wildlife information at the visitor centre adjacent to Rousay Pier.

O7 WESTRAY   OS Landranger 5

Habitat and Species

The breeding bird interest of Westray is dominated by the huge seabird colonies on the island's west coast, between the RSPB's reserve at Noup Head and the headland of Inga Ness, 5 miles (8 km) to the south. Around 60,000 Guillemot, 3000 Razorbill and 30,000 pairs of Kittiwake are estimated to nest on these cliffs, as well as smaller numbers of Shag, Puffin and Black Guillemot. Immediately inland, an area of maritime heath supports populations of up to 2000 pairs of Arctic Tern and 50 pairs of Arctic Skua. In addition, Eider, Oystercatcher, Ringed Plover and four species of gull breed. Several freshwater lochs and associated wetland areas have breeding wildfowl and waders, and these are good areas for overwintering birds. A few Corncrake still call from suitable habitat. Coastal waders are numerous in winter, especially Purple Sandpiper and Turnstone on the rocky shorelines and Sanderling on the sandy bays.

Access

Westray can be reached by both passenger ferry and air from Kirkwall (see Introduction). The following locations are recommended for initial exploration.

NOUP HEAD RSPB RESERVE (OS REF: HY 39/50)

This western promontory is approached from Pierowall by following the minor road to Noup Farm and then the track to the lighthouse—a total distance of just over 4 miles (6.4 km). The RSPB owns 1.5 miles (2.4 km) of cliff, a designated SSSI, which hold one of the highest densities of nesting seabirds in Britain. Inland, just outside the reserve, Arctic Skua and Arctic Tern breed on the heathland. Despite its westerly position, Westray occasionally receives continental migrants and these tend to be concentrated at Noup Head.

STANGER HEAD (OS REF: HY 511428)

A broad headland in the southeast of the island. It is perhaps the easiest place on Westray to see Puffin. A track leads to the coast here from Clifton, near the B9066, just over 6 miles (9.7 km) south of Pierowall.

AIKERNESS PENINSULA (OS REF: HY 45/52)

The most northerly part of Westray, upon which is situated the airstrip. Follow the minor road north from Pierowall towards the airfield, branching north to the triangulation point above the coast 3 miles (4.8 km) later. Black Guillemot is relatively easy to see along the northwest shore here.

LOCH OF BURNESS (OS REF: HY 429481)

An inland loch situated immediately west of Pierowall, and visible from several surrounding tracks. This is one of the most productive of Westray's freshwater lochs, inhabited by Britain's northernmost Little Grebe and the haunt of Mute Swan, Teal, Shoveler, Tufted Duck, Moorhen and Coot. At the margins can be found waders such as Snipe and Redshank.

Timing

A spring visit is recommended, between mid-May and mid-July.

08 PAPA WESTRAY
OS Landranger 5

Habitat

Papa Westray, or 'Papay' amongst Orcadians, is Westray's diminutive northeastern satellite, separated from it by just over a mile (1.6 km) of water.

Species

Bird interest is focused upon the maritime heath at the north of the island, which is managed as a reserve by the RSPB under an agreement with the local croft community. This area holds one of Britain's largest Arctic Tern colonies, with an average of around 6000 pairs attempting to nest in most years. Other large tern colonies, often including small numbers of Common and Sandwich Terns, are in the south of the island at Sheepheight and Backaskaill. Most of the remainder of Papay is cultivated ground, and until recently the traditional crofting practices employed here maintained a healthy population of Corncrake, perhaps numbering as many as 15 pairs. In 1995, however, only one was recorded.

Access

Papa Westray can be reached by both passenger ferry and by air from Kirkwall and Westray (see Introduction).

NORTH HILL RSPB RESERVE (OS REF: HY 49/54)

This 206-ha SSSI occupies the northernmost quarter of Papay, and represents one of the best examples of maritime heath in Scotland. The reserve is flanked by low cliffs on its east coast—possibly the last breeding site in Britain for the now-extinct Great Auk—and is otherwise bordered by a low-profile, rocky shoreline.

North Hill is reached by following the island's principal road north to its end. Between mid-April and mid-August, visitors are requested to contact the warden in advance to arrange an escorted tour of the nesting colonies, which are well viewed from the perimeter path. The warden can be found at Rose Cottage. As a consequence of its huge Arctic Tern population, North Hill supports a colony of c. 150 pairs of Arctic Skua, which specialise in pirating the terns' prey. Eider, four species of gull and several species of wader also breed. The highest section of cliff, Fowl Craig, holds a respectable seabird colony of approximately 2000 Guillemot, 1500 Kittiwake, lesser numbers of Razorbill and a few Puffin. Up to 80 pairs of Black Guillemot nest in the boulder beach surrounding the reserve.

Mull Head, at the northern tip of Papay, can be an excellent seawatching vantage in late summer and autumn—Sooty Shearwater and Long-tailed Skua have been regularly recorded in recent years.

RSPB Warden

For all Orkney reserves, please telephone 01856 850176.

HOLM OF PAPA (OS REF: HY 51/52)

The Holm is a small island situated midway off Papay's east coast, and only a few hundred metres offshore. Its ornithological significance lies in the 130 or so pairs of Black Guillemot that breed on its northeastern shore—probably the largest colony in Britain. Many gulls, terns and a small colony of Storm Petrel also breed.

LOCH OF ST TREDWELL (OS REF: HY49/51)

A large loch in the southeast of the island. This was a former breeding site of Red-necked Phalarope. It is still productive for a variety of breeding wildfowl and waders.

Timing

Mid-May to July is the ideal time to visit for the breeding species, but August to mid-October could prove interesting for seawatching and for migrants. Papay is well situated to receive spring and autumn migrants, and easterly winds in particular have produced some exciting rarities. Diligent searching of scrub vegetation and other cover is recommended.

O9 NORTH RONALDSAY   OS Landranger 5

Habitat

North Ronaldsay is the most northeasterly of the Orkney archipelago, and is separated from neighbouring Sanday by 3 miles (4.8 km) of open water. Measuring c. 3 miles by 1 mile (4.8 by 1.6 km), the island has an area of approximately 5 square miles (13 km²). The coastline is predominantly rocky, with the exception of sandy beaches on the east and south shores. Inland, the ground rises to a maximum of 18 m above sea level and is largely cultivated, the agricultural land being enclosed within a wall known as the Sheep Dyke. The island has six main lochs, some of which have fringing vegetation and associated wetlands. Overall, there are many similarities (in size, population and land use) with Papa Westray.

In 1987, the North Ronaldsay Bird Observatory was established in a modern energy-conserving building heated entirely by solar and wind energy, in the southwest of the island. Accommodation is available here, providing five four-bedded dormitories and four twin/double rooms, including one with en-suite facilities suitable for use by the disabled.

Species

A total of 51 breeding species has been recorded, of which 34 currently breed regularly. A survey of breeding birds in 1987 recorded over 200 Fulmar nests, approximately 700 pairs of Black-headed Gull, around 1000 pairs of Arctic Tern and over 450 Black Guillemot (individuals). A colony of over 50 pairs of Cormorant can be found on Seal Skerry, Orkney's most northerly extremity. Other confirmed breeding species included Mute Swan, Shelduck, Gadwall, Teal, Mallard (c. 50 pairs), Pintail, Shoveler, Eider, Water Rail, Moorhen, Coot, Oystercatcher, Ringed Plover, Lapwing, Snipe, Curlew, Redshank, Common and Herring Gulls, Sandwich Tern, Rock Dove, Skylark, Meadow and Rock Pipits, Pied Wagtail, Wren, Blackbird, Hooded Crow, Starling, House Sparrow, Twite

Leach's Petrel

and Reed Bunting. In addition, Raven has bred annually in recent years. Corncrake was at one time abundant, but is now rare and breeding has not been confirmed since 1981.

The accidental introduction of the hedgehog to the island in 1972 has led to declines in the populations of a number of ground-nesting birds. Scores of hedgehogs have now been removed from the island (mostly to SWT mainland reserves) to reduce nest predation.

A variety of wildfowl and waders 'stage' on the island during autumn. Particularly obvious are the large numbers of Golden Plover present in July–April. In recent years, these have included a few vagrant Pacific and American Golden Plovers. North Ronaldsay is ideally situated to receive continental passerine migrants. Large falls are possible in south-easterly winds, and rarities are regularly found among the more predictable passage migrants such as pipits, warblers, chats and flycatchers. Reliable scarce migrants include Icterine, Barred and Yellow-browed Warblers, Red-breasted Flycatcher, Red-backed Shrike and Common Rosefinch. In recent years, rarities such as Great Snipe, Pechora, Red-throated and Olive-backed Pipits, Citrine Wagtail, Siberian Thrush, Siberian Blue Robin, Melodious, Blyth's Reed, Booted, Sardinian, Radde's, Arctic and Bonelli's Warblers, Thrush Nightingale, Isabelline Shrike, Spanish Sparrow, Arctic Redpoll, and Yellow-browed and Pine Buntings have all been recorded. During a fall, birds can be everywhere, taking shelter in the Sheep Dyke, crops and croft gardens. The wind-lashed sycamores and fuchsias of the walled garden at Holland House tend to concentrate migrants, and this is a particularly likely location for rarities.

Seawatching can be very productive, especially from the old beacon in the northeast of the island. Large passages of Fulmar have been witnessed, Sooty Shearwater is regular in autumn and Great and Cory's Shearwaters, Leach's Petrel, Long-tailed Skua and Sabine's Gull also occur. White-billed Diver has been seen in winter.

For details of accommodation, contact: The Warden, North Ronaldsay Bird Observatory, Orkney KW17 2BE (tel: 01857 633200).

References
The Breeding Birds of North Ronaldsay. MG Pennington. *Scottish Birds*, vol. 15 (1988).

Habitat

Sanday, the largest of the northern Orkney isles, has a predominantly low-profile coastline backed by dunes and machair. Inland, the sandy soils support an agricultural regime based largely upon beef production. Although the tall sea cliffs that are such a feature of many other islands are conspicuous by their absence on Sanday and only a very limited area of moorland exists, the island is nonetheless an important place for birds.

Species

The coastal habitats support large numbers of breeding Ringed Plover, and there are substantial colonies of Arctic Tern at Westayre Loch, Start Point and Els Ness. Small numbers of Corncrake and a few Corn Bunting remain.

Access

LADY PARISH

By virtue of its position in the Orkney archipelago, the island's north-eastern arm attracts a considerable number of migrants and close scrutiny of the available cover during spring and autumn could be worthwhile. The shallow lochs around Northwall (HY 75/44) are productive for breeding wildfowl, including Teal, Wigeon, Shoveler, Tufted Duck, Red-breasted Merganser and Eider. Waders, such as Snipe, Redshank and Dunlin, also breed. North Loch is often host to large numbers of visiting Whooper Swan in early winter, as well as a variety of other northern wildfowl.

GUMP OF SPURNESS (OS REF: HY 60/35)

This hill is situated in the extreme southwest of Sanday, and is the only remaining area of heather moor on the island. It holds in the order of 25 pairs of Arctic Skua. Short-eared Owl may be found hunting here and over the dunes.

Timing

Sanday is probably of greatest interest for its visiting birds; spring and particularly autumn are likely to be productive for migrants, while in winter, the shoreline of Sanday can hold over 7500 waders, including Grey and Golden Plovers, Turnstone, Purple Sandpiper, Sanderling and Bar-tailed Godwit.

O11 EDAY

Habitat
The moorland-dominated island of Eday, some 8 miles (13 km) long and a maximum of 2.5 miles (4 km) wide, lies centrally between the extremities of Westray and Sanday.

Species
The moors hold over 100 pairs of Arctic and a few pairs of Great Skuas. Curlew, Snipe and occasionally Golden Plover also nest. A half dozen or so pairs of Whimbrel are of special interest—Eday is one of only two Orkney breeding sites. Large numbers of Fulmar and Herring Gull nest at Red Head in the north of the island, although the best seabird colonies are on The Calf, notably at Grey Head where Guillemot, Razorbill and Kittiwake breed. At the south end of the island, a large Cormorant colony is established. Black Guillemot breeds around the rocky shoreline of Eday and the small islands off the west coast; there is a small Cormorant colony on the Green Holms.

Access
During general exploration of the island, check the following localities in particular.

MILL LOCH (OS REF: HY 565368)

This probably has the highest concentration of breeding Red-throated Diver in Britain—at least eight pairs attempt to nest each year.

CARRICK HOUSE (OS REF: HY 567384)

Two small woods near the house provide ideal cover for migrants.

Timing
Visit between May and July for moorland and coastal breeding birds; either a spring or autumn visit could produce interesting migrants.

O12 STRONSAY

Habitat and Species
With the exception of an area of moorland on the southwest peninsula of Rothiesholm, Stronsay is very much an agricultural island. Though

the moorland bird community is one of the island's principal attractions, Stronsay also has considerable colonies of seabirds, concentrated on the east coast between Odness and Lamb Head.

Many of the island's lochs and associated wetlands are breeding haunts for wildfowl and waders, including Pintail, Shoveler, Snipe and Redshank. Corn Bunting, a species very much associated with traditional land-use practices, still occurs on Stronsay but is probably declining. Corncrake has not been heard for two years. Quail nest in some years.

Due to increased coverage by birders, Stronsay has gained a reputation as an excellent place for migrants. The island's wetland habitats are extremely valuable for passage waders in spring and autumn, while the fuchsia hedges that grow both within and outside the island's gardens provide cover for migrant passerines. Among an impressive list of recently recorded rarities are American Golden Plover, Semipalmated Sandpiper, Snowy Owl, Bee-eater, Olive-backed Pipit, Pied Wheatear, Subalpine, Greenish, Pallas's, Arctic, Radde's and Dusky Warblers, Rose-coloured Starling, Arctic Redpoll, Rustic, Little, Yellow-breasted and Cirl Buntings, and two new species for Orkney: White's Thrush and Tawny Pipit.

The island boasts a large wintering population of wildfowl, including up to 250 Whooper Swan and 50 Greenland White-fronted Geese, in addition to large numbers of dabbling and diving duck.

Visiting shorebirds, including important populations of Ringed Plover, Purple Sandpiper and Turnstone, are a conspicuous feature of the winter scene on Stronsay.

Access

There is a twice-daily plane service (not Sundays) to Stronsay. In addition, a twice-daily roll-on/roll-off ferry service operates from Kirkwall (not Sundays in winter).

ROTHIESHOLM PENINSULA (OS REF: HY 61/22)

(Pronounced 'Rowsum'.) During the breeding season, the moorland is the domain of 40 pairs of Arctic and several pairs of Great Skuas, five species of gull, several hundred pairs of Arctic Tern and various wildfowl and waders. Red-throated Diver and Twite also nest, making this one of the best areas in the northern islands for moorland birds. The surrounding cliffs are tenanted by Fulmar, Black Guillemot and small numbers of Shag, Guillemot and Razorbill. Leave the B9061 at the old school. Access permission should be sought at Bu Farm. Park and follow the track east of the school for 400 m south to access to moorland. There are some electrified fences in this area at present, so caution is required! Two excellent wader lochs, Mount Pleasant Loch and Bu Loch, lie adjacent to the B9061 and can be viewed en route to Rothiesholm.

MILL BAY/MEIKLE WATER (OS REF: HY 66/26 AND 66/24)

The sheltered waters of Mill Bay are excellent for sea duck and divers, while the sandy beach is productive for waders such as Bar-tailed Godwit and Sanderling. The area near the old mill is very good for migrant passerines and is most picturesque. Meikle Water holds duck throughout the year and plays host to a large winter population of Whooper Swan, White-fronted and Greylag Geese, as well as over 1000 duck. Large numbers of waders also winter in the area. To reach Mill Bay, leave the main road opposite the old mill and visit the private Stronsay Bird Reserve for local bird news. Meikle Water is best viewed from the main road which runs around its perimeter.

Timing
Visit between May and July for moorland and coastal breeding birds; either a spring or autumn visit should produce good migrant birds. Note: guided bird tours, boat trips and various types of accommodation can be arranged by contacting John and Sue Holloway, Castle, Stronsay (tel: 01857 616363).

RSPB Orkney Officer
Eric Meek, Smyril, Stenness, Stromness, Orkney KW16 3JX (tel: 01856 850176).

RSPB Senior Site Manager
Keith Fairclough, Viewforth, Swannay, by Evie, Orkney KW17 2NR.

References
Birds of Orkney. C Booth, M Cuthbert & P Reynolds (1984).
Islands of Birds: A Guide to Orkney Birds. E Meek (1985).
The Orkney Islands Reserves. RSPB leaflet.
The Birds of Stronsay. J Holloway (1991).

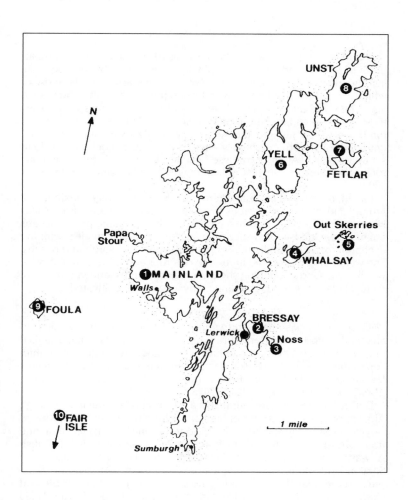

Main sites
SH1   Mainland
SH2   Bressay
SH3   Noss
SH4   Whalsay
SH5   Out Skerries
SH6   Yell
SH7   Fetlar
SH8   Unst
SH9   Foula
SH10 Fair Isle

Shetland comprises an archipelago of over 100 islands, for the most part north of 60°N latitude. Its topography is characterised by long peninsulas and deeply penetrating inlets (voes), firths and sounds, most of which are old river valleys drowned when the sea rose after the last ice age. There are many scattered sandy and gravel beaches in the sheltered 'inner' coastline and in places these have formed spits, bars and tombolas which jut into the sea, occasionally extending across the entrances of voes to completely enclose them, as at Loch of Spiggie in south Mainland. Apart from these beaches, the coast is predominantly rocky and there are several outstanding sea cliffs, some rising to over 300 m.

Inland, the rugged moorland terrain rises to an average maximum of around 250 m, the two obvious exceptions being the summits of Ronas Hill and Foula, which both exceed 400 m. Innumerable peaty lochans fragment the landscape, which is exposed and largely treeless with the exception of a few small areas of planted woodland, scrub and bushes. The weathering of exposed limestone outcrops and the accumulation of windblown sand containing shell fragments have produced patches of relatively fertile ground, enabling many areas to be cultivated.

Access

P&O operate a passenger and vehicle ferry service from Aberdeen to Shetland almost daily. Departure from Aberdeen and Lerwick is at 6.00 pm, arriving at 08.00 am the following morning. From late May to mid-September, there is a weekly service between Shetland and Orkney. Details are available from P&O Ferries, PO Box 5, Jamieson's Quay, Aberdeen AB9 8DL (tel: 01224 572615).

British Airways operate four flights a day from Aberdeen to Sumburgh Airport, on the southern tip of Shetland, Monday–Friday, with reduced service on Saturday and Sunday. The journey time is a little less than one hour. BA also operate a flight from Inverness via Orkney. Tel: British Airways at Sumburgh (01950 460345) for details. Loganair also fly to Shetland, operating a daily service from Edinburgh and Glasgow to Sumburgh. From mid-May to October, the service operates via Fair Isle and Orkney on Saturdays. Contact Loganair at Tingwall for details (tel: 01595 840246).

Public transport on Shetland is very limited, although much of Mainland can be explored in this way. Personal transport is preferable, however, as it affords the opportunity to stop and scan roadside lochans, investigate patches of scrub for possible migrants or deviate from planned routes. Cars make excellent mobile hides, both for bird photography and general birdwatching. Car hire is available as an alternative to bringing a car across on the ferry, although neither option is cheap.

There are frequent ferries to most of the other inhabited islands with drive-on/drive-off services to the islands of Unst, Yell, Whalsay, Fetlar, Out Skerries and Bressay. Advance booking is advisable, especially in summer. Loganair operate a daily (except Sunday) inter-island air service from Tingwall Airport to Whalsay, Fetlar and Unst, with weekly flights to Foula and Out Skerries, plus three flights per week to Fair Isle.

An inexpensive inter-Shetland transport timetable is published by the Shetland Tourist Organisation; this contains details of all air, sea and road services. Contact Shetland Tourist Information in Lerwick on 01595 693434.

Timing

Shetland is a magical place at any season and there is certainly much to see throughout the year. Breeding birds are best seen between late May and mid-July, migrants mid-April to early June and mid-August to late October, while wintering water- and wildfowl are present October–March. Rarities are most likely in May, September and October, depending on weather conditions. Easterly and southeasterly winds are essential for good falls of migrants, whereas northwesterlies are virtually useless.

Day length is a major asset in spring and summer, when the sun is above the horizon for almost 19 hours a day. However, by December daylight is reduced to less than six hours, and this fact should be an important consideration when planning a winter visit.

Species

An increasing population of Fulmar (currently around 150,000 pairs) breed; modest numbers of Manx Shearwater, thousands of Storm Petrel and small numbers of Leach's Petrel also breed (the latter on Foula and Ramna Stacks); Gannet first bred in 1914 and now numbers well over 10,000 pairs, mainly at Hermaness and Noss; there are an estimated 10,000 pairs of Shag breeding and 400 pairs of Cormorant; six species of gull nest, including large numbers of Herring and Great Black-backed Gulls and c. 45,000 pairs of Kittiwake; approximately 150,000 Guillemot, 20,000 Razorbill, 250,000 Puffin and 2000 Black Guillemot breed. In addition, over 5600 pairs of Great and 1900 pairs of Arctic Skuas nest on the maritime heaths and 30,000 or more pairs of Arctic Tern and smaller numbers of Common Tern nest.

Razorbill and Guillemots

The inland lochans hold more than 600 pairs of Red-throated Diver, around 15,000 Eider and small numbers of Teal, Tufted Duck and Red-breasted Merganser also breed. Between one and five pairs of Common Scoter regularly attempt to breed.

Breeding waders include large numbers of Oystercatcher, around 500 pairs of Ringed Plover, many hundreds of Golden Plover, Lapwing, Snipe, Curlew and Redshank, c. 400 pairs of Whimbrel and smaller numbers of Dunlin and Common Sandpiper. There is a small population of breeding Red-necked Phalarope and 1–2 pairs of nesting Black-tailed Godwit.

Merlins breed in small numbers, but Peregrine has not bred in recent years. Hen Harrier and Buzzard are irregular visitors but have been recorded in all months except July. Snowy Owl last bred in 1975, but one or two are still resident and can usually be found on Fetlar or Unst.

Breeding passerines include strong populations of Skylark, Rock and Meadow Pipits, Blackbird, Wheatear and the Shetland subspecies of Wren and Starling. Rook breed at Kergord and Raven and Hooded Crow are both common. Twite frequent the cliffs and a few pairs of Reed Bunting nest in areas of adjacent meadow. Species that occasionally over-summer include Great Northern Diver, Whooper Swan, Pintail, Wigeon (breeds), Shoveler (breeds), Long-tailed Duck, Velvet Scoter, King Eider, Purple Sandpiper, Turnstone, Long-eared Owl, Redwing and Fieldfare (both have bred) and Snow Bunting.

Calendar

May–July: The peak period for spring migrants is April to early June, otherwise it is the breeding birds of the moorlands and sea cliffs which are the most obvious attractions at this time of year (see above).

Passage raptors such as Sparrowhawk and Kestrel occur, with occasional records of Honey Buzzard, Marsh Harrier, Osprey and even Red-footed Falcon and Hobby. Knot, Dunlin, Bar-tailed Godwit, Curlew, Redshank, Common Sandpiper and small numbers of Sanderling pass through in May/early June; there are also passages of Purple Sandpiper and Snipe in April/May. Other migrating waders include scarcer species such as Temminck's Stint, Ruff, Black-tailed Godwit, Spotted Redshank, Greenshank and Green and Wood Sandpipers.

Arctic and Great Skuas return from April, while Pomarine and Long-tailed Skuas can very occasionally be seen offshore, sometimes in very large numbers. Lesser Black-backed Gull returns in late March/early April, followed by Common and Arctic Terns in May. Small numbers of Long-eared and occasional Short-eared Owls move through in April to early May.

Southeasterly winds produce the best number and variety of passerine migrants. These include large numbers of thrushes, chats, warblers, flycatchers and buntings, though autumn passage is generally more impressive. The occurrences of some species, however, are more frequent in spring. These include common migrants such as Tree Pipit, Dunnock, Whitethroat and Spotted Flycatcher, less numerous ones such as Grasshopper and Sedge Warblers, and scarcer species like Hoopoe, Bluethroat, Golden Oriole, Red-backed Shrike and Ortolan Bunting.

August–October: This is the peak migration period when almost anything can turn up; again, southeasterly winds are usually required.

Whooper Swan passage usually begins in late September, together with flocks of Greylag and Pink-footed Geese plus a few Barnacle and (rarely) Brent Geese. As in spring, migrant raptors are likely—Rough-legged Buzzard frequently occurs in October and may linger through the winter.

Passage waders include all those mentioned for spring, with departing Oystercatcher, Ringed and Golden Plovers and Lapwing being joined by passage birds. Sightings of Dotterel are not unusual during August; Common Sandpiper, Whimbrel and Red-necked Phalarope depart in late July/early August; a few Little Stint and Green Sandpiper usually pass through soon afterwards, with the bulk of wader passage occurring in September–October. These include small numbers of Grey Plover, Knot, Sanderling, Curlew Sandpiper, Ruff, Black-tailed Godwit, Spotted Redshank and Greenshank as well as the more numerous Dunlin, Bar-tailed Godwit, Whimbrel, Curlew, Redshank and Turnstone. There is a small Woodcock passage in mid-October. Overwintering Purple Sandpiper arrive in late September. A wide variety of chats, warblers, flycatchers, buntings and other passerine migrants can occur, including Yellow and White Wagtails, Dunnock, Robin, Redstart, Stonechat, Wheatear, Ring Ouzel, Reed and Garden Warblers, Blackcap, Chiffchaff, Willow Warbler, Goldcrest, Spotted Flycatcher, Chaffinch, Brambling, Greenfinch, Siskin, Twite, Redpoll, and Snow and Reed Buntings. In addition, large flocks of Blackbird, Fieldfare, Song Thrush and Redwing pass through in September–November.

Some of the more regular scarce migrants are Wryneck, Icterine, Barred and Yellow-browed Warblers, Red-breasted Flycatcher, Lapland Bunting and Common Rosefinch. Shetland is renowned for its rare migrants, but these can be difficult to predict—almost anything is possible! All potential cover should be checked for birds: rarities recorded in recent years include Black-throated and White's Thrushes, Lanceolated, Aquatic, Booted, Rüppell's, Radde's, Dusky, Yellow, Blackpoll and Chestnut-sided Warblers, Isabelline and Brown Shrikes and White-throated Sparrow.

Seawatching in autumn can be good, with a large passage of Sooty Shearwater in late August–September being especially noteworthy; the rarer shearwaters and skuas are also possibilities.

November–April: Offshore, up to 400 Great Northern Diver, small numbers of Red-throated Diver, and occasional Black-throated and even White-billed Divers occur. An individual of the latter which returned to the Whalsay ferry area for nine successive winters was last seen in 1990/1. Slavonian Grebe occurs in some of the voes and other grebes are sometimes recorded. Large numbers of Eider and Long-tailed Duck overwinter; smaller populations of Goldeneye and Red-breasted Merganser are also present. Very small numbers of Common and Velvet Scoters are present and King Eider is recorded most winters. Wintering Guillemot and Black Guillemot occur in many voes and Little Auk can be numerous in some years.

Wildfowl numbers greatly increase in winter, with the arrival of northern breeding birds—those seen on inland waters at this time include Whooper Swan, small numbers of Greylag Geese, 200–300 Wigeon, Teal, Mallard, 300–500 Tufted Duck, Goldeneye and Red-breasted Merganser. Occasional Shoveler overwinter, while Pintail and Scaup are infrequent. Flocks of Pink-footed, Greylag and sometimes Barnacle Geese are likely on passage in March/April. Purple Sandpiper and Turnstone are numerous, but only moderate numbers of other species overwinter. Most Oystercatcher, Ringed Plover and Lapwing start to return to Shetland in mid-February and there is a marked passage of Golden Plover from March.

Iceland and Glaucous Gulls are found in the harbours at Lerwick and Scalloway, as well as other coastal locations. Small numbers of Long-eared Owl overwinter and Rough-legged Buzzard is sometimes present. Snow Bunting and Twite regularly overwinter, but otherwise there are very few notable passerines present in winter.

SH1 MAINLAND   OS Landranger 2, 3 & 4

Access

1 SUMBURGH HEAD (OS REF: HU 40/08)

This is the southernmost point of mainland Shetland and is an excellent place for watching breeding seabirds. In autumn, some 2000–3000 moulting Eider gather offshore, while passage seabirds include regular Sooty Shearwater, Pomarine Skua and occasionally Long-tailed Skua. Park near the lighthouse (take care not to obstruct access) at the end of the minor road from Grutness. The cliffs at the head reach 80 m in height and care is needed along the cliff-top, especially in strong winds. Sumburgh Head is a good location for migrant passerines, although there is little cover to hold them. It is worthwhile checking the two small quarries. The shrub gardens of Sumburgh Hotel and Grutness provide very adequate shelter and the stone walls on the road to the lighthouse can be productive.

2 POOL OF VIRKIE (OS REF: HU 39/11)

The sheltered tidal basin of Pool of Virkie lies immediately north of Sumburgh Airport. The intertidal sand- and mudflats are of great importance for wintering and migrant shorebirds. Unfortunately, extensions to the airport have reduced its importance for breeding birds, especially Shelduck. The north shore, which can be worked from a minor road off the A970 to Eastshore, is the most useful vantage point. The gardens in this area are very good for migrant passerines.

3 QUENDALE BAY (OS REF: HU 37/12)

An extensive area of sand, backed by dunes and machair vegetation. The bay is very good for wintering divers and sea duck, and is easily viewed from the minor road on the west side.

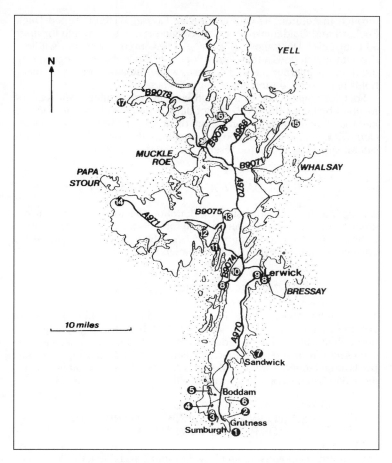

4 LOCH OF HILLWELL (OS REF: HU 376140)

A machair loch with marshy fringes situated 0.5 mile (0.8 km) north of
Quendale Bay. This is an important breeding site for several species of
wildfowl and in winter holds a large number and variety of species.
Corncrake is occasionally heard here. View from the road on the north
or west side—do not go down to the loch.

5 LOCH OF SPIGGIE RSPB RESERVE (OS REF: HU 373176)

A large, productive waterbody, blocked off from Scousburgh Bay by a
sand bar with a dune and machair system. The 115-ha reserve includes
part of the neighbouring Loch of Brow, separated from the main loch by
an area of floating marshland which is important for breeding waders.

Shelduck, Teal, Oystercatcher and Curlew nest in the area, while
Great and Arctic Skuas, Kittiwake and Arctic Tern often bathe in the
lochs. Spiggie and the neighbouring Brow form the most important winter wildfowl site on Shetland. Up to 300 Whooper Swan regularly pass

through in autumn, as well as Greylag Goose, Wigeon, Tufted Duck, Pochard and Goldeneye. In spring, Spiggie is a gathering site for up to 50 Long-tailed Duck. Loch of Brow is a less important winter wildfowl site, although it does attract many Pochard. The lochs are a regular staging area for migrant duck and geese, while the surrounding farmland holds many birds during migration periods.

Loch of Spiggie lies at the southern end of Mainland and can be reached by taking the B9122 at Boddam, turning left onto the unclassified road that follows the north shore of the loch 1.5 miles (2.4 km) later. Good views of the loch can be obtained from the road. Please park considerately and note that the reserve may not be entered.

6 BODDAM VOE (OS REF: HU 40/15)

A deep inlet in the southeast coast, Boddam Voe holds wintering divers, grebes and sea duck and can be good for gulls and waders. The slaughterhouse attracts good numbers of Great Skua and Raven, while the adjacent gardens provide significant migrant cover.

7 MOUSA (OS REF: HU 46/23)

This attractive 180-ha island lies just over 0.5 mile (0.8 km) off the east coast of Mainland, opposite Sandwick. Notable breeding species include Fulmar, Storm Petrel, Eider, Great and Arctic Skuas, several hundred Arctic Tern and many Black Guillemot. Several of the island's small pools attract migrant waders. Mousa is reached by small boat from Leebitton, Sandwick—contact the tourist office at Lerwick for details.

8 SCALLOWAY AND LERWICK HARBOURS
(OS REF: HU 40/39 AND 47/41)

Large numbers of gulls frequent the harbours, and Black Guillemot can be seen throughout the year. White-winged gulls often occur in winter, although Glaucous has been recorded in all months. In the towns, garden shrubbery provides shelter for migrant passerines.

9 LOCH OF CLICKHIMIN (OS REF: HU 465410)

On the western fringe of Lerwick, this loch is a very accessible wintering wildfowl site and can be viewed from surrounding roads and a track on the northeast shore.

10 LOCH OF TINGWALL (OS REF: HU 415425)

Both this and Loch of Asta (HU 413415) are easily viewed from the adjacent B9074. The lochs lie in a limestone valley and attract wintering wildfowl, especially Pochard and Tufted Duck. The crofts on the west side of the road are good for migrant birds.

11 WEISDALE VOE (OS REF: HU 38/49)

This voe can be worked from the A971 along the east shore or an unclassified road from the head of the loch along the west shore. The range of species is similar to that for Sandsound Voe and includes wintering divers, grebes and sea duck and Goldeneye.

12 SANDSOUND VOE AND TRESTA
(OS REF: HU 350490)

Sandsound Voe can be viewed from the minor road that heads south off the A971 Walls road at Tresta. It is a particularly good area for wintering divers, grebes and sea duck. At Tresta itself, check the gardens and sycamore trees by the chapel for migrants.

13 KERGORD (OS REF: HU 395542)

A series of mixed coniferous and broadleaved shelterbelts flanking the B9075 in the Weisdale Valley. These plantations are the longest established on Shetland and provide important cover for nesting birds including Rook and Goldcrest. It is also an excellent site for migrant and wintering woodland species. Do not enter the garden area of Kergord House. Other plantations that regularly attract migrant birds include Catfirth (HU 450542), Voxter (HU 368701), Sullom (HU 350727) and Strand (HU 432460); the latter is owned by the Shetland Bird Club.

14 SANDNESS (OS REF: HU 19/57)

This is a fertile crofting area with scattered lochs that hold numbers of wintering wildfowl. The coast here can be good for seawatching.

15 LUNNANESS (OS REF: HU 50/70)

This exposed peninsula in northeast Mainland is accessible via an unclassified road at Lunnasting, at the end of the B9071. The many lochans support breeding Red-throated Diver, while sycamore trees on the left of the road just before Lunna House and the gardens at the head of Swining Voe, west of Lunna Ness are very good for migrants.

16 SULLOM VOE (OS REF: HU 380740)

This large inlet holds good numbers of wintering Great Northern Diver, Slavonian Grebe, Eider, Long-tailed Duck and Velvet Scoter. Houb of Scatsa, immediately northeast of the airfield on the B9076, is a good wader feeding area. Sullom Voe can be viewed from the B9076 along the south shore, the A970 at the head of the voe and the unclassified road to Sullom along the north shore.

17 ESHA NESS (OS REF: HU 21/79)

West-facing old red sandstone cliffs holding Guillemot and Kittiwake colonies. The nearby Loch of Houlland has breeding terns, while the surrounding maritime moorland supports breeding Whimbrel and skuas. Red-throated Diver breed on the small lochans. Esha Ness is reached by the B9078 to Stenness, off the A970.

SH2 BRESSAY   OS Landranger 4

Habitat and Species

Bressay is the large inhabited island facing Lerwick, separated from Mainland by 0.5 mile (0.8 km) of deep water: Bressay Sound. The island is characterised by high moorland ground in the south and east (including the 226 m-high Ward of Bressay) and lower cultivated ground in the west. The crofts in the west are very good for migrants, and can be easily worked from the various unclassified roads. A colony of Arctic Skua nests in the southeast. Bressay is reached from Lerwick by a regular vehicle and passenger ferry service.

SH3 NOSS   OS ref: HU 54/40
OS Landranger 4

Habitat

The island of Noss is a 313-ha NNR lying immediately east of Bressay and separated by a narrow sound. Sandstone cliffs rise to nearly 200 m in the east/south and from these summits the island slopes to the low cliffs of the west coast. Noss is important because of its huge seabird colonies: a total exceeding 80,000 birds breeds here, including nearly 7000 pairs of Gannet, 10,000 pairs of Kittiwake, 15–20 pairs of Arctic and 200 pairs of Great Skua, 65,000 pairs of Guillemot and large numbers of Fulmar, Eider, Great Black-backed Gull and Puffin.

Access

Access is by ferry from Lerwick to Bressay, then by car or on foot across Bressay (4 miles/6.4 km) to the ferry point on the east coast. Noss is reached by inflatable dinghy by arrangement with the SNH summer warden. The island is open to visitors from mid-May to late August, 10.00 am–5.00 pm daily except Monday and Thursday. There is a regular boat

Rock Doves

from Lerwick in summer which takes visitors around the island and below the cliffs—an excellent way to see the seabird colonies. Check these details with the Lerwick Tourist Office before visiting. Once on Noss, visitors are requested to keep to the cliff-top path.

SH4 WHALSAY

OS Landranger 2

Habitat

Whalsay is a relatively compact island off the east Mainland coast. It is mostly low lying with many freshwater lochs and marshes. There is a small wader pool at Kirk Ness. Modest numbers of Kittiwake and Puffin nest at the south end of the island, and the moors and lochans hold breeding Red-throated Diver, Whimbrel, Arctic Tern and Arctic Skua.

Whalsay is an important island for migrants owing to its easterly location; the crofts in the Skaw area in the northeast are particularly good, as are those on the seaward side of Isbister in the east and around Brough in the west. A fish factory at Symbister attracts numbers of gulls in winter.

A car ferry operates from Laxo (Mainland) and there are daily flights (except Sundays) from Lerwick, operated by Loganair.

SH5 OUT SKERRIES

OS ref: HU 68/71
OS Landranger 2

This small group of exposed rocky islands lie 4 miles (6.4 km) northeast of Whalsay and are the easternmost point in Shetland. They are extremely well placed to receive continental migrants in easterly winds, and the scarcity of cover means that birds are relatively easy to find. Breeding birds include small colonies of Eider, gulls, terns and Black Guillemot. Out Skerries are served by a passenger ferry from Lerwick (a three-hour trip) on Tuesdays and Fridays (and from Whalsay on Sunday if booked in advance). There are also weekly flights in summer from Lerwick, operated by Loganair.

Black Guillemots and breeding cliffs, spring

SH6 YELL

Yell is the second largest island in the Shetland archipelago and is dominated by extensive tracts of moorland terrain, rising to a maximum of just over 200 m in the south.

Access
Access from Mainland is by car ferry across Yell Sound.

LUMBISTER RSPB RESERVE (OS REF: HU 509974)

This 1720-ha reserve is situated on the west side of Yell, between Whale Firth and the A968 to Gutcher. The moorland is dotted with many small lochans and a steep gorge that leads to the grass-topped cliffs and rocky shore of Whale Firth. The breeding species are typical of many areas of Shetland: Red-throated Diver, Red-breasted Merganser, Eider, Merlin, Golden Plover, Curlew, Lapwing, Snipe, Dunlin, Arctic and Great Skuas, Great Black-backed Gull, Wheatear, Raven and Twite. On the coast, Oystercatcher, Ringed Plover, Black Guillemot and Puffin breed. The reserve can be viewed from the A968, and access into the area is possible at all times from a lay-by 4 miles (6.4 km) north of Mid-Yell. Please take great care not to disturb breeding birds, especially divers.

YELL SOUND (OS REF: HU 43/80)

An important wintering area for divers, Eider and Long-tailed Duck. Puffin and Storm Petrel breed on the islands in the sound, several of which are owned by the RSPB (no visiting arrangements).

SH7 FETLAR

OS ref: HU 60/91
OS Landranger 1 or 2

Habitat

This diverse island is the smallest of the three inhabited northern Shetland isles. Fetlar is separated from Yell by the 2.5-mile (4 km) wide Colgrave Sound and is reached by vehicle ferry from Gutcher on Yell, or Belmont on Unst.

The western part of Fetlar, especially around Lamb Hoga, is dominated by heather moorland and peat bog; to the east, the landscape is one of grassy moorland and dry heath punctuated by many lochans, marsh-

Snowy Owl

es and patches of cultivated land. The irregular coastline is a varied mix of cliffs and beaches with boulder shores in places.

The RSPB manage 690 ha of the northern part of Fetlar as a reserve. This includes the summits of Vord Hill (158 m) and Stackaberg, plus the coastline between East Neap and Urie Ness. Most of the reserve consists of serpentine heathland, bordered by high sea cliffs to the north. This unique substrate (occurring only on Fetlar, Unst and the Lizard Peninsula in Cornwall) is characterised by extremely short, herb-rich vegetation. The presence of Whimbrel and (very occasionally) Snowy Owl can presumably be attributed to this tundra-like habitat. The reserve and other areas have been designated a SSSI.

Species

Fetlar is outstanding for breeding waders. Ten species breed annually: Lapwing, Oystercatcher and Ringed Plover near cultivated ground, Golden Plover, Dunlin, Curlew and many Whimbrel on the moorland, Snipe and Redshank in the wetter areas and Red-necked Phalarope on some lochans. Whimbrel is quite widespread—the roadside moorland west of Loch of Funzie, and moorland west of the airstrip and east of the school are the best places. Red-necked Phalarope generally returns to Fetlar in the last week in May and can be seen feeding on roadside lochs, especially Loch of Funzie. Pools and marshland are being constructed to improve phalarope habitat. A hide has been erected overlooking the Mires of Funzie. The island is also important for breeding seabirds. Lamb Hoga, in the southwest, holds breeding Manx Shearwater and a large colony of Storm Petrel, in addition to breeding Shag, Kittiwake, Guillemot and Puffin. Great and Arctic Skuas breed on the moors; around the coast 300 Arctic and a few Common Terns breed. Tern breeding success has been very poor in recent years, although the situation improved considerably in 1991 and 1992. Snowy Owl bred on

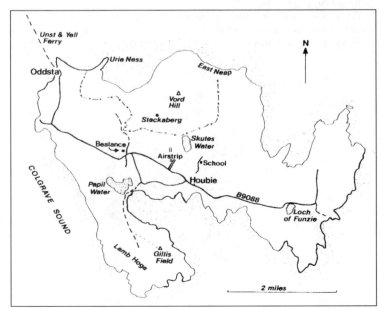

Fetlar between 1967 and 1975, but is no longer present. Around 15 pairs of Red-throated Diver breed and can be easily watched on Loch of Funzie or Papil Water. Other notable breeders include Eider, Raven (nine pairs) and Twite.

Fetlar is very well placed to receive spring and autumn migrants; the crofts in the east of the island and the Old Manse garden (do not enter) regularly produce rarities. In recent years these have included Olive-backed Pipit, Two-barred Crossbill and Greenish Warbler. Very large falls of Fieldfare and Redwing usually occur in mid-October.

Papil Water is locally important as a wintering wildfowl site. White-billed Diver has been recorded offshore at this season.

Access

Access is by ferry from Yell (Gutcher) or Unst (Belmont) then to Fetlar (Oddsta). Advance booking of vehicles on this ferry is advisable (tel: 01957 722259). A bus service from Lerwick connects with the ferry, but does not cross to Fetlar. Flights from Lerwick to Fetlar can be chartered with Loganair. In April–September the reserve is accessible only by arrangement with the RSPB's Conservation Officer, who will escort parties. Visitors should report at Bealance Croft, signposted 2.1 miles (4 km) from the Oddsta ferry terminal (HU 604916). Please respect the property of farmers and crofters on the island and do not disturb birds thought to be breeding.

RSPB Conservation Officer

Bealance, Fetlar, Shetland ZE2 9DJ.

SH8 UNST
OS Landranger 1

Habitat

Unst is the northernmost main island and is separated from neighbouring Yell by Bluemull Sound. It is a large and diverse island with a sharp ridge of high ground running north–south backing the Atlantic coastline and lower, more rounded hills to the east. The moorland terrain provides breeding habitat for many species characteristic of Shetland, especially waders and skuas. The coast holds large populations of breeding seabirds, particularly at Hermaness. Snowy Owl was a regular visitor to the island. The serpentine heathland holds good numbers of breeding waders, Arctic Skua and terns. There is an interesting sycamore plantation at Halligarth, near Baltasound and migrants are often recorded in the gardens of Norwick, Uyeasound and Baltasound. The marsh at Norwick is worth checking, as is Easter Loch in Uyeasound.

Access

There is a frequent car ferry service to Unst from Yell and Loganair flies daily (except Sunday) from Lerwick.

HERMANESS NATIONAL NATURE RESERVE
(OS REF: HP 60/16)

This 964-ha reserve is located on the northernmost peninsula of Unst and overlooks Muckle Flugga and Out Stack, the most northerly point in Britain. The cliffs rise to between 70 and 200 m high and hold, in conjunction with those at Saxavord, one of the largest seabird colonies in Britain. Fourteen species breed, including 10,000 pairs each of Fulmar and Gannet, 5000 pairs of Kittiwake, 16,000 pairs of Guillemot, 2000 pairs of Razorbill and an immense number (approximately 25,000 pairs) of Puffin. About 800 pairs of Great and small numbers of Arctic Skuas breed. Hermaness became well known among birders for its Black-browed Albatross, which returned to the cliffs annually between 1970 and 1995.

The area is accessible via the B9086 at Burrafirth—there is limited parking space near the road end. The main sea cliffs are reached by a 3-mile (4.8 km) walk from Burrafirth along a well-marked path through rough terrain inhabited by breeding Dunlin, Golden Plover, Snipe and around 800 pairs of Great Skua. A SNH summer warden lives in the ex-lighthouse buildings (shore station) at Burrafirth, where there is a visitor centre for visitors.

BLUEMULL SOUND (OS REF: HP 55/00)

Very large numbers of seabirds from Hermaness pass through the sound, especially in winter and early spring. Large numbers of Eider and Black Guillemot are often present in winter.

SH9 FOULA

OS ref: HT 96/39
OS Landranger 4

Habitat and Species

Foula is a remote 1,380-ha island situated approximately 14 miles (22.5 km) west of Mainland. The topography is dominated by the Kame cliffs in the west of the island, which soar to the height of 370 m above sea level and are even more precipitous than those of St Kilda. A ridge of high ground extends southeast from these cliffs, incorporating the Sneug, at 418 m the highest point on Foula, then the ground slopes steeply down to the low-lying crofts around Ham. A second summit, The Noup, lies in the south of the island, reaching 248 m.

Foula is an internationally important seabird station with over 125,000 pairs of breeding birds comprising 12 species, including the largest colony of Great Skua in the North Atlantic. The sheer cliffs of the north coast have few ledges suitable for nesting seabirds, although Fulmar and small numbers of Razorbill and Puffin nest here. There is a very large Guillemot colony to the northwest, however, at Nebbiefield. Puffin nests in large numbers on the grassy slopes of Little Kame, along the west coast and on The Noup. Lower cliffs on the east coast have several small mixed-seabird colonies, as have the few stacks off Ristie and below The Kame. The majority of cliff-nesting seabirds use the boulder fields, along with large numbers of Shag, notably from Western Hoevdi to The Noup and at Heddlicliff.

The small peaty inland pools are used by breeding Red-throated Diver and bathing Great Skua and gulls. The Great Skuas mostly occupy the higher western moors, leaving the lower crofting ground to the Arctic Skuas. The southeast of the island has been virtually stripped of peat, and the barren ground is now inhabited by high densities of nesting Oystercatcher, Ringed Plover, Arctic Skua and Arctic Tern. More luxuriant vegetation is principally confined to a few sheltered areas, such as The Sneck, Hametoun and the mouth of Ham Burn. It is this cover and also the stone walls and cliff-tops that inevitably tend to attract migrants.

The island's huge seabird colonies include 40,000 or more pairs of Fulmar, small numbers of Manx Shearwater, thousands of pairs of Storm Petrel, small numbers of Leach's Petrel, c. 200 pairs of Gannet, 3000 pairs of Shag, 3000 pairs of Great Skua, around 270 pairs of Arctic Skua, 6000 pairs of Kittiwake, 30,000 pairs of Guillemot, 5000 pairs of Razorbill, 60 pairs of Black Guillemot and 35,000 pairs of Puffin.

The island has hosted some remarkable rarities including, in recent years, Upland Sandpiper, Pechora Pipit, Lanceolated Warbler and Lesser Grey Shrike.

Access

Foula is served by a mail boat-cum-passenger ferry, which sails from Walls in west Mainland on Tuesdays and Fridays, weather permitting. In addition, there are weekly flights from Lerwick in the summer.

References

The Birds of Foula. RW Furness (1983).

SH10 FAIR ISLE

OS ref: HZ 20/70
OS Landranger 4

Habitat

Fair Isle is an isolated island situated more than 24 miles (39 km) southwest of Sumburgh Head, Mainland. It covers 765 ha and measures c. 3 miles by 1.5 miles (4.8 by 2.4 km). Steep sandstone cliffs reaching 200 m in places enclose sheep-grazed heather and grassy hills in the north, and crofts in the south comprise mainly improved grazing land for sheep with some cultivated areas of crops such as turnip and oats. The island is owned by the NTS and is designated a SSSI.

Access

Fair Isle can be reached by sea or air: between May and September the mail boat, *Good Shepherd IV*, sails from Grutness, Mainland at 11.30 am on Tuesdays, alternate Thursdays and Saturdays. On alternate Thursdays (i.e. the days the boat does not leave from Grutness), the *Good Shepherd IV* sails from Lerwick. In winter, the service only operates on Tuesdays. Note that rough weather frequently disrupts this schedule. Advance booking is essential—contact Mr JW Stout, Skerryholm, Fair Isle, Shetland (tel: 01595 760222).

Loganair fly from Tingwall, Mainland, on Monday, Wednesday, Friday and Saturday, May–October, and Monday and Friday for the rest of the year. There are connecting services between Tingwall and mainland Scotland. Contact Loganair—tel: 01595 840246 (Tingwall) or 0131 344 3341 (Edinburgh) for details.

Accommodation is available at the Fair Isle Lodge and Bird Observatory, April–late October. Contact Bookings Dept, Fair Isle Lodge and Bird Observatory, Fair Isle, Shetland ZE2 9JU (tel: 01595 762258). A number of crofts also cater for visitors—contact Shetland Tourism, Lerwick, Shetland ZE1 OLU (tel:01595 693434) for details.

For car hire on Fair Isle contact Mr JW Stout, Skerryholm, Fair Isle, Shetland (tel: 01595 760222).

Species

For most birdwatchers, the name 'Fair Isle' is synonymous with rare migrants. Over 345 species have been recorded here, more than at any other British location. More than 250 of these have been ringed—a total exceeding 220,000 birds. The rarity-conscious image that Fair Isle has earned, however, tends to obscure the fact that the island holds large numbers of breeding seabirds, particularly on the west and north coasts. These include around 35,000 pairs of Fulmar, almost 800 pairs of Gannet, more than 1000 pairs of Shag and c. 19,000 nests of Kittiwake. Auk populations total around 33,000 Guillemot, 4000 Razorbill, 20,000+ Puffin and c. 360 breeding Black Guillemot. In addition to Kittiwake, four other species of gull breed around the coast, while around 1100 pairs of Arctic Tern and 60 pairs of Common Tern currently nest. An unknown number of Storm Petrel breed. On the moorland, around 100 pairs each of Great and Arctic Skuas breed.

Approximately 100 pairs of Eider nest; breeding waders include Oystercatcher, Ringed Plover, Lapwing, Snipe and Curlew. Dunlin and Whimbrel occasionally breed. Nesting passerines include Rock and Meadow Pipits, Skylark, White and Pied Wagtails, Wheatear, Raven, Wren, Starling, House Sparrow and Twite.

Calendar

Resident: Fulmar, Shag, Eider, Black Guillemot, Rock Dove, Rock Pipit, Wren (Fair Isle race), Raven and Twite.

March–May: Falls of thrushes and finches can occur during southeast to east winds in March/April. In May, numbers of Bluethroat, Wryneck and Red-backed Shrike often occur; other regular migrants include Icterine and Marsh Warblers, Golden Oriole and Common Rosefinch. Lapland and Snow Buntings are often seen into late April/May. Dotterel, Quail and Corncrake regularly put in an appearance. Some of the more frequently recorded rarities include Short-toed Lark, Tawny Pipit, Thrush Nightingale, Subalpine Warbler, Red-breasted Flycatcher, and Ortolan, Rustic and Little Buntings. Early June is a good time for oddities to turn up—Lesser Kestrel, Daurian Starling and Cretzschmar's Bunting have all been recorded at this time.

June–July: Seabirds dominate the interest (see above).

August–October: Falls of migrants can occur in August but are more likely in September and October, though southeast/east winds are necessary. These occurrences are often very impressive: September falls are largely composed of Redstart, Whinchat, Wheatear, Garden Warbler and Willow Warbler, while those in October generally involve thrushes (up to 10,000 Redwing are recorded annually), finches (including Brambling), Goldcrest and Woodcock. Long and Short-eared Owls frequently occur. Migrants can turn up anywhere, but the crofting land is the best area to check. Among less common autumn migrants, Wryneck, Barred Warbler and Common Rosefinch are regular in August, while Bluethroat, Icterine Warbler, Red-backed Shrike and Ortolan Bunting are probable in September. Regular vagrants include Great Snipe (late August–late October), Short-toed Lark, Richard's and Olive-backed Pipits (October), Citrine Wagtail (late August–mid-October), Lanceolated Warbler (mid-September–mid-October), Pallas's Grasshopper Warbler (end September–mid-October), Pechora Pipit (late September–mid-October), Greenish Warbler (August), Arctic Warbler (late August/September), Pallas's Warbler (October), Yellow-browed Warbler (late September–mid-October), Red-breasted Flycatcher (September/October), Rustic and Little Buntings (late September/October) and Yellow-breasted Bunting (late August–late September)! In addition, there is always the possibility of some of the rarer Fair Isle vagrants turning up, such as Red-flanked Bluetail, Paddyfield and Blyth's Reed Warblers, and Dusky and Radde's Warblers (October/November). Red-throated Pipit is possible in spring or autumn (late September).

Skeins of Pink-footed, Greylag and Barnacle Geese can be seen overhead in late September and October. Small numbers of Whooper Swan arrive. No raptors currently breed on the island, but Sparrowhawk, Kestrel, Merlin and Peregrine are all regular spring and autumn migrants. Hen Harrier, Honey Buzzard and Osprey occasionally occur. Late migrants include Lapland Bunting and large numbers of Snow Bunting in October. Waxwing occur in November/December during irruption years. A Little Bustard was recorded in 1994.

Seawatching can be productive, but as always requires both patience and luck. Small numbers of Sooty Shearwater are seen annually from early August to early October. A few Manx Shearwater are recorded most years between May and October. Odd divers (Red-throated and Great Northern) and a few Long-tailed Duck are present offshore from mid-October. Little Auk usually occur in early spring and late autumn. On the *Good Shepherd* crossing, Storm Petrel can be seen from mid-June until mid-October. Leach's Petrel, Pomarine and Long-tailed Skuas are also occasionally seen. The crossing is a good one for views of cetaceans, including white-beaked dolphin, common porpoise and pilot whale, with occasional records of Risso's dolphin and killer whale. In addition, a number of cetaceans are recorded from the island each year.

Timing

Mid-September to late October is without doubt the prime time to visit for rare birds, although westerly winds at this time can result in disappointment. Southeasterly winds are best for migrant falls and rarities, although these are never easy to predict and rarities can appear on any wind direction. Late May–early June is the peak time for spring vagrants, yet a number of outstanding rarities have occurred in late March–April. August, too, has produced some classic rarities. To savour the true character of Fair Isle and still see some good birds, avoid both the spring and autumn twitching periods and visit in April, late June to early September or late October.

References

The Birds of Fair Isle. JF Holloway and RHF Thorne.
Fair Isle and its Birds. K Williamson (1965).
Fair Isle Bird Observatory Reports.
Fair Isle's Garden Birds. JF Holloway (1983).
The Natural History of Shetland. RJ Berry and L Johnston (1980).
Shetland Bird Report. Ed. PM Ellis/K Osborn.

RSPB Shetland Conservation Officer

RSPB Office, Sumburgh Head Lighthouse (tel: 01950 460800).

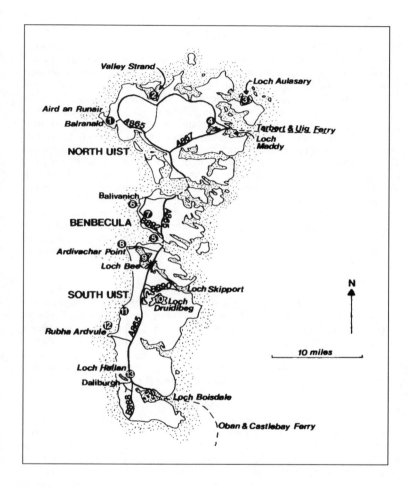

WI1 Southern Isles

1   Balranald
2   Vallay Strand
3   Loch Aulasary
4   Loch Skealtar
5   South Ford
6   Balivanich
7   Stinky Bay and West
    Benbecula Lochs

8   Ardivachar Point
    and North Bay
9   Loch Bee
10 Loch Druidibeg
11 Peninerine
12 Rubha Ardvule
13 Loch Hallan

WI1 SOUTHERN ISLES

OS Landranger 18, 22 & 31

Habitat

This group of islands embodies the quintessence of the Hebridean environment. The southern isles are arranged in a chain just over 40 miles (64 km) long from north to south. The main islands, North Uist, Benbecula and South Uist, are linked by two causeways, which make a discrete unit ideal for bird exploration. Travelling along the main north–south road, one passes through large tracts of essentially similar habitat, but a cross-section of the islands reveals a striking zonation of habitats from the low-lying western seaboard to exposed peatlands, upland moor and blanket bog, then finally the more remote eastern coast, deeply indented with intricate sea lochs. The habitat that is probably of most value to birdlife occurs as a narrow band immediately inland of the sandy beaches of the Atlantic. This area is broadly termed machair and basically comprises level grasslands formed from a mixture of wind-blown sand and peat. The drier machair is generally cultivated, the crops providing cover for many nesting species. Inland of this lie the permanently wet grasslands, shallow machair lochs and grazed 'blackland' which between them hold the highest densities of breeding waders in Britain.

Species

Some of the more interesting species likely to be seen throughout the year are Little Grebe, Grey Heron, Mute Swan, Greylag Goose, Shelduck (except autumn), Teal, Eider, Red-breasted Merganser, Hen Harrier, Buzzard, Golden Eagle, Merlin, Peregrine, Red Grouse, Golden Plover, Snipe, Redshank, Greenshank, Black-headed and Common Gulls, Black Guillemot, Rock Dove, Short-eared Owl, Rock Pipit, Stonechat, Wheatear, Raven, Twite, Reed Bunting, Corn Bunting.

Calendar

March–May: Red-throated and Black-throated Divers appear offshore by early March and quickly move inland to take up territories. By mid-March the first Lesser Black-backed Gulls are arriving. Corncrake can be heard calling from late April: between midnight and 03.00 am is the best time. In late April/early May the first Common Sandpipers arrive at their breeding lochans. Small numbers of Arctic Skua take up territories in the first part of May. At around this time, Common, Arctic and Little Terns start to arrive. Passage birds likely to be seen during this period include Pink-footed, Greenland White-fronted and Barnacle Geese, Pintail, Knot and Bar-tailed Godwit. A Broad-billed Sandpiper has occurred recently.

June–July: Great Northern Diver may linger inshore until early June, and Whimbrel passage generally continues until the end of the month. Little Tern has usually departed by the end of July. Swift may occasionally be seen at this time. Southward wader passage commences, with the possibility of Quail, Knot, Sanderling and Black-tailed Godwit.

August–November. Autumn wader passage continues, with the possibility of Little Stint, Curlew Sandpiper, Dunlin, Ruff, Bar-tailed Godwit and Whimbrel becoming more likely. There has been a good passage of Grey Phalarope from mid-September to early October off the west coast of South Uist in recent years. Rarities have included American Golden Plover and Subalpine Warbler. Wintering species start to arrive in October and November.

December–February: Great Northern Diver, Slavonian Grebe and possibly Scaup, Long-tailed Duck and Common Scoter may be seen offshore. Whooper Swan, Wigeon, Pochard, Tufted Duck and Goldeneye are all generally present on freshwater lochs. Water Rail sometimes skulks in vegetated wetlands, while Jack Snipe and Woodcock might be found on lower moorlands. Wintering shorebirds include Grey Plover, Purple Sandpiper, Dunlin, Bar-tailed Godwit and Turnstone. Fieldfare and Snow Bunting sometimes feed on the machair. An Ivory Gull was recorded recently.

Corncrake

Seawatching calendar. Seawatching can be excellent, either from promontories such as Rubha Ardvule, Aird an Runair or from the deck of the ferries to and from the Uists. Gannet and Kittiwake can be seen for much of the year, March–November. From April until August large numbers of Manx Shearwater should be seen, together with a few Sooty Shearwater from June often well into October. Arctic and Great Skuas occur throughout April–October and those moving off the west coast are joined during May/June and July/August by the rarer Pomarine and Long-tailed Skuas. Large numbers of the latter two have been recorded in recent years, especially during strong westerly winds around mid-May. Passage Leach's Petrel are regular just offshore at Rubha Ardvule in autumn, often in very good numbers.

Access

Regular car ferries operated by Caledonian MacBrayne operate on the following routes: Uig (Skye)–Lochmaddy (North Uist); Oban–Castlebay (Barra)–Lochboisdale (South Uist); and Otternish (North Uist)–Leverburgh (Harris). An additional service connects North Uist with the island of Berneray. Check the frequency of service with Caledonian MacBrayne, Ferry Terminal, Gourock PA19 1QP (tel: 01475 650100).

British Airways operate regular (Monday–Saturday) flights to Benbecula from Glasgow. A British Airways Express inter-island service connects Stornoway (Lewis), Benbecula and Barra (tel: 01345 222111).

There are several service buses (tel: 01870 620345), plus an extensive post-bus network (details at post offices). The tourist information office at Lochmaddy (tel: 01876 500321) can provide further details of public transport, car hire and taxi services.

The uniformity of much of the moorland habitat makes it difficult to single out specific birdwatching sites—basically the entire area is good for birds and diligent observation of the various habitat-types will eventually be rewarded by views of most of the area's specialities. Many of the birds mentioned here are best viewed from the roadside. Raptors, such as Golden Eagle, are most likely to be found by regularly scanning the skylines; look for Red-throated Diver flying overhead between their breeding lochans and the sea; check the fringes of lochs and marshy pools for waders; and inspect the isolated stands of trees at places like Clachan, Ben Aulasary and Newton House (North Uist) and those on the B890 Lochskipport road (South Uist) for migrants. Scan the flocks of gulls at Lochmaddy and Lochboisdale harbours and at sewage outlets such as the one at Balivanich (Benbecula) for Glaucous and Iceland Gulls. For waterfowl observation and seawatching, a telescope is almost essential.

Above all, please remember that many of the nesting birds are extremely rare in national terms and may also be very intolerant of disturbance. Nesting divers are especially at risk, as their behaviour can be very deceptive when disturbed and may mislead an observer into thinking that the bird is not in fact breeding—if you come across a diver on an inland loch, please view it briefly and from a safe distance before quickly moving away. A few outstanding areas, representative of the whole, are detailed on the following pages.

Red-throated Divers

NORTH UIST

1 BALRANALD (OS REF: NF 70/70)

This important reserve on the west coast of North Uist has been managed by the RSPB since 1966. Much of the area consists of crofts, using traditional farming methods which have created an ideal environment for many species. To the west lies a rocky headland with sandy beaches, backed by marram-stabilised coastal dunes which shelter the arable land. Behind the dunes lies the machair, planted with oats and rye as winter feed for cattle and providing cover for many nesting birds. Inland of this is a large tract of marshland, with shallow acidic pools fringed by dense emergent vegetation. Here, sedges, rushes and iris beds all provide nesting cover for wildfowl and waders. The reserve covers 658 ha and is a designated SSSI.

The entrance to Balranald is signposted 'RSPB', 2 miles (3.2 km) northwest of Bayhead on the A865 Lochmaddy–Benbecula road. A mile (1.6 km) after taking this turn, fork left to the reception cottage at Goular. No permits are required, but visitors should keep to the marked paths and respect crofting ground and churchyard. The reserve is open year-round, but a warden is present only from April to August inclusive.

Over 180 species have been recorded on the reserve, about 50 of which breed annually. Foremost among these is Corncrake, which is declining throughout most of Britain: between 10 and 15 pairs can be heard each summer at Balranald. On the lochs and marshes dense populations of duck breed, comprising mostly Mallard and Teal but including Shoveler, Gadwall, Wigeon and Tufted Duck. Waders are particularly well represented, with c. 300 pairs of Lapwing, 100 pairs each of Redshank, Oystercatcher and Ringed Plover and over 80 pairs of Dunlin on the reserve. On the drier machair, Corn Bunting and Twite breed.

The headland of Aird an Runair is an excellent seawatching point, especially in spring, extending further west than any other site in the Outer Hebrides. During spring and autumn, Fulmar, Manx Shearwater, petrels, Gannet, Arctic and Great Skuas, and various auks occur. More unusual passage seabirds also appear, such as Sooty Shearwater, Pomarine and the much rarer Long-tailed Skuas (see Calendar). In autumn, the best seawatching can be had from Rubha Ardvule where large passages of petrels and shearwaters are sometimes witnessed; many of these appear to pass west of the Monach Isles, thus missing Aird an Runair.

2 VALLAY STRAND (OS REF: NF 78/74)

This is perhaps the most accessible of the larger intertidal areas. It is most productive in autumn and winter, when large numbers of passage and wintering waders can occur. Good views over the Strand can be obtained from the main A865 road, 10 miles (16 km) west of Lochmaddy.

3 LOCH AULASARY (OS REF: NF 95/74)

Both this and Loch an Duin are important winter roost sites for Mute Swan. Approach along the unclassified road which leads east from the A865, 4 miles (6.4 km) out of Lochmaddy.

4 LOCH SKEALTAR (OS REF: NF 89/68)

This is one of the most convenient lochs on which to see Red-throated and Black-throated Divers. The loch can be viewed from the A867 immediately west of Lochmaddy.

BENBECULA

5 SOUTH FORD (OS REF: NF 77/47)

Of the fords which connect Benbecula with the Uists, the South Ford is the best both in terms of numbers of waders and viewing opportunities. Birds can be watched from the causeway or, better still, from the track which leads west, immediately south of the causeway. This joins the Ardivachar Point road at the Hebridean Jewellery shop. The locality is very good from approximately two hours before high tide when the waders are forced by the rising water into the area between the track and the island of Gualan (NF 776470).

6 BALIVANICH (OS REF: NF 76/54)

The Atlantic foreshore, accessible from the B892, holds a wide variety of divers, sea duck, waders and gulls in season.

7 STINKY BAY AND WEST BENBECULA LOCHS
(OS REF: NF 77/52 ETC.)

These lochs hold wildfowl interest, while the surrounding terrain is recommended for general birding. Stinky (NF 760525) and Coot (NF 768510) Lochs are both highly recommended.

SOUTH UIST

8 ARDIVACHAR POINT AND NORTH BAY
(OS REF: NF 74/46)

This headland in the northwest of the island is a good seawatching location. The point is c. 4 miles (6.4 km) along the unclassified road that leads west from the A865, just south of the Benbecula–South Uist causeway. In spring and autumn the entire North Bay beach is also worth a look.

9 LOCH BEE (OS REF: NF 77/44)

A very large loch extending both sides of the A865, in the northwest of the island. More than 500 Mute Swan have been recorded using the loch in winter, and other wildfowl are often numerous. Best viewed from the main road crossing the loch.

10 LOCH DRUIDIBEG (OS REF: NF 79/37)

This important NNR covers 1677 ha, and includes not only Loch Druid-ibeg but the surrounding moorland and adjacent cultivated machair. The loch has an irregular outline, is shallow in profile and is studded with islands. Although the bleak surrounding terrain appears treeless a variety of scrub woodland thrives, especially on the islands, despite exposure to the salt-laden wind. The main A865 Lochboisdale–Benbec-ula road separates the moorland part of the reserve from the more cul-tivated western section. This area encompasses the dunes, machair, shallow lagoons and marshes so typical of the western Uists.

The reserve can be adequately viewed from the A865 where there is a wooden watchtower overlooking the loch, and the B890 turn to Loch-skipport. During the breeding season, closer access is permissible only to holders of a permit issued by SNH.

Loch Druidibeg is principally renowned for its colony of breeding Greylag Geese: this has declined in the last decade but there has been a corresponding increase on North Uist and Benbecula, where almost 250 breeding pairs were counted in 1982. In addition to the geese, the res-erve has important breeding populations of wildfowl and waders; the area is also good for watching divers, raptors such as Golden Eagle, Hen Harrier and Merlin, as well as Short-eared Owl. Corncrake, Twite and Corn Bunting frequent the dry machair west of the main road. A small mixed wood on the B890 is worth checking for migrant and vagrant pas-serines.

SNH Warden
Stilligary, South Uist, Western Isles.

11 PENINERINE (OS REF: NF 73/34)

The coast at Peninerine and Loch a'Mhoil are good areas for migrant duck and waders. Quail can sometimes be heard in the rough grazing by the loch.

12 RUBHA ARDVULE (OS REF: NF 71/29)

An excellent seawatching peninsula on the central-west coast, which is particularly noteworthy in late summer/autumn when petrels—mainly Leach's—pass, sometimes only a few metres offshore in strong south-westerly winds. An added advantage is that these can be watched from your vehicle. Turn west onto an unclassified road, 8 miles (13 km) north of Lochboisdale on the A865. Rubha Ardvule is a further 2 miles (4 km). Access is very occasionally restricted by military use.

13 LOCH HALLAN (OS REF: NF 74/22)

A rich, shallow loch fringed with reeds in the southwest, near the junc-tion of the A865 and B888. Various species of wildfowl occur, often including summering Whooper Swan. The birds can be viewed without disturbance from Daliburgh cemetery, reached by taking the road west

Greenshank

from the crossroads in the village and turning north onto a track after 1 mile (1.6 km).

Timing

The Uists have something to offer at any time of year, although May and June are probably the best months to visit. Spring and autumn passage can be good on both land and at sea, while a variety of interesting wild-fowl overwinter.

ST KILDA

Habitat and Species

St Kilda is a spectacular archipelago of islands, some 41 miles northwest of North Uist. They feature the highest sea cliffs in Britain and are home to an incredible number of breeding seabirds, including the largest gan-netry in the world, and the largest Fulmar and Puffin colonies in Britain.

From Village Bay, one can either climb Conachair (430 m) to view the huge colony of Fulmar, head south towards Dun in order to see Puffin or cross over to Glen Bay on the opposite side of Hirta. The warden sometimes arranges nocturnal visits to Carn Mor, a boulder field halfway down the cliff of Mullach Bi, in order to witness the arrival of Manx Shearwater and both Storm and Leach's Petrels. A sail around Boreray, Stac Lee and Stac an Armin will produce spectacular views of Gannet, and is highly recommended. St Kilda is very good for migrants. Village Bay is probably the best area to seek these, although they can turn up anywhere.

Access

Several boats are licensed to operate charters to St Kilda. Most operate out of Oban, although pick-up points in the Outer Hebrides can usually be negotiated. Demand for these trips is high and it is therefore essential to book well in advance. One option would be to find enough people (usually 12) to charter the boat outright. Trips are weather dependent, and seasickness a certainty! The following vessels can be recommended.

Vessel	Owner	Passengers	Contact
Annag	Western Edge Ltd	6	01224 210564
Isle of Harris (60' motor)	Roddy Campbell		01859 511255
Jean de la Lune (96' motor/sail)	JDL Marine Ltd	12	01501 742414
Ocean Bounty (70' motor)	G Scott-Watson	12	01573 224641

Visitors should report to the NTS warden immediately upon landing in Village Bay on Hirta, the largest island. Near the landing point there is a small museum that provides information concerning the history of the islands, the archaeology, people and wildlife.

St Kilda is occupied by an Army Detachment, but visitors are made welcome in certain areas of the camp and may use the public telephones, shop and bar (the 'Puff-Inn'). There is a small campsite, bookable through the NTS. There is no other accommodation, nor is food or fuel available. Note that the weather can be ferocious, even in summer. Warm clothing, good footwear and a good tent are therefore essential.

References

Outer Hebrides Bird Report, nos. 1 and 2. Ed. T Dix and P Cunningham.
Birds of the Outer Hebrides. P Cunningham (1983).
Birdwatching in the Outer Hebrides. P Cunningham, T Dix & P Snow (1995).

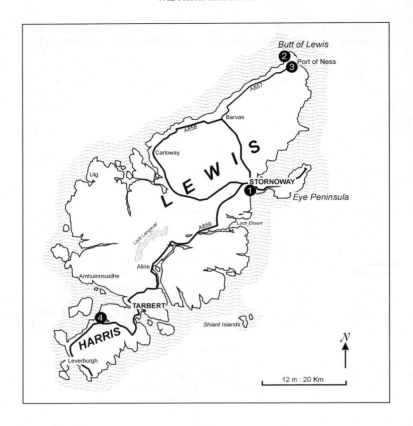

WI2 Harris and Lewis

1 Stornoway

2 Butt of Lewis

3 Loch Stiapavat

4 Laxdale River

WI2 HARRIS AND LEWIS

OS Landranger
8, 13, 14 & 18

Habitat

Harris and Lewis is actually one island, 60 miles (95 km) in length and up to 30 miles (50 km) wide. The mountains of Harris and southern Lewis rise to nearly 800 m and are generally rugged and precipitous, whereas the remainder of Lewis is characterised by low-lying undulating moorland with deep peat deposits. Long, fjord-like sea lochs penetrate the coast, particularly in the east. A fringe of arable land, formed by the deposition of wind-blown sand, extends along the Atlantic coastline and the east coast north of Stornoway.

Species

Breeding birds of interest include Red-throated and Black-throated Divers, Fulmar, Greylag Goose, Red-breasted Merganser, Golden Eagle, Merlin, Peregrine, Red Grouse, Greenshank, Dunlin, Golden Plover, Great and Arctic Skuas, Black Guillemot and Raven.

Access

Regular car ferries operated by Caledonian MacBrayne work the following routes: Ullapool–Stornoway (Lewis); Uig (Skye)–Tarbert (Harris); and Otternish (North Uist)–Leverburgh (Harris). An additional service connects Harris with the island of Scalpay. Check the frequency of service with Caledonian MacBrayne, Ferry Terminal, Gourock PA19 1QP (tel: 01475 650100).

British Airways operate regular (Monday–Saturday) flights to Stornoway from Glasgow and Inverness. A British Airways Express inter-island service connects Stornoway, Benbecula and Barra (tel: 01345 222111).

There are several service buses (tel: 01851 704327), plus an extensive post-bus network (details at post offices). The tourist information office at Stornoway (tel: 01851 703088) can provide further details of public transport, car hire and taxi services.

All of Harris and Lewis are worthy of exploration. Regular scanning of mountain skylines, moorlands and freshwater lochs should produce views of specialities such as birds of prey, breeding waders and divers. The following locations are listed as good examples of the various contrasting habitats present.

1 STORNOWAY (OS REF: NB 42/33)

The woods surrounding Lewis Castle (NB 419333) hold both the only rookery and the largest tree heronry in the Outer Hebrides. Furthermore, a unique range of breeding passerines is found that are absent elsewhere in the islands, including Grey Wagtail, Blue, Great and Coal Tits, Spotted Flycatcher, Treecreeper, Siskin, Whitethroat, Wood Warbler and Mistle Thrush. The harbour (NB 422328) holds Iceland and Glaucous Gulls, Turnstones and Purple Sandpiper. Rare gulls such as Ross's and Ivory Gulls have been recorded. The airport (HB 45/33) hosts up to eight calling Corncrake each spring.

Some 4 miles (7 km) from Stornoway on the A866 is the Braighe, a narrow isthmus containing a small freshwater loch. This attracts a wide variety of waterfowl at all times of year, and is a favoured bathing and loafing site for Kittiwake which breed at nearby Chicken Head. Red-throated and Great Northern Divers are present year-round, and up to 20 Black-throated Diver can be present in August. Large rafts of Long-tailed Duck and Red-breasted Merganser gather offshore in autumn. Wintering wildfowl include Long-tailed Duck, Scaup, Common Scoter, Goldeneye and Teal. Rarities seen include Spoonbill and White-rumped Sandpiper.

The mouth of the Coll river, 5 miles (8 km) north of Stornoway on the B895, is a good place to find migrant waders. A track leads to the shore on the north side of the river. Further along the B895 at Gress Moor (NB 50/43), Arctic and Great Skuas breed and can be watched without disturbance from the old road.

2 BUTT OF LEWIS (OS REF: HB 520665)

Some 24 miles from Stornoway, the island of Lewis ends abruptly in spectacular cliffs. It is possible to park by the lighthouse and observe the breeding seabirds, which include Shag, Fulmar, Kittiwake and Black Guillemot. However, it is the birds offshore that are of principal interest: Gannets ply constantly to and from their feeding grounds, while Manx and Sooty Shearwater may be seen during passage periods. The Butt is also a good location from which to observe cetaceans, including occasional killer whales.

3 LOCH STIAPAVAT (OS REF: HB 528643)

Of interest throughout the year, this loch regularly produces ducks, waders and other birds unusual in the Hebrides, e.g. Shoveler, Green-winged Teal, Garganey, Spotted Crake, Wood Sandpiper, Ruff and Grey-headed Wagtail. The loch can be viewed from either the B8013 or B8014 to the south and north, respectively.

4 LAXDALE RIVER (OS REF: NG 07/98)

Ten miles (16 km) south of Tarbert on the A859 is the estuary of the Laxdale River. A road along the north side permits extensive views of feeding duck and waders. The road ends at the township of Luskentyre, from where a short track through the dunes accesses the Sound of Taransay, which is frequented by fishing terns in summer and large numbers of Eider and Common Scoter in autumn and winter, when Surf Scoter and Slavonian Grebe may also be present.

LOCAL BIRD RECORDERS & REPORTS

All bird records should be sent to the appropriate recorder, although in cases of difficulty they can be sent to the editor of the *Scottish Bird Report*, 4 Bellfield Crescent, Eddleston, Peebles, Borders EH45 8RQ. Records should be on one side of a sheet of paper, well spaced and, if possible, in Voous order (as per most current field guides).

Most recording areas in Scotland now produce a local bird report. These are generally available from the Scottish Ornithologists' Club, 21 Regent Terrace, Edinburgh EH7 5BT, or from the local distributors listed below. The following list is taken from Murray, R, 1999. *Scottish Bird Report* (Number 32, June 2001). Scottish Ornithologists' Club.

Region: **Argyll & Bute**
Recording area: Argyll & Bute (except Clyde islands and former Dumbarton)
Local recorder: Paul Daw, Tigh na Tulloch, Tullochgorm, Minard, Inveraray, Argyll PA32 8YQ; 01546 886260; monedula@globalnet.co.uk
Local bird report: *Argyll Bird Report* from Bill Staley, 16 Glengilp, Ardrishaig, Argyll

Region: **Ayrshire & Clyde**
Recording area: Ayrshire (not Cumbraes)
Local recorder: Angus Hogg, 11 Kirkmichael Road, Crosshill, Maybole, Ayrshire KA19 7RJ; 01655 740317; dcgos@globalnet.co.uk
Local bird report: *Ayrshire Bird Report* from Recorder

Region: **Ayrshire & Clyde**
Recording area: Clyde
Local recorder: Iain Gibson, 8 Kenmure Drive, Howwood, Johnstone, Renfrewshire PA10 2EB 01505 705874 c/o jim.val@btinternet.com
Local bird report: *Clyde Birds* from Jim & Val Wilson, 76 Laigh Road, Newton Mearns, Glasgow G77 5EQ; 0141 635 2516

Region: **Ayrshire & Clyde**
Recording area: Clyde Islands (Arran, Bute and the Cumbraes)
Local recorder: Bernard Zonfrillo, 28 Brodie Road, Glasgow G21 3SB 0141 557 0791 b.zonfrillo@bio.gla.ac.uk
Local bird report: in *Clyde Birds*

Region: **Borders & Lothians**
Recording area: Scottish Borders
Local recorder: Ray Murray, 4 Bellfield Crescent, Eddleston, Peebles, Borders EH45 8RQ; ray.d.murray@ukgateway.net
Local bird report: *Borders Bird Report* from Malcolm Ross, The Tubs, Dingleton Road, Melrose

Region: **Borders & Lothian**
Recording area: Lothian (Edinburgh, E & W Lothian, Midlothian, Bass Rock, Inchmickery and Craigleith
Local recorder: David Kelly, 149 High Street, Prestonpans, East Lothian EH32 9AX
Local bird report: *Lothian Bird Report* from Recorder

Region: **Central Scotland**
Recording area: Perth & Kinross
Local recorder: Ron Youngman, Blairchroisk Cottage, Ballinluig, Pitlochry,
                    Perthshire PH9 0NE; 01796 482324; blairchroisk@aol.com
Local bird report: Available by e-mail on request from Recorder

Region: **Central Scotland**
Recording area: Forth (Clackmannanshire, Falkirk and Stirling)
Local recorder: Dr Cliff Henty, 7 Coneyhill Broad, Bridge of Allan, Stirling FK9
                    4EL
Local bird report: in *Forth Naturalist & Historian* from L Corbett, University Lib-
                    rary, University of Stirling, Stirling FK9 4LA

Region: **Central Scotland**
Recording area: Fife
Local recorder: Douglas Dickson, 2 Burrelton Court, Bankhead, Glenrothes,
                    Fife KY7 4UN; 01592 774066
Local bird report: *Fife Bird Report* from Recorder

Region: **Central Scotland**
Recording area: Isle of May
Local recorder: Ian English, 21 Grant Court, Avon Grove, Hamilton, South
                    Lanarkshire ML3 7UT; i.english@talk21.com
Local bird report: *Isle of May Bird Observatory Report* from Recorder

Region: **Dumfries & Galloway**
Recording area: former Nithsdale, Annandale & Eskdale, Stewartry & Wigtown
Local recorder: Paul Collin, Gairland, Old Edinburgh Road, Minnigaff, New-
                    ton Stewart, Wigtownshire DG8 6PL; 01671 402861
Local bird report: *Dumfries & Galloway Bird Report* from Recorder, also Joan
                    Howie, 60 Main Street, St John's Town of Dalry, Castle Dou-
                    glas, Kirkcudbrightshire

Region: **Highland**
Recording area: Caithness
Local recorder: Stan Laybourne, Old Schoolhouse, Harpsdale, Halkirk, Caith-
                    ness KW12 6UN; 01955 290501; stanlaybourne@talk21.com
Local bird report: none at present

Region: **Highland**
Recording area: excluding Caithness and Moray
Local recorder: Colin Crooke, 6 George Street, Avoch, Ross-shire IV9 8PU;
                    01381 620566
Local bird report: *Highland Bird Report* from Recorder

Region: **Northeast Scotland**
Recording area: Northeast Scotland (City of Aberdeen & Aberdeenshire)
Local recorder: Andy Thorpe, 30 Mearn Gardens, Milltimber, Aberdeen,
                    Grampian AB1 0EA; 01224 773296; andrewthorpe3@aol.com
Local bird report: *Northeast Scotland Bird Report* from Dave Gill, Drakemyre
                    Croft, Cairnorrie, Methlick, Aberdeenshire AB41 0JN

Region: **Northeast Scotland**
Recording area: Moray & Nairn
Local recorder: Martin Cook, Rowanbrae, Clochan, Buckie, Banffshire AB5
2EQ; 01542 850296; martin.cook9@virgin.net
Local bird report: *Moray & Nairn Bird Report* from Recorder

Region: **Northeast Scotland**
Recording area: Angus & Dundee
Local recorder: Dan Carmichael, 2a Reres Road, Broughty Ferry, Dundee
DD5 2QA; 01382 779981; dan_a_carmichael@email.msn.com
Local bird report: *Angus & Dundee Bird Report* from Recorder

Region: **Orkney**
Recording area: Orkney
Local recorder: Tim Dean, Echa View, Burray, Orkney KW17 2SX
Local bird report: *Orkney Bird Report*, Mildred Cuthbert, Vishabrack, Evie, Orkney

Region: **Shetland**
Recording area: Shetland—except Fair Isle
Local recorder: Kevin Osborn, Inkleholm, Swinister, Sandwick, Shetland ZE2
9HH; 01950 431286; k.o@virgin.net
Local bird report: *Shetland Bird Report* from Martin Heubeck, Sumburgh Light-
house, Virkie, Shetland ZE3 9JN; 01950 460760

Region: **Shetland**
Recording area: Fair Isle
Local recorder: The Warden, Bird Observatory, Fair Isle, Shetland ZE2 9JU
Local bird report: *Fair Isle Bird Report* from Fair Isle Bird Observatory

Region: **Western Isles**
Recording area: Outer Hebrides (including Uists and Barra)
Local recorder: Andrew Stevenson, Mill House, Snishival, South Uist, Western
Isles HS8 5SG; 01870 620317; andrew.stevenson@SNH.gov.uk
Local bird report: *Outer Hebrides Bird Report* from Brian Rabbitts, 6 Carnish,
Lochmaddy, North Uist, Western Isles HS6 5HL

Immature Sea (White-tailed) Eagle

British Trust for Ornithology
The Nunnery
Nunnery Place
Thetford
Norfolk
IP24 2PU

Caledonian MacBrayne
Ferry Terminal
Gourock
PA19 1QP
(tel: 01475 650100)

Forestry Commission
231 Corstorphine Road
Edinburgh
EH12 7AT

National Trust for Scotland
5 Charlotte Square
Edinburgh
EH2 4DU

Scottish Natural Heritage
12 Hope Terrace
Edinburgh
EH9 2AS

Royal Society for the Protection of Birds
17 Regent Terrace
Edinburgh
EH7 5BN

Scottish Ornithologists' Club
21 Regent Terrace
Edinburgh
EH7 5BT

Scottish Wildlife Trust
25 Johnston Terrace
Edinburgh
EH1 2NH

Wood Sandpiper, spring

SELECT BIBLIOGRAPHY

Twites

Angus, S (ed.) (1983) *Sutherland Birds*. The Northern Times.

Berry, RJ (1985) *The Natural History of Orkney*. Collins

Berry, RJ and Johnson, L (1980) *The Natural History of Shetland*. Collins.

Booth, CG (1981) *Birds in Islay*. Argyll Reproductions Ltd.

Booth, C, Cuthbert, M and Reynolds, P (1984) *The Birds of Orkney*. Orkney Press.

Collet, PM and Manson, SAM (1987) *Birds of Caithness*. Caithness SOC.

Cunningham, P (1983) *Birds of the Outer Hebrides*. The Melven Press.

Cunningham, P, Dix, T and Snow, P (1995) *Birdwatching in the Outer Hebrides*. Saker Press.

Dennis, R (1984) *Birds of Badenoch and Strathspey*. Roy Dennis Enterprises.

Elliott, R (1989) *The Birds of Islay*. Christopher Helm.

Eggeling, WJ (1960, reprinted 1985) *The Isle of May: a Scottish Nature Reserve*. Oliver & Boyd.

Fuller, R (1982) *Bird Habitats in Britain*. T. & A. D. Poyser.

Furness, RW (1983) *Birds of Foula*. The Brathay Hall Trust.

Hogg, A (1983) *Birds of Ayrshire*. Glasgow University.

Holloway, J (1991) *The Birds of Stronsay*. Privately published.

Hywel-Davies, J and Thom, VM (1984) *The Macmillan Guide to Britain's Nature Reserves*. Macmillan.

Jardine, DC, Clarke, J and Clarke, PM (1986) *The Birds of Colonsay and Oransay*. Privately published.

Lack, P (1986) *The Atlas of Wintering Birds in Britain and Ireland*. T. & A. D. Poyser.

Madders, M and Snow, P (1987) *Birds of Mull*. Saker Press.

Madders, M., Snow, P and Welstead, J (1992) *Birds of Mid-Argyll*. Saker Press.

Meek, E (1985) *Islands of Birds: a Guide to Orkney Birds*. RSPB.

Murray, R (1986) *Birds of the Borders*. Borders SOC.

Nethersole-Thompson, D (1978) *Highland Birds*. Highlands & Islands Development Board.

Ogilvie, M (1992) *Birds of Islay*. Lochindaal Press.

Omand, D (ed.) (1984) *The Ross and Cromarty Book*. The Northern Times.

Prater, AJ (1981) *Estuary Birds of Britain and Ireland*. T. & A. D. Poyser.

Redman, N and Harrap, S (1987) *Birdwatching in Britain: a Site by Site Guide*. Christopher Helm.

Rhead, J and Snow, P (1994) *Birds of Arran*. Saker Press.

Sharrock, JTR (1976) *The Atlas of Breeding Birds in Britain and Ireland*. T. & A. D. Poyser.

Smout, AM (1986) *Birds of Fife*. John Donald.

Thom, VM (1970) *Loch of Lowes*. SWT.

Thom, VM (1986) *Birds of Scotland*. T. & A. D. Poyser.

CODE OF CONDUCT
FOR BIRDWATCHERS

Today's birdwatchers are a powerful force for nature conservation. The number of those of interested in birds rises continually, and it is vital that we take seriously our responsibility to avoid any harm to birds. We must also present a responsible image to non-birdwatchers who may be affected by our activities and particularly those on whose sympathy and support the future of birds may rest.

There are 10 points to bear in mind:
1. The welfare of birds must come first.
2. Habitat must be protected.
3. Keep disturbance to birds and their habitat to a minimum.
4. When you find a rare bird think carefully about whom you should tell.
5. Do not harass rare migrants.
6. Abide by the bird protection laws at all times.
7. Respect the rights of landowners.
8. Respect the rights of other people in the countryside.
9. Make your records available to the local bird recorder.
10. Behave abroad as you would when birdwatching at home.

Welfare of birds must come first
Whether your particular interest is photography, ringing, sound recording, scientific study or just birdwatching, remember that the welfare of the birds must always come first.

Habitat protection
Habitat is vital to a bird and therefore we must ensure that our activities do not cause damage.

Keep disturbance to a minimum
Birds' tolerance of disturbance varies between species and season. Therefore, it is safer to keep all disturbance to a minimum. No birds should be disturbed from the nest in case opportunities for predators to take eggs or young are increased. In very cold weather disturbance to birds may cause them to use vital energy at a time when food is difficult to find. Wildfowlers already impose bans during cold weather: birdwatchers should exercise similar discretion.

Rare breeding birds
If you discover a rare bird breeding and feel that protection is necessary, inform the appropriate RSPB Regional Office. Otherwise it is best in almost all circumstances to keep the record strictly secret in order to avoid disturbance by other birdwatchers and the attentions of egg collectors. Never visit known sites of rare breeding birds unless they are adequately protected. Even your presence may give away the site to others and cause so many other visitors that the birds may fail to breed successfully. Disturbance at or near the nest of species listed on the First Schedule of the Wildlife and Countryside Act 1981 is a criminal offence.

Copies of Wild Birds and the Law are obtainable from the RSPB, The Lodge, Sandy, Bedfordshire SG19 2DL (send two second-class stamps).

Rare migrants

Rare migrants or vagrants must not be harassed. If you discover one, consider the circumstances carefully before telling anyone. Will an influx of birdwatchers disturb the bird or others in the area? Will the habitat be damaged? Will problems be caused with the landowner?

The Law

The bird protection laws (now embodied in the Wildlife and Country-side Act 1981) are the result of hard campaigning by previous genera-tions of birdwatchers. We must abide by them at all times and not allow them to fall into disrepute.

Respect the rights of landowners

The wishes of landowners and occupiers of land must be respected. Do not enter land without permission. Comply with permit schemes. If you are leading a group, do request visits in advance, even if a formal permit scheme is not in operation. Always obey the Country Code.

Respect the rights of other people

Have proper consideration for other birdwatchers. Try not to disrupt their activities or scare the birds they are watching. There are many other people who also use the countryside. Do not interfere with their activities and, if it seems that what they are doing is causing unnecessary disturbance to birds, do try to take a balanced view. Flushing gulls when walking a dog on a beach may do little harm, while the same dog might be a serious disturbance at a tern colony. When pointing this out to a non-birdwatcher be courteous, but firm. The non-birdwatchers' good-will towards birds must not be destroyed by the attitudes of birdwatch-ers.

Keeping records

Much of today's knowledge about birds is the result of meticulous record keeping by our predecessors. Make sure you help to add to tomorrow's knowledge by sending records to your local bird recorder.

Birdwatching abroad

Behave abroad as you would at home. This code should be firmly adhered to when abroad (whatever the local laws). Well-behaved bird-watchers can be important ambassadors for bird protection.

This code has been drafted following consultation between the British Ornithologists' Union, British Trust for Ornithology, the Royal Society for the Protection of Birds, the Scottish Ornithologists' Club, the Wildfowl and Wetlands Trust and the editors of British Birds.

Further copies may be obtained from The Royal Society for the Protec-tion of Birds, The Lodge, Sandy, Bedfordshire SG19 2DL.

INDEX OF SPECIES

Index of species

AB4, AC1, AC5, BL3,
BL9, BL11, BL13, BL15,
C1, C13, DG7, DG8,
DG9, H10, H11, H14,
H16, H17, H19, H23,
H31, NE6, NE12, NE13,
NE15, NE18, NE19,
NE22, NE24, NE27, O1,
O4, O10, SH6, SH7, SH8,
SH10, WI1, WI2

Dunnock BL10, BL16, O12

Eagle, Golden AB3, AB4,
C6, C23, H5, H6, H7,
H10, H11, H12, H15,
H24, H25, H26, H27,
NE15, NE16, NE24, O4,
WI1, WI2
White-Tailed AB3, H12,
NE15

Egret, Great White NE6
Egret, Little DG7, NE6
Eider AB1, AB2, AB3, AB4,
AC1, AC5, AC7, BL1,
BL9, BL10, BL11, BL15,
C9, C10, C11, C13, C14,
DG4, H10, H19, H21,
H23, H24, NE1, NE2,
NE3, NE5, NE6, NE7,
NE8, NE9, NE10, NE11,
NE12, NE13, NE17,
NE19, NE21, NE22, O2,
O6, O7, O8, O9, O10,
SH1, SH3, SH5, SH6,
SH7, SH8, SH10, WI1,
WI2
King BL1, DG4, H19, NE3,
NE5, NE6

Falcon, Red-Footed C14
Fieldfare AB2, AB3, AB4,
AC2, AC7, BL4, BL10,
BL13, BL16, C2, C4, C6,
C8, C16, C18, DG1, H8,
NE18, SH7, WI1
Firecrest BL1, BL16, C11
Flycatcher, Pied BL2, BL8,
BL16, C6, C23, DG2,
DG3, H8, NE4, NE17
Red-Breasted BL1, BL16,
C11, C14, H29, NE17,
NE21, O9, SH10
Spotted AB4, BL8, BL10,
BL13, BL16, C4, C6, C7,
C16, C18, C19, C20, H1,
H24, NE26, WI2
Fulmar AB1, AB2, AB3,
AB4, BL1, BL10, BL11,
BL12, BL14, BL16, C9,
C14, C16, DG6, DG9,
H20, H21, H22, H23,
H24, H30, NE1, NE2,
NE3, NE6, NE8, O1, O2,
O4, O6, O9, O11, O12,
SH1, SH3, SH8, SH9,
SH10, WI1, WI2

Gadwall AB2, BL8, BL9,
BL10, C1, C10, C12, C16,
NE6, NE7, NE26, O9,
WI1
Gannet AB1, AB2, AB3,
AB4, AC1, BL1, BL9,
BL10, BL11, BL14, BL16,
C1, C11, C13, DG5, DG6,
H10, NE4, NE13, NE20,
SH3, SH8, SH9, SH10,
WI1, WI2
Garganey AC4, BL9, C15,
NE6, NE7, NE17, WI2
Godwit, Bar-Tailed AB2,
AB3, AB4, AC1, BL9,
BL10, BL11, BL15, C1,
C13, DG9, H10, H14,
H16, H17, H19, NE6,
NE18, NE19, NE26, O1,
O10, O12, WI1
Black-Tailed AB2, AB3,
AB4, AC1, AC4, AC5,
AC6, BL9, BL10, BL11,
BL15, C1, C13, C16,
DG7, H14, H17, NE3,
NE6, NE7, NE13, NE18,
NE19, WI1
Goldcrest BL1, BL16, C3,
C14, H19, H26, NE4,
NE14, NE17, NE26, SH1,
SH10
Goldeneye AB2, AB3, AB4,
AC1, AC2, AC3, AC5,
AC6, BL1, BL3, BL4,
BL5, BL6, BL7, BL8, BL9,
BL10, BL11, BL15, BL16,
C1, C2, C5, C6, C7, C9,
C10, C13, C16, C20, C21,
DG2, DG4, H1, H2, H3,
H7, H8, H10, H11, H13,
H14, H17, H19, H21,
NE3, NE4, NE6, NE7,
NE14, NE18, NE19,
NE24, NE27, O1, SH1,
WI1, WI2
Barrow's AC5
Goosander AB3, AC2, BL2,
BL3, BL4, BL5, BL6, BL7,
BL8, BL9, BL10, BL16,
C1, C2, C4, C5, C6, C13,
C16, C18, C20, C24,
DG2, H2, H3, H12, H14,
H15, H24, H26, H27,
NE1, NE4, NE6, NE7,
NE10, NE14, NE22, NE24
Goose, Barnacle AB1, AB2,
AB3, AB4, AC4, BL3,
BL6, BL9, BL10, BL14,
C11, C13, C16, DG7,
DG9, H10, H23, H24,
H25, NE6, NE7, NE17,
NE26, O4, SH10, WI1
Bean DG2, NE17
Brent AB2, AB4, BL3,
BL9, BL10, BL14, C1,
C11, C16, NE6, NE7,
NE17

Canada AB4, BL8, BL10,
C16, C18, C20, NE6
Greylag AB1, AB2, AB3,
AB4, AC2, BL3, BL6,
BL7, BL8, BL9, BL10,
BL12, BL13, BL16, C5,
C7, C12, C13, C15, C16,
C17, C18, C20, C21,
DG2, DG8, DG9, H2, H8,
H10, H16, H17, H19,
H23, H24, H26, NE6,
NE7, NE11, NE14, NE17,
NE18, NE22, NE24,
NE26, NE27, O1, O12,
SH1, SH10, WI1, WI2
Pink-Footed AB3, AB4,
AC4, BL3, BL6, BL7,
BL8, BL9, BL10, BL14,
BL16, C1, C5, C12, C16,
C17, C18, DG2, DG7,
DG8, DG9, H8, H17,
H23, NE4, NE6, NE7,
NE17, NE18, NE22,
NE24, NE26, SH10, WI1
Snow AB1, AB4, BL3,
C12, NE6, NE7, NE17
White-Fronted AB1, AB2,
AB3, AB4, BL3, C7, C12,
C16, DG2, H10, H21,
NE6, NE7, NE17, O1,
O12, WI1
Grebe, Black-Necked BL8,
BL10, BL11, C16, DG4,
NE7, NE26
Great Crested AC1, AC2,
BL5, BL10, BL11, BL12,
BL13, BL16, C1, C2, C5,
C8, C9, C10, C12, C13,
C16, C18, C20, DG2,
NE7, NE18, NE19, NE20,
NE24, NE26, NE27
Little AB2, AB3, AC2,
AC6, BL1, BL4, BL8,
BL9, BL10, BL12, B13,
C1, C2, C8, C15, C10,
C12, C18, C21, H14,
NE24, NE26, O7, WI1
Red-Necked AC7, BL10,
BL11, C2, C9, C10, C13,
DG4, H19, NE3, NE4,
NE7
Slavonian AB3, AB4,
AC1, AC7, BL8, BL10,
BL11, C2, C10, C13, C16,
DG4, H13, H16, H19,
NE3, NE4, NE7, O3, SH1,
WI1, WI2
Greenfinch BL10, C16,
NE11, O12
Greenshank AB3, AB4,
AC1, AC2, BL3, BL5,
BL7, BL9, BL10, BL11,
BL13, BL15, BL16, C1,
C12, C13, C15, C16, C18,
H3, H10, H17, H19, H22,
H23, H24, H25, H26,
H27, H31, NE6, NE7,

NE10, NE13, NE18,
NE26, WI1, WI2
Grosbeak, Pine C14
Grouse, Black C6, C23,
DG2, H3, H13, H15,
NE15, NE16, NE24
Red AB3, BL3, BL13, C22,
H10, H11, H12, H22,
H23, H24, H25, H26,
NE6, NE24, O1, O4, WI1,
WI2
Guillemot AB1, AB2, AB3,
AB4, AC1, BL1, BL9,
BL10, BL11, BL14, BL16,
C1, C14, DG4, DG6,
DG9, H14, H20, H21,
H22, H23, H24, H30,
NE2, NE8, NE11, NE12,
O1, O2, O4, O6, O7, O8,
O9, O11, O12, SH1, SH3,
SH5, SH6, SH7, SH8,
SH9, SH10, WI1, WI2
Black AB3, AB4, AC1,
AC7, BL10, BL11, C14,
DG4, DG6, DG9, H21,
H22, H23, H24, H30,
NE8, NE12, O2, O4, O7,
O8, O9, O11, O12, SH1,
SH5, SH6, SH8, SH9,
SH10, WI1, WI2
Gull, Black-Headed AC1,
AC2, BL3, BL10, BL11,
BL13, BL16, C1, C16, H2,
H8, H13, NE19, NE26,
O6, O9, WI1
Common AB3, AC1, BL3,
BL11, BL13, H13, NE19,
O9, WI1
Franklin's BL11
Glaucous AB3, AB4, AC3,
BL10, BL11, BL14, BL16,
C1, C10, DG4, H14, H19,
H21, NE3, NE4, NE9,
NE11, NE12, NE17, O1,
SH1, WI1, WI2
Great Black-Backed BL3,
BL10, BL11, C18, NE19,
SH3, SH6
Herring AB4, AC1, BL1,
BL10, BL11, C14, C18,
NE1, NE2, NE6, NE19,
O1, O9, O11
Iceland AB3, AB4, AC3,
BL11, C10, DG4, H14,
H19, H21, NE3, NE4,
NE9, NE12, NE17, O1,
WI1, WI2
Ivory WI1, WI2
Lesser Black-Backed
BL10, BL11, BL13, C14,
C16, C18, O1, WI1
Little BL1, BL9, BL10,
BL11, BL14, BL16, C9,
C10, C11, C1, C15, NE3,
NE6, NE19, NE20
Mediterranean AC3, AC7,
BL1, BL11, BL14, C10,

NE3, NE4
Ring-Billed AC3, AC7,
BL11, NE4, O1
Ross's WI2
Sabine's AC7, BL14, C11,
DG5, O9
Gyrfalcon AB4, H6

Harrier, Hen AB1, AB3,
AB4, AC4, BL9, BL13,
C11, DG2, DG7, DG8,
DG9, H7, H8, H9, H10,
H11, H12, H13, H19,
H28, H31, NE6, NE15,
NE16, NE24, NE26, O1,
O4, O6, SH10, WI1
Marsh AC4, BL10, H8,
NE7, NE17, NE26
Montagu's BL10, NE22
Hawfinch BL8, BL9, BL16,
C3, C19
Heron, Grey AB3, AB4,
AC6, BL3, BL8, BL12, C1,
C2, C3, C16, DG9, H10,
NE14, NE24, NE27, WI1
Night BL1, BL12, C8
Purple NE7
Hobby O12
Hoopoe BL1

Ibis, Glossy NE7, O1

Jackdaw AB3, C16, C18
Jay AB4, BL2, BL8, BL15,
C7, C19

Kestrel AB2, AB3, AC2,
BL1, BL3, BL10, BL13,
C1, C16, C22, C23, H10,
H12, H15, NE4, NE14,
O1, SH10
Lesser SH10
Kingfisher AC1, AC6, BL4,
BL8, BL9, C1, C18, C19,
C21, DG2, NE20, NE24
Kittiwake AB2, AB3, AB4,
BL1, BL9, BL10, BL11,
BL14, BL16, C1, C9, C11,
C14, DG5, DG6, DG9,
H20, H21, H22, H23,
H30, NE2, NE6, NE8,
NE20, O1, O2, O4, O6,
O7, O8, O11, SH1, SH3,
SH4, SH7, SH8, SH9,
SH10, WI1, WI2
Knot AB3, AB4, AC1, BL3,
BL5, BL9, BL10, BL11,
C1, C10, C13, C16, DG4,
DG7, DG8, DG9, H10,
H14, H16, H17, H19,
NE6, NE13, NE19, NE22,
WI1

Lapwing AB1, AB2, AB4,
AC1, AC5, AC6, BL3,
BL6, BL7, BL9, BL10,
BL11, C1, C13, C16, C18,

DG4, DG7, DG9, H11,
NE6, NE14, NE18, NE22,
NE27, O5, O6, O9, SH6,
SH7, SH10, WI1
Lark, Shore BL9, BL10,
NE17
Short-Toed SH10
Linnet AB3, AC1, BL1,
BL10, BL11, BL12, BL16,
C1, DG9, NE11, NE19

Mallard AB2, AB3, AB4,
AC1, AC2, AC5, AC6,
BL2, BL3, BL4, BL5, BL6,
BL7, BL8, BL9, BL10,
BL12, BL13, BL15, BL16,
C1, C2, C5, C7, C8, C12,
C13, C16, C18, C20, C21,
DG2, DG3, DG4, H14,
H16, H19, NE6, NE7,
NE14, NE18, NE22,
NE27, O1, O9, WI1
Mandarin BL8, C18
Martin, House NE14
Sand AB3, AC6, BL4, BL6,
BL7, BL8, C16, C18,
NE18
Merganser, Red-Breasted
AB2, AB3, AB4, AC1,
BL9, BL10, BL11, BL15,
BL16, C1, C6, C7, C10,
C13, C18, C21, C24,
DG4, H2, H11, H15, H19,
H21, H24, H26, H27,
NE1, NE6, NE7, NE10,
NE13, NE19, NE22,
NE23, O1, O6, O10, SH6,
WI1, WI2
Merlin AB1, AB2, AB3,
AB4, AC5, BL1, BL9,
BL10, BL11, BL13, C1,
C13, C14, DG7, DG8,
DG9, H7, H9, H10, H11,
H12, H15, H16, H23,
H24, H26, H31, NE6,
NE7, NE15, NE16, NE17,
NE22, NE24, O1, O4, O6,
SH6, SH10, WI1, WI2
Moorhen AB2, AC6, BL4,
BL8, BL9, BL10, BL13,
BL16, C1, C2, C3, C8,
C12, C16, NE14, NE26,
O7, O9

Nightingale C11, C14, H29,
NE3, NE21, O9, SH10
Thrush C14, H29, NE21,
O9, SH10
Nuthatch BL8

Oriole, Golden BL1, C11,
SH10
Osprey BL14, C2, C20,
DG2, H1, H2, H3, H8,
H11, H12, H15, H17,
H19, NE10, NE13, NE14,
NE22, NE26, SH10

Index of species

Wigeon AB2, AB3, AB4, AC1, AC2, AC5, AC6, BL1, BL4, BL5, BL6, BL7, BL8, BL9, BL10, BL11, BL13, BL15, BL16, C1, C2, C7, C8, C12, C13, C16, C18, C20, C21, DG2, DG4, DG8, H3, H8, H10, H11, H14, H16, H17, H19, H24, NE6, NE7, NE14, NE22, NE24, NE26, NE27, O1, O10, SH1, WI1

American BL8, C2, C8, H19, NE7
Woodcock AB3, C2, C6, C14, C20, DG1, DG3, H2, H3, H4, H24, NE16, NE24, SH10, WI1
Woodpecker, Great Spotted AB3, AB4, BL2, BL4, BL8, BL9, BL15, BL16, C2, C4, C6, C7, C18, C19, C20, C21, C23, DG1, DG2, DG3, H1, H2, H7, H8, H10, H26, NE14,

NE26
Green BL2, BL4, BL8, C8, C19, DG1, DG2, H1, NE26
Woodpigeon C16, O1
Wren H10, O9, SH10
Wryneck BL1, BL16, C11, C14, H29, NE6, NE17, SH10

Yellowhammer AB2, AB3, AC1, BL1, C16, NE19
Yellowlegs, Lesser NE7